DEDICATION

To the brilliant, brainy and occasionally bonkers
team at Propellernet, without whom this book
could never have been written.

Your stories are our success; keep them coming.

ACKNOWLEDGEMENT

There are a lot of theory books out there about how to run an organisation. Fortunately, this is not one of them. It is a practical playbook, written by someone who has created one of the most exciting company cultures anywhere, packed with tips and advice on how to do it yourself.

Imagine a workplace where people are energised and motivated by being in control of the work they do, where they are trusted and given freedom, within clear guidelines, to decide how to achieve their results. Imagine they have managers who support and coach them, rather than telling them what to do. Wouldn't you want to work there?

As Chief Happiness Officer of a company called Happy, my passion is for creating workplaces like these and indeed for creating joy at work. There is a stack of evidence that great cultures lead to improved productivity and better returns. And the benefits of this kind of approach reach far wider than the finance department.

That is why I was so excited to meet Nikki, a woman with real passion and energy for creating an environment in which her people are not just engaged, but superengaged. Not only because of the numbers, but also because it is the right thing to do.

Superengaged will explain how to create this kind of environment for yourself, as well as giving you plenty of 'nickables' to take away and action. I guarantee that you will be inspired by this book; you will be making notes as you read along and, if you put the ideas into practice, you will see dramatic changes in what your business and your people achieve.

I know from my own book, *The Happy Manifesto*, that ideas like these can make a difference. One CEO read it, implemented the ideas and came top of the Sunday Times Best Workplace list. Another saw their share price triple in the three years after they started putting the concepts to work.

Superengaged will have that kind of impact. Indeed, it will probably have far more. It will show you how to create a culture where people can not only fulfil their potential but fulfil their dreams – inside and outside of work.

That dream could be ending street homelessness in Brighton by 2020. Or supporting a safari company in Namibia. Or creating a weird alternative reality, including fake kidnappings, in the French Alps. Or putting on one of the most popular late-night experiences at Glastonbury.

You might ask, what does any of this have to do with the success of a marketing agency in Brighton? A hell of a lot, as it turns out. *Superengaged* shows the unexpected outcomes which come from putting people and purpose first, ranging from the increased motivation of those involved to the radical ideas inspired by tearing up the standard business blueprint.

So, do you want to create a truly great organisation, one that gets the best out of its people every single day, that you feel proud to be part of? Then read on.

I love these ideas. I love this book. Make sure you read it but, even more importantly, make sure you use the ideas. And then pass it on to somebody you want to inspire.

Henry Stewart

Chief Happiness Officer, Happy Ltd, and author of *The Happy Manifesto*

ABOUT THE AUTHOR

Nikki Gatenby is a force to be reckoned with (in a good way).

She spent the first 12 years of her career experimenting with entrepreneurial ways of working across international teams in competitive digital agencies in London and Paris. She then brought her skills to the growing digital hub in Brighton, becoming MD of Propellernet eight years ago and, more recently, a co-owner.

During her time at Propellernet, Nikki has overseen its transformation from a small, Brighton-based digital marketing agency to a globally operating powerhouse. She has led a team that has tripled margin, quadrupled revenue and generated ten times more profit. And she has proved beyond all doubt that putting people first creates genuine business success.

Under her leadership, Propellernet has become known for its culture of inclusion, personal responsibility and creative freedom. It has been showcased for the way it works, as well as the work it does, by the BBC, the Guardian, Management Today, the Parliament Trust and the Chamber of Commerce. The company has had a top fifteen listing in the Great Place to Work® awards six years in a row and was voted one of the top five medium companies in Campaign's Best Places to Work 2018. It also boasts one of the lowest staff turnover rates in the industry.

Nikki is known for combining a no-bullshit approach to business with a passion for helping people be the best version of themselves. When she's not making life better for her staff, clients and community, she is usually to be found at the top of a mountain or the bottom of the ocean. But not at the same time.

DON'T JUST TAKE OUR WORD FOR IT...

"Propellernet is the UK's answer to Zappos. Nick as many of their ideas as you possibly can."

LISA PANTELLI. FOUNDER, BECOME COMMUNICATIONS

"Nikki is the real deal, creating a culture of happiness and purpose, to deliver lasting business benefits. Propellernet is proof that you can drive business results through employee engagement."

ANDY BUDD. FOUNDER, CLEAR LEFT

"I challenge you not to be inspired by Superengaged. This is not just a book, it's a radical, revolutionary, whoop in the face of the outdated presumptions that fuel a demoralising corporate life, and strangle productivity. Easy to read, and full of examples, stories and practical suggestions of how you can start to move towards a superengaged company culture in your business."

ANN BOOTH-CLIBBON. BAFTA NOMINATED STORY COACH

"Superengaged distils the processes that Propellernet devised, as well as the hard lessons learned in turning themselves from a boutique business into a multi-million pound service company, becoming No. 1 in the Guardian Best Places to Work list. Packed with useful examples and key insights, it's a must-read for anyone looking to grow their business."

MIKE SOUTHON. CO-AUTHOR OF THE BEERMAT ENTREPRENEUR AND OTHER BEST-SELLING BUSINESS BOOKS

"Whether you're a growing business or a fledgling start-up this is the book to read if you want to create an organisation that is built to last."

CARLOS SABA. CO-FOUNDER THE HAPPY START UP SCHOOL

"Superengaged is the missing manual when it comes to running a happy, profitable agency. Essential reading if your heart sinks at the thought of conducting yet another exit interview."

IAN HARRIS. FOUNDER, AGENCY HACKERS

"Too many businesses think they understand their employees, and assume that they just want bigger, better, more. Superengaged explodes these outdated views, getting to the heart of what motivates today's workforce, and setting out innovative ways to deliver it, within a successful business."

KAREN MATTISON, MBE. CO-FOUNDER, TIMEWISE

"An energetic argument for the business case of a happy team. Written with inspirational brio and pace, it makes you want to jump up and start making changes right away."

EUGENIE TEASLEY. CEO, THE GOODALL FOUNDATION

"If you run an agency beg, borrow, steal or even buy a copy of Superengaged. I wish Propellernet had existed during my agency career. I'd have joined without question, assuming they'd have me."

CHRIS MERRINGTON. FOUNDER, SPRING 80:20. AUTHOR 'WHY DO SMART PEOPLE MAKE SUCH STUPID MISTAKES?'

"Nikki Gatenby is a force to be reckoned with. Her drive, purpose and integrity are infused in this book from start to finish. If you want to know how to create a successful start-up and how to fail forwards and upwards, let Nikki tell you how. A must read!"

RIFA THORPE TRACEY. MENTOR AND SHE SAYS CURATOR

"Superengaged tracks the progress of a company who refused to play by the traditional and exhausting rules of success and invented better ones. No earthly sum of investment capital can buy this. But you can build your own and Superengaged shows you exactly how."

CARRIE BEDINGFIELD. FOUNDER OF ONEFISH TWOFISH, 50TH GENERATION, LOMO AND RUN FOR YOUR LIFE

"Reading Superengaged was like having a series of repeated slaps across the face – in equal measure: buckets of inspiration, genuinely stop and make you think examples, actually helpful references, plus a few unexpected wakeup calls – all combined with totally out there real-life proven examples of how to propel your staff engagement levels through the roof! What's not to like?"

CHRIS FREELAND. CEO RAPP

"In a word? Brilliant! If you are looking for ways to make work fun, this is for you."

JOOST MINNAAR. CO-FOUNDER, CORPORATE REBELS

CONTENTS

SUPERENGAGED

/ˌs(j)uːpərɪnˈgeɪdʒd/

adjective: superengaged

According to engagement experts
Then Somehow, a superengaged employee:

- Knows their organisation cares for its people and is doing its utmost to ensure their emotional and psychological wellbeing.

- Has complete faith that the organisation will tell them the truth, while being faithful to its own core principles (which, in turn, they feel deeply aligned to).

- Feels genuinely challenged, with the appropriate training and support to take on those challenges, and has a clear sense of how they will progress.

How do you make that happen?
Keep reading to find out and visit:

www.superengaged.co.uk

Section 1

UPFRONT

(and why you should read this book)

1. HELLO.

Welcome to our not-too-rough guide to building a successful, profitable, purposeful business which is also a brilliant place to work. It's the true story of how we've created genuine business success by putting people first and propelling them forward, both personally and professionally.

This book is for anyone who wants to know how to create and maintain a company culture that manages to drive performance, boost enthusiasm, reach world-class engagement levels, and generally make life better all round, all at the same time. That's some juggling act – but we're doing it, and now we want to help you do it too.

Back in 2003, when we started our marketing agency, we didn't have it all worked out. We just knew we wanted to attract some great people and enable them to do great work for great clients. 15 years later, despite a huge amount of social, economic and political turbulence, we've achieved all that and more, and managed to make a healthy profit while we were at it.

Along the way, we've taken brave decisions, implementing ideas that have caused a few raised eyebrows or indeed, led people to question our sanity.

Like letting our people have a say in the clients we work with, or the way the business is run. Or like trying to say "*Let's give it a try*" more often than we say "*No*". Madness, say some; quite the opposite, we reply – and our staff retention rates back us up.

EMBRACING CHANGE TO MAKE LIFE BETTER

In the intervening years, things have changed more than any of us could have expected. When we started in 2003, there was no Facebook, no Twitter, no YouTube even. The iPhone was four years away, and the iPad seven years. Bonkers, but true.

And these changes in technology have underpinned fundamental disruption to the status quo. WikiLeaks, fake news, the sharing economy, the gig economy, the growing number of jobs being lost to robots and the increasing amount of people demanding to work flexibly... the list goes on too long to keep your attention, but you get the idea.

As Mark Stephenson, an entrepreneur, author, broadcaster, expert on global trends and all round clever bloke, once said:

"Technology is accelerating five times faster than management."

Yet, despite this radical shake-up that we've all been living through, too many businesses haven't moved with the times. They're still wedded to old-school ways of squeezing as many hours as possible out of their employees, who they see as 'assets to be sweated' (urgh). It's no wonder so many employees feel so disengaged.

The daft thing is, there's a whole bunch of evidence to suggest that engagement pays. For example, research has shown that, in the context of engagement, the top 25% of companies enjoy 200% more annual profit than the lowest 25%[i]. And businesses that ignore this evidence, that put profit before people, with managers who aren't equipped to adapt and innovate to the changing world, are increasingly getting left behind.

PUTTING PEOPLE AND PURPOSE FIRST

We were always determined that we weren't going to become one of those; and we've stuck to our word, fronting up to changes and challenges as our business has grown and developed.

We've created a clear purpose, backed up by living and breathing values, to guide us on the right way to succeed. We've put the freedom and democracy of our team at the heart of what we do. And we've taken the best available technology and used it to give our clients and their customers what they want, before they even knew they wanted it.

So, the question you're no doubt asking yourself is, did it work? Luckily (otherwise this book would be a bit on the short side), the answer is yes.

Our people-first approach has led us to deliver award-winning work with massive revenue and profit growth for our clients, whilst earning double-digit margins. And the combination of this approach with our technological insight has allowed us to create a profitable software company, CoverageBook, and a free app, AnswerThePublic, used by hundreds of thousands of people around the world.

We've also been celebrated as a UK Best Workplace™ by the Great Place to Work® Institute, with a place in the top 15 for six years running. And we've triggered the creation of a whole new category in Then Somehow's *Culture Catalyst* engagement survey[ii] – Superengaged – just for us.

We've had some bright ideas, some rubbish ideas, some totally madcap ideas. Some have led us to make fantastic decisions and taken our business to a new level. Others, frankly, have stunk.

But even the ones that didn't work out have helped get us to where we are now. And we've got a bucketload of other ideas about how to make life better, currently being nurtured in our beachside hub in Brighton, ready to launch on an unsuspecting world.

NICK OUR IDEAS AND LEARN FROM OUR MISTAKES

In the meantime, lots of people have asked us about our journey and what we've learnt along the way. And lots more have asked us why we haven't written a book about it. So, we thought it was about time we did just that.

What follows is our story. We've set it out in bite-sized chunks, with examples, ideas and tools for you to try, rather than a story to read from beginning to end. So feel free to start wherever you want (we did).

But however you approach it, we hope you'll get stuck in and enjoy reading about what we've got up to. And we also hope you'll feel inspired to nick some of our ideas, learn from our successes and avoid some of our mistakes.

We'd love to know what you think, what you agree and disagree with, and what you might use to propel your people and your business forward.

We'd also love to hear what else you've been up to, so feel free to get in touch and share your ideas with us, by emailing the team behind this book at superengaged@propellernet.co.uk

You might not believe everything we say. In fact, we're often asked, *"Where's the catch?"*

There isn't one. That's a promise.

Welcome to Propellernet.

Nikki

Nikki Gatenby, Co-Owner and Managing Director, Propellernet

www.superengaged.co.uk   www.propellernet.co.uk

SUPERENGAGED IN NUMBERS

Our staff turnover rate is just 7% (sector average: 30%).[iii]

They average just 1 day off sick a year (sector average: 5 days).[iv]

90% of them are ranked as fully engaged[v] (global average 30%).[vi]
(yes, really!)

98% of them would recommend working here.

In 10 years, we've tripled our margin, quadrupled our revenue, and generated 10 times more profit.

We love our people, they love us, and we all do better as a result.

NOTES

---

i   *Employee Engagement – The Evidence, Rayton Dodge and D'Analeze, 2012.*

ii   *Culture Catalyst was designed by Then Somehow, who invent, pilot and help deploy tools and programmes that help organisations become better places to work. www.thensomehow.com*

iii   *IPA Census data www.ipa.co.uk/news/ipa-2015-census-highlights-three-key-agency-employment-trends-#.WO3zmPnyubg*

iv   *Personnel Today Occupational Health & Wellbeing Survey 2015 www.personnelto-day.com/hr/sickness-absence-rates-and-costs-revealed-in-uks-largest-survey/*

v   *Taken from our most recent Culture Catalyst survey, designed by Then Somehow www.thensomehow.com*

vi   *Taken from a global survey quoted in The Happy Manifesto by Henry Stewart.*

TEN OF THE IDEAS WE'RE GLAD WE DIDN'T SAY NO TO

1. Putting people before profit and making wellbeing central to how we run the business, not external shareholder value (right from our bootstrapped start in a spare bedroom).

MORE IN SECTION 3

2. Limiting our size to 60 people, to force innovation in growth.

MORE IN SECTION 7

3. Being deadly serious about making dreams come true, including having our own Dreamball Machine and building our team's dreams into our business plan.

MORE IN SECTION 6

4. Funding the development of new technology products such as coveragebook.com and answerthepublic.com (without a penny of external investment) which are currently making life better for the PR industry, globally.

MORE IN SECTION 6&7

5. Having an outpost in the French Alps, so our team can enjoy an alpine experience whilst cooking up new ideas in our CEO's treehouse.

MORE IN SECTION 6

6. Raising awareness and donations for charities, with a focus on helping Brighton Housing Trust achieve their mission of no one being street homeless.
MORE IN SECTION 2

7. Putting fun on the agenda, getting our staff to try things like jet-skiing to work, learning to draw in caricature style, sculpting portraits and tuk tuk racing around Brighton.
MORE IN SECTION 3

8. Starting a housing project that helped some of our team get onto the property ladder.
MORE IN SECTION 6

9. Launching a band of renegade creative freedom fighters into the world to put on immersive theatrical events at Glastonbury and elsewhere – just for kicks.
MORE IN SECTION 6

10. Encouraging our team to go on sabbatical and helping them act on the dreams and ideas they bring back (such as collaborating with a Namibian safari company to help preserve life).
MORE IN SECTION 6

2. REWIND

Now, that all sounds very jolly and uplifting, doesn't it? But you didn't buy this book to hear us bang on about how lovely life is.

We've promised you some epic fails, and we're going to stick to our promise, however uncomfortable that may be.

When founders Jack and Jim set up Propellernet, they were clear that they wanted it to be a brilliant place to work. Having worked with various captains of industry, and been disappointed each time, they wanted to create a company that was good for all the people who worked there, rather than for faceless shareholders or unapproachable bosses.

Businesses are created by people, after all; so why shouldn't the people benefit?

PROPELLERNET 1.0

However, this kind of ambition isn't easy to work towards, let alone achieve. So, despite their enthusiasm, Propellernet wasn't always a brilliant place to work. In the early days, if we're honest, it was all a bit chaotic.

We were a small, unremarkable, search marketing agency. Just 15 of us, with no real game plan apart from holding on to enough clients to make the next payroll run, and avoiding being swallowed up by unnecessary processes. The focus on people and purpose was there, but it was latent, rather than clearly defined; building the client base was our sole priority.

We pitched a lot, and we won a lot – but we didn't really have a strategy around who we wanted to work with. And while staff retention was high, largely because people were having too much fun to look elsewhere, recruitment was tough, as we had yet to make a mark on the industry ("Propeller-who?"). We could have disappeared, and no one would have cared.

It wasn't all bad, of course; in fact, in those early days, we came up with some of the core ideas that still drive the way we work today. Such as being the first agency in the world to add PR into our technical expertise, and so earning our clients their SEO visibility, rather than just bulk-buying links. We called it Authentic Search, and it was game-changing for us and our clients.

But the problem was, we weren't making consistent, sustainable profit. In fact, some months we weren't making any profit at all. And it wasn't until we got a proper handle on the commercials that we began to understand why.

FINANCIAL FAILS

It's fair to say that we let out a few juicy words when we (belatedly) worked out that only 30% of our time was being billed to clients.

!?%$£*!

!?%$£*!

Based on the people we had in the building and the number of hours we were charging, we were only working on client projects for one and a half days a week. No, we're not joking; it's not a laughing matter. One and a half days a week. *!?*%$£*!

It's no wonder staff retention was high; we were having a smashing time filling the other three and a half days with brainstorms and blue sky thinking, which we either neglected to turn into client impact, or just gave away for free. In too many cases, our so-called brilliant ideas ended up resembling a firework display; each one sparking and kicking off with a bang, but failing to land, fizzing out as we moved on to the next one.

In our desire to avoid being slaves to profit, we had created the opposite problem. We had some great people on board who wanted to do good work, but it was only happening in pockets. We were coasting, instead of focusing on driving the business forward.

And this relaxed approach to client hours and billability was working against us in terms of being sustainable. We were breaking the golden rules of having three months' salary cover in the bank, and no client worth more than our profit margin. The whole company could quite easily have collapsed, if the perfect storm of cashflow hits had fallen against us. To be blunt, we were winging it.

STRATEGIC FAILS

But it wasn't just the finances that were in bad shape. We also didn't have sufficient clarity on what we were doing, where we were going or how we were going to get there.

Jack could sell anything, but he was the only person who could sell what we were offering, and the rest of us weren't entirely sure what that was.

It was hard for us to create a unique offer that appealed to a strong base of clients, because we hadn't got it out of Jack's head and into a proposition that we could all understand.

On top of which, our client portfolio was unbalanced, and precarious to boot. Our new business approach was to play the volume game; keeping the wolf from the door by pitching for everything we could, and taking on anyone who would have us. And while we did win a lot of new business, we ended up with a scattergun portfolio of small clients, underpinned by two massive ones.

The smaller ones were impossible to service properly, let alone nurture into long-term sustainable relationships; the large ones dominated our culture, and would have caused the business to fold if they had upped and left. Lots of agencies run on a knife edge, but ours was a bit too sharp; it felt as if we were one call away from catastrophe.

COMMUNICATION FAILS

Unfortunately, this lack of strategic vision was matched by a lack of internal communication. We had mapped out our values, and we felt they were strong, but they had never really made it off the PowerPoint and into people's hearts and minds.

Our teams didn't communicate as well as they should; people tended to be focused on their own parts of the business, without strategically connecting the dots, wasting hours replicating similar tasks. And even our newest recruits were affected. Sometimes, a team member would arrive for their first day without most of us knowing who they were; their enthusiasm somewhat squashed by the lack of welcome, desk or consensus around what they should be doing.

What's more, the lack of clarity around the numbers meant that the people on the ground didn't know what they needed to do to keep the business afloat. We didn't have a revenue forecast; it was hard for team leaders to make decisions, because they didn't have the numbers to back them up.

And bear in mind, we were a small outfit at the time, which should have made communication easy. We needed to nail it if we wanted to grow; if you can't communicate as a start-up, you don't stand a chance when you scale up.

HOW WE TURNED IT AROUND

So, it's fair to say that we weren't the business we had set out to be.

The kick-bollock-scramble of getting anything through the front door felt like we were permanently in start-up mode. The commercial pressures and lack of vision meant the founders were at odds, the consultants didn't have a strong direction to go in, and clients came and went.

Our unwillingness to be driven by process meant we didn't have time to be properly creative. We were exhausted just trying to keep up with ourselves, let alone articulate what we did, or do it properly.

But we knew we wanted to be something. We wanted to show the world that you can run a sustainable, people-first business, breaking the mould of how business can work and giving new ideas room to breathe. We had big dreams, but dreams don't come for free; if we wanted to bring them to life, we needed to bring in the money. And that meant getting some help to professionalise our business.

In short, we had some growing up to do. We just needed to knuckle down and get on with it.

What follows is how we grew up, on our journey from being unremarkable to superengaged, from mayhem to one of the best places to work in the UK. Our hope is that by sharing our story, we can help you avoid some of our mistakes, and benefit from our experiences.

Some of it has been tough; we're not without our battle scars. And we have to admit that sharing our mistakes so openly, while good for the soul, isn't great for the ego. But if we can make your life, and that of your employees, better, it will have been worth it.

TEN OF OUR ~~FALIS~~, *FAILS* WHICH WE HOPE YOU CAN LEARN FROM:

1. **Lacking clarity on our foundations.** Not articulating our purpose clearly. Thinking that just having an ambition to be a brilliant place to work was enough to make it happen. Then getting frustrated that our team didn't think "this democracy thing" was working.

MORE IN SECTION 1

2. **Putting the business at risk by failing to have a firm grasp of the numbers.** Such as not having a revenue forecast, nor knowing how much time we were billing to clients. And having two clients who were worth more than our margin and dominated our portfolio, without having the contingency of three months' worth of salaries in the bank. Doh!

MORE IN SECTION 8

3. **Confusing chaos with creativity.** Foolishly thinking process is evil, rather than understanding that it unlocks quality thinking time, creates space for deep work and ultimately releases creativity.

MORE IN SECTION 1

4. **Recruiting in haste, repenting at leisure.** Being more slapdash than strategic didn't really serve us well; neither did thinking the recruitment process stops as soon as someone accepts a job, or that anyone who had a few years of work under their belt would be a great manager.

MORE IN SECTION 4

5. **Working with unreasonable people, just for the money.** The irony being, they were profit vampires who took way more of our time and attention than they were paying for, at the expense of our other clients and our people..

MORE IN SECTION 8

6. **Missing what was right under our noses.** Deciding to spend time and money trying to grow the business internationally. Taking a madcap trip to Hong Kong to interview a potential Head of Propellernet Down Under. Then realising on the flight home that developing an innovative growth plan for the UK business was a much better idea.

MORE IN SECTION 7

7. **Placing too much value on ideas, rather than execution.** An idea means nothing unless you can bring it to life, and too many ideas can paralyse you from creating that one amazing thing. Blue skies may look pretty, but you can't do much with them.

MORE IN SECTION 7

8. **Giving up on potentially valuable new areas of our business too early.** Sometimes it's the timing or the dynamic that's wrong, not the concept. Even the most brilliant, well-planned projects don't always come up trumps first time; you need both expertise and tenacity to see them through.

MORE IN SECTION 6

9. **Getting carried away with our focus on fun.** Such as deciding to throw a party to raise money for charity, in a house we'd bought to renovate, without checking in with the council. Which could have led to a hefty fine or even time in the clink. Ooops.

MORE IN SECTION 6

10. **Being rubbish at difficult conversations.** Enough said.

3. INTRODUCTION

◀◀REWIND

Back in the day, the concept of engagement and the value it could add to a business wasn't on our radar. We certainly knew how to have a good time, our people got on, we threw some epic parties... but creating and measuring a deeper sense of engagement just hadn't occurred to us.

On the journey from starting up to growing up, we began to understand how few companies were really engaging their people, and the difference that it could make to us if we did. So, we decided to make engagement a priority – and it's one of the best things we've done to date.

> **"** *We find people with great skills and abilities who care about our mission of making the world more open and connected and who share our core values: Be open, focus on impact, and move fast.* **"**

Sheryl Sandberg, Facebook's COO and author of influential women in the workplace book Lean In.

WHAT IS ENGAGEMENT?

The world of work is in the middle of an engagement crisis.

Back in 2009, a global survey quoted in Henry Stewart's *The Happy Manifesto* reported that only 21% of staff were fully engaged at their workplace. The other 79%, presumably, were just turning up and trying to make it through the day without making mistakes.

Fast forward to 2018, and the figures haven't got much better. Glenn Elliot and Debra Covey's *Build it: The Rebel Playbook* quotes a report from global research gurus Gallup, which suggests that full engagement has only inched up to 30%. That still leaves 70% of employees, more than two thirds, who aren't properly engaged in their jobs, almost a whole decade on.

And while clearly this isn't much fun for the 70%, there's a more serious business issue at stake. How much potential and innovation are we missing out on, if so many of us are just going through the motions? And how brilliantly could we all be doing if that 70% were fully engaged too?

THE SECRET INGREDIENT THAT DRIVES SUCCESS

To start with, let's be clear about what we mean by engagement. For us, it's the degree to which an employee feels personally involved in the success of the business: eager and able to drive change, have a positive effect on

33

those around them and be the best version of themselves.

It's a physical, emotional and mental state of being, created by the work they do, the people they work with and the way their business operates. It may mean something different to you – each business has its own engagement drivers – but at Propellernet, it's driven by purpose, values, camaraderie, transparency, autonomy and trust.

But make no mistake: engagement isn't some fluffy nice-to-have, just there to keep HR happy. Engagement matters as much on a business level as a personal one, because it drives performance and profit.

Don't believe us? Then believe Gallup, whose 2016 employee engagement vs bottom line survey of 1.8 million employees[i] concluded that **business divisions scoring in the top half of reported employee engagement had nearly double the performance impact, compared with those in the bottom half.**

> A RECENT INDEPENDENT SURVEY PUT OUR ENGAGEMENT LEVELS AT A STAGGERING 90%. SO HIGH, IN FACT, THAT THEY HAD TO CREATE A NEW SUPERENGAGED CATEGORY, JUST FOR US.

And this is regardless of the organisation, industry or company; regardless of changes in the economy or even massive changes in technology. In simple terms, on a global scale, people who are engaged are natural brand ambassadors and deliver high quality outcomes. So, if performance and profit are important to you, your people are the place to start.

Of course, your own engagement figure may be well above the current 30% average. But there's a real opportunity here that savvy businesses should be taking: in a global engagement crisis, companies that nail engagement will have a sustainable competitive advantage.

SO WHAT IS SUPERENGAGEMENT THEN?

At Propellernet, staff engagement is so tangible you can almost touch it. It feeds into the vibe in our offices, the relationships with our clients and the new business ideas that we try not to say no to, as well as radiating from our engagement figures.

We don't take it for granted though, so we track our engagement levels every 12-18 months using an internal survey called *Culture Catalyst[ii]*, run by workplace culture specialists Then Somehow. And the last time we did so, we found that 90% of our team are engaged, bringing their enthusiasm, imagination, enterprise and talent into work with them every day.

This figure was so high, and so unprecedented, that Then Somehow created an extra category on the engagement scale, just for us: Superengaged. We're pretty proud of that.

Propellernet Employee Engagement Data

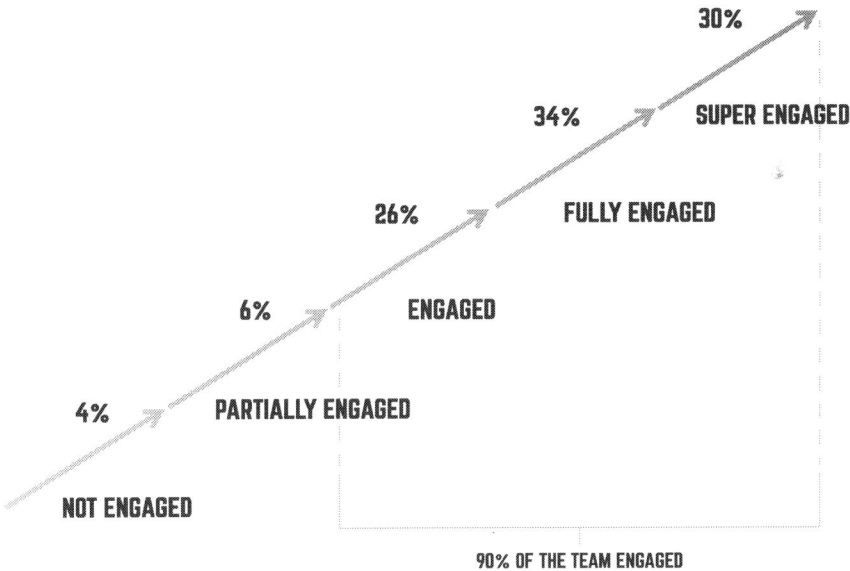

30%

34%   SUPER ENGAGED

26%   FULLY ENGAGED

6%   ENGAGED

4%   PARTIALLY ENGAGED

NOT ENGAGED

90% OF THE TEAM ENGAGED

Source: Culture Catalyst, 2017

In our experience, being superengaged means living our values of innovation, creativity, adventure, fun and wellbeing. It allows us to achieve more collectively than we could individually, as we strive to make life better.

Being superengaged also means valuing people and purpose more than profit (though remember, as Gallup proved, when you get the first two right, profit follows.) We're a people-first business, because any value we deliver to clients begins with our people, and because we believe value works both ways.

And to be specific, being superengaged means that we have tripled our margin, quadrupled our revenue and generated ten times more profit in the last decade.

So, if you're looking to drive more profit in your business, being superengaged is the answer. It's so fiendishly clever, and yet so absolutely simple, that we feel everyone should know about it.

Spreading the word starts right here.

END NOTES

---

i   *www.gallup.com/services/191489/q12-meta-analysis-report-2016.aspx*
The survey examined 49 industries across 73 countries, covering 82,000
business units and 1.8m employees.

ii   *Culture Catalyst was designed by Then Somehow, who invent, pilot and*
help deploy tools and programmes that help organisations become
better places to work. www.thensomehow.com

Section 2
AMBITION
& PURPOSE

4. OUR AMBITION

◀◀REWIND

If Propellernet had a founding ambition, it was that Jack and Jim wanted to be their own bosses. They didn't want to work for anyone else (in their words, "We weren't very good at it"). Instead, they wanted to create freedom for themselves and others to work in a different way, whilst making a decent living, having a good time and giving new ideas room to breathe.

That's how it started. Over the years the ambition has grown into something significantly more aspirational.

HOW TO BE THE BEST PLACE TO WORK IN THE WORLD

Let's kick things off by talking about our biggest ambition. And that doesn't mean trotting out a bunch of jargon-filled nothings about pushing envelopes and leveraging synergies. It's pretty simple really; we want to be the best place to work in the world.

Yep, the world. Not Brighton and Hove. Or England, the United Kingdom or even Europe. The world. Why? Because our people are worth it.

We spend a massive chunk of our lives working (almost as much as we spend sleeping, and even more than we spend watching Netflix). So, we owe it to ourselves and our people to make it as much fun as possible.

Here's the dream:

- *Picture a workplace where Monday morning is greeted with a grin, not a groan.*

- *Where people come in full of energy and raring to get started.*

- *Where they are trusted to take control of their own careers and supported to think about their futures, on company time.*

- *Where they are actively encouraged to talk about their life goals and dreams, knowing they will be taken seriously.*

- *Where engagement levels are sky-high and "Let's give it a try" is heard far more often than "No".*

- *Where they win awards for the way they operate, as well as the work they do.*

- *Where, when asked if they would recommend working there, pretty much everyone says yes.*

Wouldn't you want to work there? Could such a place even exist?

Well it does, and it's called Propellernet. It's our dream brought to life; a living, breathing example of a brilliant place to work, which we are continuing to refine and develop. Our staff love working here (how do 90% engagement and 98% recommendation rates sound?) and lots of others wish they could; having heard about what we do and how we work, people regularly send in speculative CVs[i], either their own or others'.

We're making this happen by setting our 'best in the world' ambition as our top priority. And we'd encourage you to do the same, whatever your role in your company; to build a place not just to work but to be, where people enjoy spending productive and purposeful time and are encouraged to achieve whatever mix of fun, fame and fortune is right for them.

MORE IN CHAPTER 13
So how do we do it? Well, it's not about funky bean bags, table football and free Dolly Mixtures. It's about creating an environment which encourages individual growth and personal connections, with a culture to shout about. A company in which employees have a sense of pride and investment, and which they excitedly describe as *"The best I've ever worked for"*. A place which recognises that we are human beings first and foremost, with lives on the other side of the office door, and which seeks to make these lives better in every way possible.

THE BUSINESS IMPACT OF THE HAPPINESS ADVANTAGE

And it's not just about the feel-good factor. A people-first culture has a strong commercial rationale: when people are happy, they are more creative and productive, which should positively impact every aspect of your business. Including the bottom line.

Really? Yes, really. As we've already mentioned, American research giants Gallup directly link employee engagement to company performance[ii] – no matter what industry, location, size or number of employees, and regardless of changes in the economy or technological advances. It applies to anyone and everyone.

Or to put it another way, according to Shawn Achor, researcher, Harvard lecturer and CEO of Good Think Inc.:

"If you're happy, your brain has a happiness advantage over when it is negative, neutral or stressed. Your intelligence rises, your creativity rises, your energy levels rise and business outcomes improve."

This happiness advantage is a powerful thing. Very simply, happy people do better work than miserable people. It's not rocket science – but it's surprising how rarely it's factored into the business plan.

So, by promoting individual and collective happiness at Propellernet, we've grown in ways we never could have anticipated. Back in 2010 there were 15 of us selling our services to a small number of mainly UK businesses. We are now a global company, selling our products and services to thousands of businesses in more than 3,000 cities worldwide (and counting).

And this massive growth has happened while we've deliberately chosen to be people-centred. Not in spite of it, we'd argue, but because of it.

Now, we're aware that the idea of promoting happiness flies in the face of traditional capitalism, which is too often about driving more and more profit out of fewer and fewer resources at the bottom end, whilst those at the top take the lion's share of the rewards.

But, put like that, traditional capitalism doesn't sound like much fun; and it certainly doesn't sound like a win, from either a financial or social capital returns perspective. As well as generally creating bad karma, this kind of approach can lead to real problems with staff turnoverand sickness, which are costly in terms of time, money and HR department resources.

So, start by asking yourself this. Are you and your colleagues happy or miserable? We don't mean right now, in this specific moment (everyone has good days and bad days) but generally.

More specifically, does the way your organisation operates actively promote their happiness, freeing them up to do better work? Are your colleagues productive? Do they tend to stay in the business or move on quite quickly? Are they well and present or are sickness and absence rates an issue? Essentially, could you do better?

At Propellernet, we see the benefits of our way of working every single day. We have a staff turnover rate lower than a quarter of our industry average (7% vs an industry average of 30%)[iii] and sickness rates five times lower than the national average (1.1 days vs 5.7 days)[iv].

There's no place in our organisation for trying to squeeze more out of less, or other similarly chaotic management practices. Instead, we've set out to create a positive, people-focused environment – and we're proving without any doubt that being human pays off. We may not be the best place to work in the world quite yet, but we're well on the way.

BE SUPERENGAGED

What's your ambition? Is it clearly understood, and are your people on board with it? Do you have a plan, however flexible, of how you're going to get there?

We're always up for a bit of healthy competition so if your ambition matches ours, we'd love to hear about it. Maybe we can share some ideas and spur each other along.

YOU WIN SOME, YOU LOSE SOME

Surprisingly, you may come across the odd person who doesn't want to work in a people-first business. That's fine; there are plenty of other places where they'll feel more comfortable, and it's better to be Marmite than bland and invisible. Stick to your guns and make it work for the people whose ambitions chime with yours.

FURTHER READING AND VIEWING

Sean Achor's Ted Talk:

https://www.ted.com/talks/shawn_achor_the_happy_secret_to_better_work

Blogs:

https://www.fastcompany.com/3048751/happy-employees-are-12-more-productive-at-work

https://www.forbes.com/sites/stevecooper/2012/07/30/make-more-money-by-making-your-employees-happy/#7a7d94bb5266

https://good.co/blog/workplace-happiness

5. OUR PURPOSE

◄◄ REWIND

Working to live, not living to work, was our driver
from the start. But when you're busy hustling your
start-up, and there's no money coming in, a sense
of purpose can feel like a luxury.

We'd hit on search marketing at the right moment
in time; there was a huge potential pool of clients
out there who needed our skills and we were
focused on finding and keeping them. So, while our
sense of what we stood for and how we wanted
to operate was always there, under the surface, it
took at least five years for us to give it the time and
attention it deserved.

PEOPLE + PURPOSE = MAKE LIFE BETTER

Successful, inspirational businesses aren't only profit driven. They are purpose driven too. And the way they achieve this isn't by focusing on egos, bank balances or bottom lines.

Creating a purposeful business is about doing something that matters; taking something you've dreamed about and making it real. And if you believe, as we do, that people-first businesses are the best businesses, then it should also be about keeping your people front and centre.

Our purpose draws on all of the above, and it's simple. It's to Make Life Better. For everyone. And it's so important, we put it in title case.

Now admittedly, that's rather broad. You might even say it's a bit woolly; indeed, a senior marketing professional once said to us that it was *"so vague as to be meaningless"*. If it was our proposition (what we do), he might have had a point but it's not. It's our purpose (why we do it) and it's more powerful than it might seem at first glance.

Making life better has always been part of our company culture, but we really pinned down its value to the business in 2013, after hearing rower Ben Hunt-Davis speaking about his journey from being a sporting underdog to winning Olympic gold for Team GB in the men's eight.

Ben described how, for two years in the run-up to the 2000 Sydney Olympics, he and the rest of the crew decided to change the way they worked, by asking themselves the following question before making any decision, large or small:

"Will it make the boat go faster?"

We mean ANY decision; from how they approached their diet and training to how to behave off the water and where to focus their attention. In fact, they didn't even attend the 2000 Olympics opening ceremony, because the answer to the question was no. No, we couldn't believe it either.

Yet, as history shows, it paid off. Watch it and see; it's inspiration on water.[v]

So, as we watched Ben handing his gold medal around the audience, it hit us; we too needed a mantra, a guiding principle, to help us bring our vision to life. And ours is also framed as a question:

'Will it Make Life Better?'

As we said, it's deceptively simple, but it works on many levels and guides our thinking, in everything we do:

1. Will our work Make Life Better for our clients?
2. Will our work Make Life Better for our clients' customers?
3. Will the way we work Make Life Better for each other?
4. Can we work to Make Life Better for those in our community?

And, just like Ben and his teammates, asking these questions helps us stay true to our vision, and run our business based on our people and purpose, rather than profit alone, with a clear sense of the outcome that we want to achieve. If being a brilliant place to work was an Olympic sport, we'd be aiming for a podium finish.

We'll talk more about how we answer each of these questions in the next few chapters.

BE SUPERENGAGED

Think about who inspires you; what can you learn from them? Listen to people's stories of how they've achieved success and see what you could apply to your business.

Putting commercial success to one side, what drives you? Try and articulate your purpose, in a single sentence. Then work out the questions you'll need to ask yourself to make sure you're sticking to it.

YOU WIN SOME, YOU LOSE SOME

Not everyone will buy into your purpose and that's OK; but people who are planning on staying with you will need to be onside. So be clear about what it is, particularly when you're recruiting. As Ben might have said, you'll never make the boat go faster if you're pulling in different directions.

FURTHER READING

Will it Make the Boat Go Faster? Ben Hunt-Davies, 2011

6. MAKING LIFE BETTER FOR OUR CLIENTS

◀◀REWIND

Whilst we have always been able to get clients through the door, keeping hold of them used to be much more of a challenge. Our lack of strategy meant that we took on whatever came our way, even if it wasn't a proper partnership and we were treated like any old supplier. We certainly hadn't drilled down that having fewer, well-matched clients is better than lots of random ones.

It wasn't a total disaster; we're still here, and still working with a couple of the very first clients we took on. But the realisation that relationships are everything was a big lesson for us. If you have a great relationship, your client will forgive the odd mishap – we're human after all. If you don't, there is nothing to keep you together when things get tough.

MAKE YOUR CLIENTS FEEL LIKE PART OF THE TEAM

As the musical philosopher Jessie J once said, *"It's not about the money, money, money"*. And while we do factor the finances into new business decisions, it's certainly not our top priority.

Before we take on a new client, we ask ourselves the following questions:

- Can we Make Life Better for them by working with them?

- Will we be able to deliver strong results and build lasting relationships?

- Can we help them achieve their personal, professional and/or organisational objectives, now and in the future?

It's only if we have a yes to all three that we start looking at whether the finances add up.

ORE IN
HAPTER
57

As a result, we sometimes make the seemingly radical decision not to take a potential client on, either because we're not right for them or, even more radically, because they're not right for us.

It's best to get that decision out of the way early on; allowing a client to have a consistently negative impact on our staff doesn't just affect them, it affects their ability to deliver for our other clients too. And that sounds suspiciously like making life worse.

95%
OF OUR CLIENTS SAY THEY WOULD RECOMMEND US

80%
OF OUR NEW BUSINESS COMES FROM REFERRALS

THAT'S A LOT OF SATISFIED CLIENTS

But when we get it right, and we're working together towards shared goals, it feels like they're not clients at all, but rather that we're all part of the same team.

And it works both ways. One of our clients calls us *"our secret weapon"*, another *"my growth engineers"*, and we win around 80% of new business through referrals.

THE TOP FIVE QUESTIONS ALL CLIENTS SHOULD BE ASKED

Of course, this kind of relationship doesn't happen overnight; building trust and creating honest, open working relationships is an ongoing activity. But we know the effort we put in is appreciated, as 95% of our clients say they would be happy to recommend us.

How do we know? It's simple, really; we ask them, using a set of five questions that provoke honest conversations:

1. *How's business?*

2. *What's the biggest impact we've had on your business?*

3. *What should get more of our time and attention?*

4. *If we could do one thing to make your life better, what would it be?*

5. *On a scale of 1-10, with 1 being low and 10 being high, how likely would you be to recommend us to others?*

Top marks if you've spotted that the last one is similar to the Net Promotor Score® question, considered by author Fred Reichheld to reveal how well companies will thrive in the modern world.

In his book, *The Ultimate Question*, he suggests that elevating customer metrics to the same level of importance as financial metrics is essential for business health. As he explains on his blog:

"This single question allows companies to track promoters and detractors, producing a clear measure of an organization's performance through its customers' eyes – its Net Promoter Score®.

Bain & Company analysis shows that ... companies that achieve long-term profitable growth have Net Promoter Scores two times higher than the average company. NPS leaders outgrow their competitors in most industries, by an average of 2.5 times."

Who wouldn't want some of that? We certainly do. So, we ask the questions and we really listen to the answers, sharing both the good and the bad news with our team.

When it becomes clear that things aren't working as well as they should, we all take responsibility and seize the opportunity to solve any problems, which usually has a direct impact on profitability. And when it's positive, we use it as a springboard for what we do next. Either way, the answers give our staff a deeper understanding of the client's business, which *always* means a better working relationship.

As David Ogilvy, founder of advertising agency Ogilvy & Mather, said when talking about how clients treat agencies, *"Clients get the advertising they deserve."* We think agencies get the clients they deserve, based on how they choose to work with them. And so, by focusing on making life better for our clients, it becomes better for us too.

BE SUPERENGAGED

What questions would you ask your clients to make sure you're working as a team? A good client relationship can be a gamechanger, so make sure you're asking the right questions, at the right time, and acting on the answers.

YOU WIN SOME, YOU LOSE SOME

If you don't ask how things are going, some unhappy clients won't tell you – they'll just put their business up for repitch instead. It's easy, when you're busy, to miss the fact that things could be veering towards wrong; but our five questions have saved a number of client relationships from turning sour – and in one near-miss, when we failed to communicate our achievements properly, saved a client from walking away.

FURTHER READING

Confessions of an Advertising Man, David Ogilvy, 2013

The Ultimate Question – How Net Promoter Companies Thrive in a Customer-Driven World, Fred Reichheld, 2006

WHAT IS THE NET PROMOTER SCORE®?

The Net Promoter Score®, or NPS®, is a brilliant tool which measures customer experience and predicts business growth. This proven metric now provides the core measurement for customer experience management programmes all over the world – and can be applied to any business or customer group.

You can calculate your NPS from the answers to a key question, using a 0-10 scale: *"How likely is it that you would recommend [brand] to a friend or colleague?"*

NICK THIS

Respondents are grouped as follows:

Promoters (score 9-10) are loyal enthusiasts who will keep buying and refer others, fuelling growth.

Passives (score 7-8) are satisfied but unenthusiastic customers who are vulnerable to competitive offerings.

Detractors (score 0-6) are unhappy customers who can damage your brand and impede growth through negative word-of-mouth.

Find out more at
https://www.netpromoter.com/know/

7. MAKING LIFE BETTER FOR OUR CLIENTS' CUSTOMERS

◀◀ REWIND

Billions of online searches happen every day. For search agencies who know their stuff, these searches can provide exceptionally insightful data about what customers are looking for; the kind of data that brands and advertising agencies dream of having.

But to start with, we (along with our clients and pretty much every other search agency) took a narrowly product-focused approach to how we answered those search queries. By not focusing on the other things that people ask for online, such as personal advice, practical help and a million other bits of seemingly random information, we were missing out on the good stuff.

Our approach to making life better for customers has evolved considerably since then.

MAKE YOUR CLIENTS' CUSTOMERS COME BACK FOR MORE

Like many companies in the service industry, we have two sets of clients; the brands we work with, who pay our bills, and their customers, who pay theirs. So, as well as thinking about how we can Make Life Better for our direct clients, we ask the same question about their customers too.

The more we know about the company, product or challenge, the better job we can do, so we strive to cram our briefs with as much insight as possible. This means everyone involved has a clear understanding of what motivates our clients' customers, how they behave and what they want or need.

"Well OK," you may be thinking, *"nice picture, but what if my clients don't know the answers?"* Don't panic: technology can tell you. People share what they are looking for through search engine queries and social media interaction, as well as direct customer feedback and specific research. It's all there, hiding in plain sight, for us to see.

So, by identifying what the end customers are looking for, we enable our clients to give it to them. We do this by creating insight-driven content that helps them find, choose or buy what they want or need. And we follow up by measuring how well it's worked, to inform our clients' next steps.

Of course, there's a lot more to it than that, but this isn't a book about search; we'll go into it in more detail later, but you get the general idea. The key takeout is that we listen, then we use what we've learned to engage customers, and it works.

MORE IN SECTION 8

CASE STUDY: LONG TALL SALLY

Long Tall Sally specialise in clothing and footwear for tall women, who are often unable to find well-fitting pieces elsewhere. And it's not just how the clothes are designed but also how they're displayed that's an issue for customers; in shop windows and even on Microsoft Windows, the mannequin is too often a petite size 0. This can make tall women feel invisible, as they never see themselves represented in the shopping sphere.

So, we set out to challenge the fashion industry by creating the first mannequin based on a 3D scan, using a Long Tall Sally customer, Harriet, who is six feet tall and size 14. The company committed to using the mannequin to design, display and detail their clothing, and we used the hashtag #MadeTall to share the news. And it went down a storm.

Global media coverage meant that sales increased and the return on investment for the campaign hit over 700%. But just as importantly to us, was the response of the customers, all over the world, who shared feedback such as:

"Clearly this company has real people in mind as its customers - bravo!"

*"I would love to see more realistic mannequins in all stores.
This is fantastic."*

"Yay, I'm a US size 10 and 5'11" and this makes me so happy!"

*"So refreshing to see a mannequin embody the shape of a REAL woman!
Go Harriet, may your story trigger a change in how the fashion industry
sells us clothes and bravo Long Tall Sally for making it happen."*

I think it's fair to say we made their lives better. We also made sure they'll come back for more.

To be frank, we get a real kick out of this part of our work. It's hugely satisfying to give people what they want, and of course, it makes our clients happy too. It also means we get regular trophy-shaped pats on the back from the industry, scooping up multiple awards each year.

So, by making our clients' customers' lives better, we make our clients' lives better, which makes our team's lives better. It's not just win-win, it's win-win-win.

BE SUPERENGAGED

How much do you know about your or your clients' customers? Listen to direct feedback to help shape both the product you're selling and the way you sell it. The more you engage with them, and speak their language, the better they'll respond.

Mine the search data to get other, non-verbal insights and act on what they're telling you – it can help you refine products, target marketing and hit commercial goals. If you're not sure where to look, or how to interpret online searches, try www.answerthepublic.com.

MORE IN CHAPTER 37

And if you want to know what people are enjoying and sharing right now, www.buzzsumo.com is a great place to start.

YOU WIN SOME, YOU LOSE SOME

If you're carrying out customer research, don't try to steer the people involved to say what you want to hear, and don't just latch on to the good stuff. You'll usually learn more from what they don't like than what they do.

8. MAKING LIFE BETTER FOR EACH OTHER

◀◀ REWIND

Once we'd fixed on Make Life Better as our core purpose, there was a danger that it might come across as a bit insular and self-centred; selfish, even.

We picked up pretty quickly that we needed to explain the holistic meaning of our purpose, so our team understood that it wasn't just about making life better for themselves, but also for our clients, their customers, our community and each other.

MAKE YOUR STAFF
LOVE COMING TO WORK

You may have spotted by now that one of the ways we set about making life better is by constantly asking ourselves questions. And we always make sure that the people factor is part of any decision we're trying to make:

- *Are we inspiring each other to be the best version of ourselves, whilst doing the best work of our careers?*

- *Will the decision we're about to make enable us to be more creative, innovative and productive?*

- *Are we challenging ourselves; will this shape our adventure and increase the fun factor?*

- *Are we looking after each other to maintain a strong sense of wellbeing?*

This shouldn't come as a surprise to anyone who knows us. As a people-first business, we try to see everything through a human-shaped lens. That doesn't mean we think we're perfect; on the contrary, we're well aware that things sometimes get messy and, dare we say it, a bit stressful.

Neither do we think we're the only organisation to know that the quality of our work is directly linked to how happy and engaged our people are; our heads aren't that big. But what's different about us is how seriously we take it, and how often we check back in to see whether the messiness is winning.

As we explained all the way back in Chapter 3, we run an internal survey called *Culture Catalyst*[vi] every 12-18 months, with the aim of keeping tabs on how engaged our staff are. And the most recent survey flagged up that 90% of our team are *Engaged, Wholly Engaged* or *Superengaged*.

When you compare this to the global survey quoted in Henry Stewart's *The Happy Manifesto*, in which only 21% of staff reported that they were fully engaged at their workplace, you can see why we're so chuffed (full disclosure: we mention it again later). But hopefully you can also see that we're not just bragging; we're demonstrating the impact of making life better for our team.

IT'S OFFICIAL; WE'RE A 'GREAT PLACE TO WORK'

Another external measure we are proud to have nailed is the Great Place to Work® awards. The first time we entered in 2013, we did so just to benchmark ourselves, and we were as surprised as anyone when we were named as the UK's Best Small Workplace. We've been named as one of the Best Workplaces™ every year since.

So, what can you learn from all that? Well, the Great Place to Work® Institute uses something called the Trust Index© to decide who's punching above their engagement weight. As they explain:

> *Employees need to trust their employer and their colleagues to be engaged at work. The UK Best Workplaces™ demonstrate this; on average, they score 86% on the Trust Index© compared with just 55% for average organisations. Trust and engagement are influenced by organisations' approaches to values and ethics, communication and involvement, teamwork, recognition and empowerment and accountability.*

Great Place to Work® Institute

Trust on this level doesn't just happen. It needs to be encouraged and nurtured, through working practice, regular feedback, mentoring and development. And it needs to be supported by a culture which treats making mistakes as a learning experience, and so encourages aiming high and taking risks without the fear of failure. It's an ongoing process, not just a once-a-year-for-the-appraisal add-on.

But it works; and here's the proof. Because we put our people first, and work hard at making their lives better, the sense of trust within our business is strong across all Trust Index© categories:

TRUST INDEX® SURVEY DIMENSIONS OVERVIEW

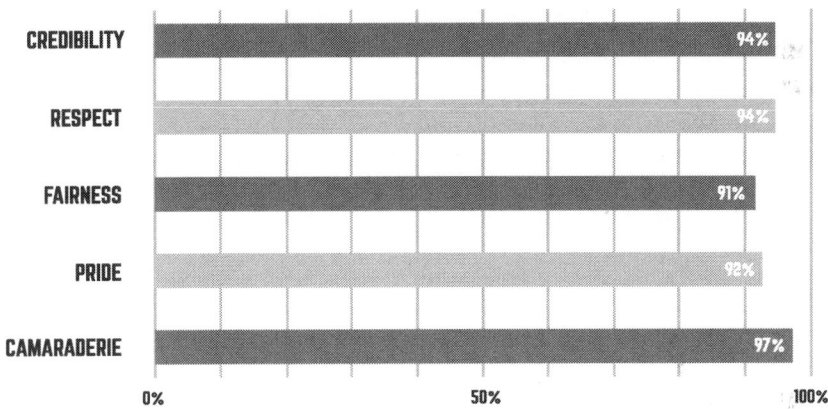

CREDIBILITY	94%
RESPECT	94%
FAIRNESS	91%
PRIDE	92%
CAMARADERIE	97%

Propellernet Trust Index© Scorecard from the Great Place to Work® Institute

We'll talk more specifically about the different ways that we make their lives better throughout this book. But for now it's just worth noting that, while being this people-focused may take a great deal of effort and enthusiasm, the impact it has is off the scale. Happy, productive people stay, and Make Life Better for others along the way.

⊕ BE SUPERENGAGED

MORE IN SECTION 9

Tools like Culture Catalyst and external awards are good ways to benchmark your engagement levels, but there's no substitute for talking directly to your team. Feel free to pinch or adapt these questions for your own company, and make sure you ask them regularly.

NICK THIS

1. Do your leaders provide a clear view of your mission and goals?

2. Does everyone have the right tools to do their job well?

3. Is everyone treated as a full member of the company, regardless of their position?

4. Are you all trusted to do a good job without being micromanaged?

5. Are people willing to go the extra mile to get the job done?

6. Based on experience, would you say your company is a brilliant place to work, and would you recommend it to others?

👍 YOU WIN SOME, YOU LOSE SOME

We love the fact that 90% of our people are engaged, but that still means that 10% aren't. That number has got smaller as we've taken on feedback and made changes to our business, but we're not giving up until it hits zero. So, we'll keep asking questions, keep identifying any issues, and keep doing something about them.

We include everyone in our cultural surveys, even if they've just started or are about to leave. Don't leave these people out; first impressions and exit insights are a vital piece of the jigsaw, and you'll be surprised by what they teach you.

9. MAKING LIFE BETTER FOR OUR COMMUNITY

◀◀ REWIND

We like to think of ourselves as a generous bunch, so community work was always going to be part of the plan. But in the early days, we didn't do it very well; partly because our finances were too precarious, and partly because, instead of a having a CSR strategy, we just hopped between one-off events.

As a result, anything we did do didn't have much impact. And when asked whether they felt good about the way we contribute to the community, as part of the 2015 Great Place to Work® survey, only 60% said yes (our lowest ever score on this kind of question).

Since then, we've become much more focused. Our impact has grown exponentially, and our scores have gone up to match.

GIVE SOMETHING BACK AND MAKE LIFE BETTER ALL ROUND

If you're really, truly focused on trying to Make Life Better, then why stop at the people you know? Who else could you make a difference to by being people-focused? And what might that mean for your own team?

A little while ago, we took the collective decision to regularly donate time and experience to people or businesses in our local community. We've done one-off events such as running marathons or cycling to Amsterdam to raise money for charity; we also offer educational, developmental and business support to help others build more sustainable futures.

Part of our motivation was our feeling that our city, and the spirit of community that exists here, have really helped us to thrive. Brighton is fast becoming a digital hub and we've benefitted from that as much as we have contributed to it. That's why, despite being asked on a regular basis, we're not opening a London office.

And although the starting point was to help our city thrive in return, we've learned that our parents were right and it really *is* as good to give as to receive, with 94% of our team now saying that they feel good about the ways we contribute to the community.

We do so in a number of different ways; too many to include here. So instead of giving you a long list, here's a snapshot of three of the projects we've brought to life in the last couple of years.

1. BRIGHTON HOUSING TRUST

We chose BHT as our focus charity after realising that the homelessness problem in Brighton seemed to be growing in front of our eyes. Our work with them includes awareness-building and fundraising, all in support of their aim to have no one street homeless in Brighton by 2020.

Combating Homelessness
Creating Opportunities
Promoting Change

MORE IN CHAPTER 38

One of our most recent projects was an awareness campaign to highlight how homeless people often feel ignored by society, telling inspirational stories of those who the charity has supported back from extreme poverty.

2. BEYOND YOUR HORIZON

We always take part in the Brighton Digital Festival, seeing it as an opportunity to connect with and support local people with all things tech. But for the last two years, we've also used it to support and inspire children from some of the most deprived parts of the city.

Staggered to learn that one in three children in Brighton are living in poverty, and to hear that many of the city's children have never even been to the seaside[vii], we took pupils from three primary schools down to the beach and from there on a VR tour to Rio de Janerio via Paris, Mont Blanc, Holland and South East Asia.

As well as expanding their view of the physical world, we hope to have broadened their personal horizons and inspired some tech stars of the future.

3. TRUST FOR DEVELOPING COMMUNITIES

When we found out about the Trust for Developing Communities (TDC) and the brilliant work they do in changing the lives of children in hardship, we wanted to do more than just support them. So I became a Trustee, and got busy trying to help them increase their profile.

Realising that they are very much a 360° charity, who are good at looking at the big picture, and noting that the British Airways i360 was in the process of going up in Brighton, I persuaded BAi360 to let us pitch for TDC to become their charity partner.

We were rank outsiders; but we won it all the same, and the resulting partnership has raised awareness of TDC across the city. This has encouraged our business community to support the charity as well as helping raise funds to improve the sustainability of local community projects over time.

One of the first things to happen was the auctioning of the hoardings that had been placed around the BAi360 while it was being built. They had been (legally) spray-painted by Aroe Musk, an influential local graffiti artist, and so had the potential to raise quite a bit of money. The proceeds went towards paying for community street workers, who identify vulnerable youngsters and help them come off the streets and get care and support from the right places.

It's fair to say that this way of living Make Life Better has been the most challenging of them all. It may not be something that you'll be taught about on your MBA, or experience in your average company; we've had to learn it on the hop.

But in addition to delivering real change for the people we're supporting, our community work ranks as some of the most rewarding work we've done to date – and we wouldn't be us without it.

BE SUPERENGAGED

Who or what could you support in your local area? What expertise, facilities or business skills could you share? Remember, it's not just about raising money, although if you can motivate your team to do some fundraising, it can be a great bonding exercise.

In our experience, teams see this kind of work as a bonus, not a chore; but expecting them to do it all in their own time could quickly deplete their goodwill. Make sure you make time in the working week for your pro bono activities.

YOU WIN SOME, YOU LOSE SOME

We haven't always got it right. When we first started working on community projects, we were so enthusiastic about the potential of our plans that we took too many on, and spread ourselves too thinly.

We then chose to make Brighton Housing Trust our focus charity, which has allowed us to deliver profound, demonstrable change. So much so that our colleague Dan was recently crowned BHT Fundraiser of the Year for his dedication to the charity and the amount of money he's raised.

10. OUR LONG-TERM STRATEGY

◀◀ REWIND

Ten years ago, a sale was very much on our radar; every agency was on the same path. Start up. Grow up. Grow more. Look for a buyer and a fancy multiple. Sell out and live on a yacht in the Caribbean for the rest of your life.

But as time went on, we clocked that when something sounds too good to be true, it usually is. We realised that we're not very good at being told what to do, and that we couldn't face dancing to the beat of somebody else's drum. Even the thought of being handcuffed into an earn-out made us all shudder.

So, we decided to take a different path. It's not right for everyone, but it's right for us.

WE ARE NOT FOR SALE

"What's your exit strategy?" We get asked that a lot.

"Would you consider selling?" We get asked that a lot too.

But we're not for sale and we don't have an exit strategy – we have a rolling business model instead.

It's rolling in that it's constantly moving and changing, to create sustainable success in a constantly moving and changing world. We innovate and take a different path when exciting new possibilities and challenges pop up, not because a spreadsheet tells us to.

It's this kind of thinking that made us one of the first agencies in the world to incorporate PR into search marketing (and now, wouldn't you know it, everyone's having a go). It enabled us to free up some of our best people to create an innovative new product, www.coveragebook.com, which is currently making life better for PR people all over the world.

MORE IN CHAPTER 56

MORE IN CHAPTER 47

It's also the reason our personal dreams are part of our collective business plan. And why that plan is nothing like any business plan you've ever seen; in a rare correct use of the word, it's unique.

MORE IN SECTION 6

All of this, this original thinking, planning and doing, all stems from the fact that we want to Make Life Better, not just sell stuff. And we know that the best way to do that is to stay true to ourselves, by staying independent. We're not in the business of selling off our time, our people and our souls. We don't lock down, rinse and repeat, or spend our lives chasing a big payout. We evolve, and evolve, and evolve.

And despite evolving, and growing (but not too big, just 60 precious seats), we've held onto our core principle of putting people first in the knowledge that the money will come, rather than making money the be-all and end-all. Our people are our biggest assets; but unlike other pieces of kit, they appreciate over time, by developing their skills, their relationships, their knowledge and their innovative genius.

MORE IN CHAPTER 46

SELLING UP = SELLING OUT = SELLING YOUR SOUL

The blueprint for marketing agencies is to groom themselves for a buyout from a multinational corporation, eking out as much profit as possible from the company in the run-up to the sale, and trimming off any fat (aka people) to get the highest valuation possible.

If this was our plan, we'd have to spend all our time focusing on the numbers, ignoring the needs of the business today for the promise of a cash prize tomorrow. Our first question wouldn't be *"Will it Make Life Better?"*; it would be *"Will it make the P&L look better?"*

And any company who bought us out would rightly have an opinion on how the business is run – but that feels like a recipe for disaster. Culture clashes are common in these situations; given the strength of our own culture, it would make *Game of Thrones* seem like a game of cops and robbers. We'd love to see what an Alan Sugar-a-like would have to say about 'Dream Budget Accrual' appearing on the P&L each month, for a start.

MORE IN
SECTION 6

As everyone who's worked in a pressure-cooker business knows, it's hard to innovate when you're a slave to aggressive short-term sales figures, and it's hard to think freely when you're afraid. That's probably why some big businesses form innovation units, which aren't under the cosh from broader commercial pressures[viii].

At Propellernet, our whole business is an innovation unit. We love what we do, so we're happy to pour our time, our energy (and, where necessary, our money) into it. And we never want to lose our people-first approach or turn into a place where people are stuck on a treadmill, counting the years until they can retire. Instead, we bring the fun forward, by including the kind of things people save until retirement in our rolling business plan.[ix]

When we talk about this, we're often met with sceptism, and told that everyone has a price. And while that may be true, we can say with absolute confidence that selling up and cashing out is not on our radar. As we've said, we can't imagine dancing to the beat of someone else's drum. We think it would knock the soul out of our organisation, and essentially Make Life Worse.

Nile Rodgers, a man who knows a lot about soul, talked about his love of music at the 2015 Amsterdam Music Festival. He said that although his guitar, the Hitmaker, has played on a billion pounds worth of records, he didn't set out to make money – he set out to make great music and everything else followed. The purpose, the soul of his music, was in the stories he told, not the royalties he earned. Without soul, there would be no music; or as he put it:

"Music without soul is just noise."

We couldn't agree more. And if music without soul is just noise, business without purpose is just admin.

We don't want a life of noisy, soulless admin.

So no, we don't have an exit strategy. And no, we're not for sale.

BE SUPERENGAGED

What if you had no exit strategy? Whether you are a business owner or not, imagine for a moment that leaving or retiring wasn't an option. What would you do differently? What would you stop worrying about? What would you focus your attention on? How would you make your time at work as enjoyable and fulfilling as possible – for you and for others?

YOU WIN SOME, YOU LOSE SOME

Don't be restricted to traditional blueprints. Look at your business, your purpose and your culture and create a pathway that works for you.

When you go off-piste, it can be scary for some – so you need to lead from the front. Make sure you have a united attitude to risk at board level, and invest the time in taking people with you.

TL;DR

11. FOR THE SKIM READERS AMONG YOU...

Make Life Better isn't just a whizzy phrase, nor is it an empty promise. It's hard-wired into the DNA of Propellernet, and it runs through everything we do, from how we work with our clients to how we treat our people and others. And it's a big part of the reason why we won't put the business up for sale.

It's about putting people before profit and setting out to create an environment in which people have the time, space and freedom to achieve and thrive. It's about asking the right questions, listening carefully to the answers, and acting on what we learn.

Having such a clear purpose allows us to make sound, coherent decisions for the good of our organisation, rather than focusing on short-term business gains. And it's allowed us to find and keep some absolutely brilliant people who make coming to work a pleasure.

We don't just believe it, we know it; if you put people first, the money will come. If you put money first, people will leave. So, for the more hard-nosed readers among you, it adds up commercially too.

END NOTES

i   *We always try to reply to people who send in CVs – and it pays off. Once, when I was at a Talent Summit with over 100 other agency people, one of the competitor recruiters came over to me and said, "Oh I've always wanted to meet you. I applied for a job with Propellernet in 2015 and you sent me the kindest, most personal response. Even though I didn't even get an interview, I'm always raving about Propellernet."*

ii   *www.gallup.com/services/191489/q12-meta-analysis-report-2016.aspx*

iii   *IPA Census data www.ipa.co.uk/news/ipa-2015-census-highlights-three-key-agency-employment-trends-#.WO3zmPnyubg (You'll need a log in)*

iv   *Personnel Today Occupational Health and Wellbeing Survey, 2015 www.personneltoday.com/hr/sickness-absence-rates-and-costs-revealed-in-uks-largest-survey/*

v   *Sydney Olympics 2000, GB men's eight winning gold https://www.youtube.com/watch?v=Wo12muzAHKk*

vi   *Culture Catalyst was designed by Then Somehow, who invent, pilot and help deploy tools and programmes that help organisations become better places to work. www.thensomehow.com*

vii   *www.theargus.co.uk/news/9787829.Deprived_children_in_Brighton_who_have_never_been_to_the_beach*

viii   *Many big businesses want to be nimble and fast-acting, yearning for the speed of innovation of their smaller counterparts. Being a big enterprise can stifle innovation, so they try to encourage it by creating micro-cultures within the business which operate with more freedom. For example, Unilever are bringing the outside in with their 'Open Innovation' approach, in which they invite applications from anywhere in order to deliver progress. Unilever bring the commercial clout, reach and customers to the innovation and ideas of any applicant; in their words "...be they established suppliers, start-ups, academics, designers, individual inventors – anyone with a practical innovation that can help us meet our challenges". www.unilever.co.uk/about/innovation/open-innovation/*

ix   *Volunteering in the community; brewing our own beer; going on safari; making time for ourselves and living out our dreams: these are all "When I retire" kind of projects that we're enjoying right now.*

Section 3
VALUES

12. VALUES: INTRODUCTION

◄◄ REWIND

Having values wasn't a priority when we started out. Having fun, cutting deals, signing contracts and generally scrambling around like start-ups do, didn't leave much time to focus on what we stood for. And even once we had mapped out our values, they tended to only make guest appearances in PowerPoint presentations or induction folders, rather than being a living, breathing part of our organisation.

Everything changed when we started to explore the value of values, and how they could cement our company into something more than a soulless cycle of clients in, work out. We certainly haven't regretted it.

BRING YOUR VALUES OUT TO PLAY

Values? How very old-school. Why would a 21st century business need those?

Well, if your purpose is what you're working towards, your values are how you'll get there. Each one should be carefully chosen to create a strong cultural force that will drive your organisation in the right direction.

Values communicate what is important, give you principles to align to, help you focus on your end goal and inspire people to act in the right way. They also make you stand out, by setting out what you stand for.

The thing is, they have to be real, and they have to be true.

People have well-honed bullshit detectors these days. We are bombarded with thousands of sales messages every waking hour and are used to questioning the authenticity or otherwise of a brand, its mission and values. Most of us understand the power of fake news (bad!) and know that just because someone says something, it doesn't make it true.

The same goes for the workplace. If the only time people encounter your company's values is on a PowerPoint slide at their induction, they're never going to stick. Values must be lived to be believed, and if they aren't, they'll simply fade away. Along with the motivation and engagement of the people you've worked so hard to recruit.

What a waste – when the impact of living your values to the full can be so, well, valuable.

Our values are at the heart of our culture at Propellernet, and as we have evolved and grown, they've evolved with us, shaping the way we work. We make them real by hiring people who share them, and by taking every opportunity to reinforce them. We don't make our staff stand on chairs and recite them on a Monday morning (yeuch), but we do expect them to embrace our values and build them into everything they do.

MORE IN CHAPTERS 18 & 23

THE FIVE WORDS WE LIVE BY:

INNOVATION

CREATIVITY

ADVENTURE

FUN

WELLBEING

So, what are your values?

Here are ours, and why we chose them:

INNOVATION

We value **innovation** as a way of embracing the ever-changing world around us and using it to our advantage, allowing us to reinvent what we do as a business and keep working towards a better tomorrow.

CREATIVITY

We value **creativity** because it's an irresistible, life-enhancing human force. Music, design, story, colour, film, comedy, dance – these all bring magic into our lives and ideas into our heads. Without them, life would be hollow, and our business would risk becoming boringly unsuccessful.

ADVENTURE

We value **adventure** because fear of the unknown stifles innovation and creativity, leading to a cycle of diminishing returns. But by facing change or challenges with a spirit of adventure, we can turn them into opportunities.

FUN

We value **fun** because we are more creative when we are in a playful state. A culture of fear wastes energy by focusing the mind on negativity, whereas laughing, smiling, playing and having a good time allow us to build stronger working relationships and improve our performance, as well as making life better for everyone.

WELLBEING

We value **wellbeing** because it provides us with the inner strength to fulfil our potential. If our mind and body are healthy, and our relationships are harmonious, we have rock-solid foundations from which to come up with ideas that might just set the world on fire.

We've deliberately chosen values that share some common themes, as we believe they are stronger and more durable as a result. Read on to find out how we incorporate them into our everyday working lives.

BE SUPERENGAGED

If you were writing a brutally simple job ad for your company, for sharing only with your friends, with the truth of how you feel about work at its core, what would it say?

Use this as a platform to think about what you stand for, and how you could verbalise this into core values that your employees can understand. Then make sure you bring them to life and evolve them along with your business.

YOU WIN SOME, YOU LOSE SOME

Too many businesses use the same bland words to describe themselves; don't fall into that trap. Your values should be distinctive and make you stand out. And don't keep adding new ones as you evolve; too many can mean too shallow a focus on each.

MORE IN THE NEXT FEW CHAPTERS

Build your values into every stage of your working practice. Ours live and breathe in our recruitment, our onboarding and throughout the employee experience, from personal development conversations to visual expression on the walls of the agency. If values are to be valued, they need to be brought out to play.

FURTHER READING

www.propellernet.co.uk/our-blog/2015/9/20/ extreme-innovations-in-employee-welfare

www.propellernet.co.uk/our-blog/2015/9/20/ our-health-is-our-wealth

13. THE VALUE OF INNOVATION

◀◀REWIND

We value innovation as a way of embracing the ever-changing world around us and using it to our advantage, allowing us to reinvent what we do as a business and keep working towards a better tomorrow.

NO STRAITJACKET REQUIRED

The business world is developing at lightning speed, which means we all need to innovate just to stay ahead. And innovation is particularly powerful when wielded by companies who invest in their people.

But there's a big heap of barriers that can get in the way of innovation if you're not careful. Here are some of our (least) favourites:

- Worrying about what you might lose if you try something new.
- Settling for what's worked before, hoping it'll work again.
- Writing off a new development by thinking *"It'll never last"*.

At Propellernet, we've recognised these barriers, and tackled them head on, ensuring that innovation runs through our business like the words in a stick of our local rock. Here's how:

Looking ahead, not behind
It's all too easy to get sucked into the *"This is how we do it, because this is how we've always done it"* way of working. Top tip: Don't!

It makes you too easy to commoditise, and too tempting to imitate. And that can trigger a race to the bottom, with businesses rivalling each other to cut costs, throwing their values and people-focus out along the way. Instead, we deliberately and continually evolve and improve what we offer.

Being brave
Once a company becomes successful, and its leaders feel they have something to lose, risk-taking can feel too, errrm, risky; that's a one-way ticket to stagnation.

Instead, we accept that we don't know exactly what our business will look like three years from now, and that we will need to step out into the unknown from time to time if we want to remain compelling. It helps that we have built a culture in which making mistakes is seen as a way of learning, not failing.

MORE IN CHAPTER 35

Planning to improvise

That said, we're not totally free-wheeling it. We have a rolling business plan, and a damn good one. But it's not a rigid, straitjacket of a plan; it's got flexibility built in.

There are so many things beyond our control – market conditions, our competition, broader economic, social and cultural forces – and we need to be ready to respond. So we've made space in the plan for capitalising on new opportunities when they come up, because that's what we do.

Keeping our ears to the ground

We can all think of former giants who failed to keep up with the rest of the world and fell by the wayside as a result. Popped to Blockbusters to rent a DVD recently? No, us neither. Kodak, MySpace, Woolworths, Borders... the list of companies who didn't adapt to change or embrace new technology is tragically long.

We're not keen to join that list, so we actively ask our team to keep us up to speed and tell us what they would do to make the business more successful (and, importantly, listen to the answers). We build in time for making life better and regularly develop new products and services as a result, some of which have gone global.

MORE IN CHAPTERS 28 & 47

And as a result of all the above, we have maintained our uniqueness and held on to our talented people, while continuing to make a healthy profit.

When people apply to join Propellernet, they often ask, *"Where is the company going?"* It's a great question, but they don't always like the answer, which is that our goal is not a fixed point. And whereas some embrace the intellectual freedom that this brings, others find the sense of uncertainty too great, and can't re-wire their thinking to be part of our journey.

But when people do come on board, and embrace our sense of innovation and the places it takes us, they do so with an enthusiasm that surprises even us sometimes. Like the time our colleague Sam posted on LinkedIn to encourage his connections to come and join us:

Sam Zindel
Insight Director at Propellernet
2d

Open invite to come to Brighton and be our Head of PR!! Seriously exciting time to join the best company I've ever worked for. If you're even 1% intrigued give me a nudge and let's go for a beer/coffee and I'll tell you more about the film we're making, the safari company we're partnered with, the craft beer company we co-own, our playground in the Alps and how we got booked to play Glastonbury this year. Oh and our shit-hot digital marketing campaigns that won us a PR Moment award a couple of weeks ago, and the PR product business we launched (CoverageBook)... and our office next to the sea. Ok. I'll stop – but seriously...get in touch.

| propellernet | Head of PR |
| make life better™ | propellernet.co.uk |

This is just a snapshot of what it feels like to work in a place where innovation is the air we breathe. It allows us to build growth through uncharted territory, to embrace change through improvisation. It's quite an experience and is sometimes a bumpy ride; you could never describe it as dull. We wouldn't have it any other way.

BE SUPERENGAGED

What barriers are holding you back from innovating? You need to identify them before you can overcome them. That means taking a good hard look at the way you make decisions and assess risks.

Having an open dialogue with your staff about new ideas and developments is critical if you're going to stay ahead of the pace of change. Keep asking the questions that will help you answer the big one: "What's next?"

YOU WIN SOME, YOU LOSE SOME

It can be tempting to think that innovation, by definition, requires a massive game-changer of an idea, delivered on a huge scale. That's certainly how our team used to approach it.

But in fact, everyday innovation can be as powerful, such as changing the format of a report, or taking a different approach to presenting creative, and so making it easier for clients to understand and make decisions.

NICK THIS

One of the ways we try and capture this kind of low-level innovation is by asking ourselves four questions at the end of every project:

- *What went well?*
- *What could have gone better?*
- *What did we learn?*
- *What still puzzles us?*

The answers often lead to small but perfectly formed innovations in how we go about our business.

FURTHER READING

Make Your Mark, 99U, 2014

14. THE VALUE OF CREATIVITY

◀◀REWIND

We value creativity because it's an irresistible, life-enhancing human force. Music, design, story, colour, film, comedy, dance – these all bring magic into our lives and ideas into our heads. Without them, life would be hollow, and our business would risk becoming boringly unsuccessful.

THINKING DIFFERENTLY EN ROUTE TO THE FUTURE

Our second core value is closely linked to our first; creativity and innovation make a great team. Together, they form the backbone of the work we deliver for clients and the way we operate as a business, as we visualise and bring to life our innovations for the future.

We challenge every member of our team to be a creative thinker, and sometimes they surprise themselves with how creative they can be.

Now, this might sound a bit airy-fairy for a business with its roots in technical, data-driven search. But in fact, data and creativity go hand in hand. The most brilliant idea targeted at the wrong people would be destined to fail; but combined with accurate data, it can lead to even more powerful innovation.

And the awards we've won from creative industry bodies such as The Drum are proof that we've cracked it.

Creativity is particularly important when you work in a medium that evolves every day. Millions of new conversations happen each moment online; new content is created, new ideas gather momentum.

To keep up, Google changes its search algorithm around 500-600 times a year, which is more than once every 24 hours. It takes some highly creative thinking to beat that.

And true creativity isn't about being good with pictures or words. It's a conceptual, ideas-based world, driven by connecting unconnected things, and thinking differently. It's the realm of our imaginations and we all have an innate ability to play here. We just need to feel free to do so.

CREATIVITY NEEDS SPACE AND TIME TO DEVELOP

So how do we give our people that freedom? Well, it doesn't happen by accident. It's hard to be creative when you're sitting at the same desk looking at the same things, with a big deadline hanging over your head, even in an office as lovely as ours. So, we create space and time, physically and metaphorically, to free up creative thought.

MORE IN CHAPTER 48

One way we do this is through the Propellernet Academy, which we started back in 2012 as a forum for sharing our skills with each other. Like everything at Propellernet, it's evolved and grown over the years, and is now a forum for being curious and exploring new ideas, concepts or skills – critically, on company time and money. Learning a new talent, a language, an instrument, to drive... all of these things create new connections in our brains[i] and expand our horizons. So, we expect our teams to give their creative minds a workout, as part of their working week.

Even more radically, we've introduced Propel Days, to support our staff's career development and further encourage innovative thinking. Every member of our staff can take a day a month, 12 days a year, to go and *propel themselves forward*. Yes, 12 extra days a year, on top of a generous holiday entitlement, for their own personal development; that's how seriously we take it.

MORE IN CHAPTER 28

Last year, this added up to 600 Propel Days taken across our team. That's a lot of time and space safeguarded for creativity and innovation, and we've all benefitted from the results.

Of course, there are logistical challenges to making sure staff take their Propel Days, and they do have to slot in around client work. We also know from feedback from the team that it can feel emotionally challenging to take a whole day, just for themselves. But on every level, it's absolutely worth it.

As Dan Pink said in his book, *A Whole New Mind*, if your job can be replaced by a computer, a robot or outsourced to a different cost base, you need to think differently. To paraphrase his thinking:

"Artificial intelligence is here; code, contracts and number crunching may well fall into the realm of the robots. The future belongs to creators, empathisers, meaning makers, artists, inventors, designers, storytellers, care givers, big picture thinkers. Creativity is essential for survival if you don't want to become a commodity in the near future."

Big picture thinkers? Check. Creators and inventors? Check. The future belongs to our team, and we're giving them the tools they'll need to thrive when they get there.

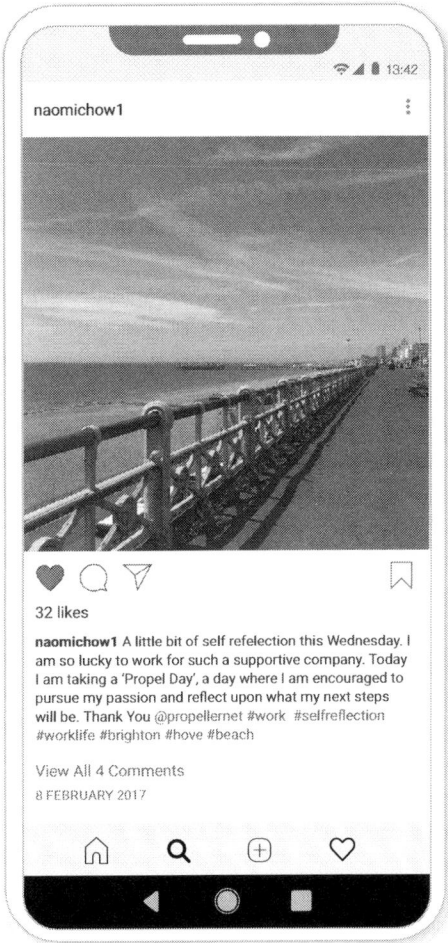

WHEN YOU MAKE IT INTO YOUR TEAM'S SOCIAL MEDIA SPACE, YOU KNOW YOU'VE CREATED ROOM FOR THEM TO BREATHE.

BE SUPERENGAGED

How much would you be prepared to invest in your staff's personal development? If 12 days a year isn't yet achievable, what is? Encouraging them to spend time away from their core roles may have a financial impact, but the return on your investment in terms of loyalty will be high – and the gains to your business from what they learn even higher.

YOU WIN SOME, YOU LOSE SOME

Sometimes encouragement isn't enough; people need to be empowered to try something new. In our case, while the idea of Propel Days floated everyone's boat, only a quarter of them were taken in the first year. A change of approach has led to a much higher uptake.

MORE IN ← CHPATER 28

FURTHER READING

Whatever You Think, Think the Opposite, Paul Arden, 2006

TODAY'S CREATIVITY IS TOMORROW'S REALITY

None of us know what the future holds – but the movie makers are pretty good at coming up with creative ideas which then become reality:

- In 2002's *Minority Report*, Steven Spielberg's vision of the year 2054 contained seemingly radical ideas that are mainstream today, more than 35 years ahead of schedule. Gesture control and touch sensitivity, anyone?

- In 1985, *Back to the Future* showcased hoverboards in the film's future version of 2015. Lexus put themselves up for the challenge of creating them in time for the real world catching up, followed by many others, including Zapata Racing with their Flyboard 2016[ii].

- Looking ahead from our present, the 2015 fantasy *Ex Machina* gave a terrifying prediction of how artificial intelligence could penetrate our homes in the future. Think it's never going to happen? How many of us have welcomed Alexa into our homes?

And it's not just the creative industries that are showing creative, innovative thinking. Pharma companies are radically transforming the way medicines are created:

- 3D printing of pharmaceuticals sounds like something space-age, but it's happening today. Spritam, an epilepsy seizure control, is the first FDA approved drug to be available for printing at home.

- Companies like Organovo are already bio-printing functional human tissue – blood vessels, heart valves, skin, bionic ears – right now.

When mobile phones were first introduced, who would have predicted that one day they would evolve into mini computers, and that we'd become almost physically attached to them? And what's the next step in the development of phone technology? Micro-chip implants? It's not as far-fetched as you'd think; in fact, it's already happening[iii].

The pace of change and the inventiveness of creative thinkers brings new ideas, new products, new services to market every day. We refuse to be left behind.

15. THE VALUE OF ADVENTURE

◀◀ REWIND

We value adventure because fear of the unknown
stifles innovation and creativity, leading to a cycle
of diminishing returns. But by facing change or
challenges with a spirit of adventure, we can turn
them into opportunities.

SETTING THE DIAL AT ADVENTUROUS

This one certainly raises a few eyebrows, especially when we ask it at interviews (which is why we prep our candidates beforehand). But it's one of the most important questions we ask:

> *"Do you have a sense of adventure? Are you happy to go where others may fear to tread? Tell us about your adventurous side."*

It's vital for our business that we are flexible and nimble; it's how we stay ahead, and it requires an adventurous streak. That's why it has a place at our recruitment table: the people who respond with enthusiasm are the ones we know will fit right in.

MORE IN CHAPTER 23

ADVENTUROUS PEOPLE THINK, WORK AND ACT BOLDLY

Our clients pose us challenging deadlines; that's just how it is in marketing. Many also think innovation should be part of every project (we couldn't agree more). And they often need us to work closely with their other agencies, which can be combative at times, though we work hard to make those relationships as collaborative and fulfilling as possible. All of which requires a certain boldness.

What's more, people who set themselves interesting challenges and embrace new experiences are less likely to say *"No"* and more likely to say *"Let's give it a try"* if, for example, we suggest they hop on a plane and come out to our alpine playhouse to open up new ways of thinking and connecting.

MORE IN CHAPTER 29

So, by embracing adventure, we can be bolder in the way we work with our clients and their partners, bolder in the way we think, and bolder about the way we push the boundaries. All of which helps drive high impact results.

MORE IN CHAPTER 6

That's not to say we want to employ a bunch of foolhardy risktakers. We're not anarchists. But something we all have in common is that we're not afraid of the unknown, and we approach the new with total and utter enthusiasm.

For some, this is just too far out of their comfort zone – and it's good to find that out early, for everyone's sake. It's our responsibility to manage expectations around our values, and that's why we talk about them from the off.

But for those whose eyes light up when we ask the question, it allows us to engage them right from the start of their Propellernet journey. It's the first step to bringing their whole selves to work, to being more creative and productive; the first step to being superengaged.

BE SUPERENGAGED

How adventurous do you want to be? Not all businesses or leadership teams would feel comfortable with the way we approach this value. That's OK – the important thing is to set your dial in the right place for you and make sure everyone is on board.

What unusual questions could you ask at interview to assess how well a candidate will fit in with your company's values? Don't be afraid to veer from the typical script. If you have a strong company culture, you'll need your staff to be onside with it if you want to superengage them.

YOU WIN SOME, YOU LOSE SOME

One thing we've learned is how important it is to discuss values like adventure during the recruitment process; it means the people you bring on board are up for the challenge. So, for example, one team-member who hadn't been through that process viewed our inspiration-building trip to the Alps as wasted time, which could be better spent selling to clients. It's not that he was wrong, but he was wrong for us.

16. THE VALUE OF FUN

◀◀REWIND

We value fun because we are more creative when we are in a playful state. A culture of fear wastes energy by focusing the mind on negativity, whereas laughing, smiling, playing and having a good time allows us to build stronger working relationships and improves our performance, as well as making life better for everyone.

> *Laughter... releases endorphins that are already in there... Laughter is such a social thing, it's who we are, it pre-dates language – it's a gift.*

Jimmy Carr, stand-up comedian, actor, writer and radio & TV presenter.

LETTING THE GOOD TIMES ROLL

This is the one where leaders with a more traditional business model start thinking we've lost the plot. Fun? FUN? How does that work with the bottom line?

Well, right back atcha, people! We've developed our formula for profitability and it factors in time for fun. Or, as Stephen Hawking might have said, if he'd come and hung out with us:

HAVING FUN = DOPAMINE HIT = HIGHER PERFORMANCE.

Laughter is an important part of our working day, and not just because we like it; there's a reason it's called the best medicine.[iv] It has been proved to decrease stress hormones, increase immune cells and infection fighting antibodies, and so in turn improve our resistance to disease. (Remember how our sickness rates are a fifth of the industry average?)

It also triggers endorphins, which boost drive, focus and concentration and, in big doses, inspire optimism and contentment. And it shows; in our team's feedback from the most recent Great Place to Work® survey:

✴ **98% said Propellernet is a fun place to work**
98% said they would recommend working here to others

Either the other 2% have exceptionally high standards, or we've not hit the right formula of enjoyment for them yet – we'll have fun trying. And if they decide they'd prefer to spread their wings and find fun in the next stage of their career, we're committed to helping them make that happen too.

→ MORE IN CHAPTER 32

PUT YOUR MONEY WHERE YOUR SMILE IS

But as with everything, creating a sense of fun doesn't happen by chance; we plan for it, and budget for it. 5% of our profits go into our Fun & Wellbeing Fund, which is democratically run by our Fun Ministers (each in post for a maximum of six months, so we all get to have a go). Their brief is to create experiences and interactions across the team that wouldn't otherwise happen.

Here's some of the organised fun we've said yes to so far:

Comedy nights | Caricature drawing and portrait sculpture classes | Quiz nights | Games nights | Charity events | Trips to the Alps | Taking part in the Brighton Fringe | Photo competitions | Creating time and space for on-site massage, reflexology and Pilates

Clearly, these experiences are designed to be enjoyable. But it's also worth noting that our focus on this value isn't just about having fun for fun's sake. We're big fans of Paul Dolan's book *Happiness by Design*, and his definition of happiness as *"experiences of pleasure **and purpose** over time"*.

As you can imagine, this kind of thinking is right up our street. Yes, we prioritise fun as one of our values but not just for the hell of it; it's part of our purpose to Make Life Better. And not just for us, for everyone. Our clients can feel it too, which may explain why they tend to stay with us for a long time (and find excuses to come and visit us as often as they can).

Go on. Try it. We dare you.

BE SUPERENGAGED

What's the atmosphere like in your office? How often do you hear laughter? How often do your clients hear it?

Ask yourself, if something doesn't excite you and it's not much fun, are you going to be able to dedicate yourself to it for a sustained period, AND do an amazing job? It's hard to feel amazing when you're frowning (try it). It's equally hard to perform at your best when enjoyment isn't part of the plan. That's why fun needs to be factored in.

YOU WIN SOME, YOU LOSE SOME

One person's fun is another's idea of hell, so make sure you offer plenty of options. One of our Fun Ministers came up with improv classes; it filled some of us with horror, but others loved it so much they ended up debuting on the stand-up circuit. Repeat after us: Compulsory fun is NO FUN.

FURTHER READING

Happiness by Design, Paul Dolan, 2014

17. THE VALUE OF WELLBEING

◀◀ REWIND

We value wellbeing because it provides us with the inner strength to fulfil our potential. If our mind and body are healthy, and our relationships are harmonious, we have rock solid foundations from which to come up with ideas that might just set the world on fire.

> *Long hours, excessive busyness and lack of sleep have become a badge of honour for many people these days. Sustained exhaustion is not a badge of honour; it's a mark of stupidity. Companies that force their crew into this bargain are cooking up dumb at their employees' expense.*

Jason Fried, Founder & CEO, Basecamp. (Taken from The Calm Company[ix]).

LOOKING AFTER NUMBERS 1-60

The importance of wellbeing at work isn't new – but it's increasingly making the news, as a problem of epidemic proportions[v]. And closer to home, many of us have felt the impact of stress-related health problems, via friends, family or business associates who have had early heart attacks due to pressure at work or, in one extreme case, lost a life due to depression.

When did it become acceptable for marketing, a cerebral, highly engaging career, to be life-threatening? And it's not just confined to our industry. All over the planet, businesses are pushing people too hard and too far. Lawyers, city bankers, junior doctors and tech startup employees are all renowned for being overworked, or outworking each other. Treating people like battery hens, aiming for high productivity over long hours in confined spaces, is too often the norm.

At Propellernet, we know that squeezing more and more out of tired people isn't going to light anyone's fire. For us, wellbeing isn't a string of tactical activities that tick the CSR box. It's the core of what we stand for; the foundation to our people-first strategy. It's not just what we do on our staff jollies but also how we work, day in, day out. It's Make Life Better in action.

We could fill another book about how we approach wellbeing, and maybe one day we will, but in the meantime, here are the headlines:

WELLBEING REQUIRES INVESTMENT

We make no apologies for prioritising wellbeing in our strategic and financial planning. Our aim is for no more than 70% of an individual's time to be billed out to clients, and the target number is even lower for team members who have management or mentoring responsibilities.

This leaves a minimum of 30% of our time for team connection, personal growth and development. Of course, from time to time our workload makes this a challenge, but we aim for that to be the exception, rather than the rule.

And linked to the way we approach the value of fun, we also fund and support a whole load of wellbeing activities, from regular massage days and in-house Pilates classes to drop-in sessions with our resident coach.

But we don't just take a scattergun approach to it. We've invested the time in pinning down the relative values of the different kinds of wellbeing, using Maslow's hierarchy.

And, being us, we make a point of asking how people are – and actively listening to the answers (something that is nowhere near as common as it should be in many workplaces).

As a result, we can be confident that we're supporting and fixing the things that people actually want and need help with. Which leads neatly on to...

jess_leader

12 likes

jess_leader Forgot it was #massageday at work today #zen #lookafteryourself #ontopoftheworld thanks @propellernet

View 1 Comment

8 FEBRUARY 2017

There are five key factors that drive personal wellbeing, which every company should have on their HR agenda. We've taken the principles and overlaid them with the plans we've made to bring them to life. How would your company complete the pyramids?

NICK THIS

SELF ACTUALISATION

- Engagement Tracking - Culture Catalyst
- Resident Coach
- Dream Valley
- Brighton Housing Trust Partner
- Propel Days
- Integration Stations
- Stunning Colleague
- Dream Balls
- Industry Awards
- Supporting the Community
- Soldout Kats
- Red Stars
- Namibia 365
- Happiness Tracking & Big Ups
- Transparent Finances
- Loyalty Holiday

ESTEEM

- Run and Wellbeing Fund & Fundraisers
- Weekly Tone News & other Get Togethers
- Enhanced Induction including Buddies
- 360-Degree Feedback
- Referral Payments
- Birthday Propel Day & Prosecco
- Pre-Payday Lunch
- Free Beer, Wine & Soft Drinks

LOVE & BELONGING

- Equal Company Bonuses
- Interest Free Loans
- Brighton & Hove Albion Season Tickets
- 25-30 Days Holiday + Bank Holidays
- Wellbeing Check-Ins
- Collaboratory Version
- Staff HomeWork
- Health Cash Plan
- Enhanced Maternity, Paternity & Childcare Vouchers
- Safe & Fun Environment
- Dream Ball Consultations
- Fresh Eyes Meetings

SAFETY

- Saver Travel Loans
- Flexible Working Hours
- Brighton Cycle network
- Food, Breakfast Tea & Coffee
- Subsidised Massage & Pilates
- Ride 2 Work Scheme
- Legal Support

PHYSIOLOGICAL NEEDS

WELLBEING ISN'T THE SAME FOR EVERYONE

If you really want to help people personalise their everyday wellbeing, you need to know what makes them tick.

For example, our business is home to lots of very different people: paid media specialists, techies, creatives, PRs, strategists. The techies are never going to want to pick up the phone and cold call journalists; the PRs would shudder at the thought of spending a day coding. But we all need to work together to create high impact results for our clients. We just need to do so in the best way for us.

And it's not just about different skills and experiences. It's about different ways of being too. The fascinating findings of *Quiet – The Value of Introverts in a World That Won't Stop Talking* by Susan Cain, has taught us a lot.

So, we've used a variety of working style analysis tools to look at who leans towards being more expressive, more driven, more analytical or more amiable, mapping each of us together so we can see preferences in working style, and learn how to get the best from each other.

And we've made sure our office has different kinds of workspaces to suit the different characters in our team: quiet rooms with no phones for thinking; open plan areas with no desks, just for lounging and sharing; focused rooms with ON AIR signs for uninterrupted concentration; communal eating areas for breaking bread together and catching up.

WELLBEING DOESN'T STOP AT THE OFFICE DOOR

At risk of stating the blindingly obvious, it's hard to focus on work if your home life isn't going well. Plus, we genuinely care about our people, and want the best for them. So, if someone has an issue with their landlord, a partnership has gone wrong, or they find themselves in a legal dispute, we can get involved and help them solve the problem.

We've pulled together a strong support network for people to draw on – from coaches and mentors through to doctors, counsellors and legal aid – and we regularly pick up the bill. Make Life Better goes way beyond the walls of the agency, consistently.

MANAGERS NEED TO CHECK THEIR PEOPLE ARE LIVING IT

Of course, there's no point offering loads of lovely stuff if no one takes advantage of it. We do expect our people to take responsibility for using the wellbeing tools we provide, but we also know that sometimes people need nudging.

With this in mind, Winnie, our People Manager, schedules in six-monthly Wellbeing Check-ins with everyone on the team, to find out whether they're getting what they're entitled to. For example:

- Are they taking their **holidays** regularly?
- Have they used at least three **Propel Days** in a year?
- Are they making the most of their **Health Insurance**, for non-critical things like eye exams, dental care and acupuncture as well as more serious illnesses?
- Are they taking advantage of their **coaching** sessions?

NICK THIS

It's an informal conversation, but by making it a formal part of Winnie's role, we prove that wellbeing is a priority for us, and help our team do the same.

WELLBEING DOESN'T MEAN ENTITLEMENT

The flip side of all this, and one we've learned from experience, is that it's very easy to get used to, and to start thinking that the way we operate is just normal business practice. This is usually identified by a visceral howl when a crisis of epic proportions takes place, such as there being *NO CEREAL LEFT* or *THE COFFEE MACHINE BEING BROKEN.*

It's human nature to take things for granted, and we get it, but we do like to keep an eye on it all the same. The good news is, it only takes a new starter or a Foundry visitor to remind everyone how unusual our approach to wellbeing is.

MORE IN CHAPTER 48

LEADERS SHOULD PUT THEIR OWN
OXYGEN MASKS ON FIRST

When it comes to wellbeing, the people at the top *really* need to set a good example; it's no good shooing everyone out of the office on time if you then settle in for another few hours. If you don't take care of yourself, you make it harder for everyone else to, not least because you're likely to take your stress out on them.

But if you create an environment that radiates wellbeing, and practise what you preach, you'll be doing everyone a favour, including yourself.

We all need to take care of ourselves, emotionally, mentally **and physically**; our health really is our wealth. By putting wellbeing front and centre, you'll empower your people to play their part to the best of their abilities, creating the future as they go.

As a parting comment, we'll come back to Jason Fried, who can say so much with so few words:

> "IF IT'S CONSTANTLY CRAZY AT WORK,
> WE HAVE TWO WORDS FOR YOU:
> FUCK THAT. AND TWO MORE:
> ENOUGH ALREADY."

Quite.

BE SUPERENGAGED

Do you know how much profit you made last year? Do you know how much the wellbeing of your people improved last year? Too many leaders know the first but not the second; try caring more about your stakeholders than your shareholders and see where it takes you.

How much have you invested into looking after your people? It needs to be accounted for, and planned in, or it won't happen. Of all the investments you make, it's probably the most important.

If you're one of your business's leaders, are you setting a brilliant example? Do you live the values of your organisation, or just expect everyone else to? Hint: the latter won't work.

YOU WIN SOME, YOU LOSE SOME

By taking wellbeing into the core of our business, we've deliberately gone in the opposite direction to many of our peers; we never forget that it's OK to do things differently. We want to be the best place to work in the world, and it doesn't bother us that those who don't share our ambition don't value wellbeing as we do.

We're frequently challenged about the opportunity cost of not billing 100% of our time to clients. We're open about the fact that it runs into the millions and we're fine with that; our experience has shown that it's worth every penny.

FURTHER READING

The Calm Company, Jason Fried and David Heinemeier Hasson, 2013

Quiet: The Power of Introverts in a World That Can't Stop Talking, Susan Cain, 2013

18. RECRUITING THROUGH OUR VALUES

STARTING AS WE MEAN TO GO ON

For our values to have real impact, they have to be living, breathing drivers of behaviour. And the way we make that happen is by putting them front and centre from day one. Or indeed, from day minus-one, by incorporating them into our interview process.

ORE IN
PTER 23

MORE IN
SECTION 4

It's important to note, though, that it's not about asking trick questions or trying to trip people up. We genuinely want to hear interview candidates' take on our values, so we make sure they've had some time to think about their answers. Here's the brief we send out before we meet:

Your interview – it's for the both of us.

Your interview – it's for the both of us.

Welcome to how work could feel in the future.

We're delighted you're coming in for an interview. To give you an insight into how we work, we'd like you to think about these questions, as we'll be asking you about them (and others) when we meet.

1. We hold our values close. They are innovation, creativity, adventure, fun and wellbeing.
   - Share with us how you embrace innovation. Do you enjoy changing stuff and making it better?
   - Do you have a passion for creativity? Do you get a kick out of making stuff; what have you made, how did it work? Tell us how you've creatively approached a challenge.
   - Do you have a sense of adventure, are you happy to go where others may fear to tread? Tell us about your adventurous side.
   - Do you value your wellbeing, and will you bring more value to a brilliant place to work?
   - Are you fun to be with? Of course you are. Talk to us about how you work well with others.

2. If you were given 12 days per year to propel yourself forward, how would you use them?

Looking forward to seeing you.

propellernet
make life better™

NICK THIS

We never forget that they are interviewing us as much as we are interviewing them, and we want them to feel excited about coming to work with us. Starting as we mean to go on, and engaging them with our values from the off, is a great way to achieve it.

BE SUPERENGAGED

Once you've pinpointed your values, the next step is to assess how present they are in the day-to-day life of your business. Are they brought to life by your policies, strategies and staff? And are you yourself breathing them – are you setting the tone with your own behaviour?

We've mapped out the first one to start you off. Be as honest as you can.

OUR VALUES	LIVING IT Is this value alive in your business? How does it live?	BREATHING IT How are you breathing it? What do you do that epitomises this value?
Wellbeing	*Time allocated for personal growth and wellbeing.* *Support, mentorship, coaching and guidance.* *Healthcare and pensions for everyone.*	*Taking care of my own health & fitness.* *Active participation in and connection with weekly company gatherings.* *Taking my Propel Days.* *Booking regular time off so I don't run myself into the ground.*

(You can download a blank A4 version at www.superengaged.co.uk)

YOUR VALUES	LIVING IT Is this value alive in your business? How does it live?	BREATHING IT How are you breathing it? What do you do that epitomises this value?

YOU WIN SOME, YOU LOSE SOME

It's easy to focus on your values when you define them, and to share them with new team members, but don't forget to keep it up; values need regular airspace. A year or so after we first defined our five values, we realised that we weren't prioritising them enough. So, we invested some time out as a leadership team to examine our own motivational drivers, personal intent and values, together.

In the process, we learnt a great deal about each other, which strengthened our relationships, and helped us take both the business and our values forward. We increased our focus on innovation and creativity, upped our sense of adventure, maximised the fun factor and enhanced our collective wellbeing.

19. BRINGING OUR VALUES TO LIFE

◄◄ REWIND

No one wants to dread turning up to work. And the people you work with are a massive part of how you feel about your working day; toxic colleagues can bring everyone down to their level.

So, having a great bunch of people and a warm friendly vibe means you've nailed the workplace relationships thing, right? Wrong, as we discovered.

BE A STUNNING COLLEAGUE. THAT'S IT.

We pride ourselves on being a pretty nice bunch, and so were delighted when the Culture Catalyst survey concurred. Except – wait, what's that you say, Culture Catalyst? Too nice? TOO NICE? How can we be TOO NICE?

But once we stopped huffing around the office and thought about it, we realised they had a point. Our internal relationships are unusually strong, which is brilliant, but there's a risk that being so friendly makes it harder to give constructive criticism.

Now clearly, being too nice is better, on balance, than being too nasty. As some recent Harvard Business School research claimed, *"One toxic colleague wipes out the value of two superstars."*[vi] But the flip side is, we all need honest, thoughtful feedback if we're to grow and develop, both as individuals and as colleagues. If we don't embrace different perspectives and challenge each other, we're in danger of standing still.

OUR PRINCIPLES FOR STUNNING BEHAVIOUR

So, as part of our work towards defining our values, we also took the time to evaluate the behaviours we ought to be displaying if we're to really live and breathe them. And we took inspiration from (or you could say, blatantly stole from) a presentation by Netflix[vii] in which they shared the concept of being a Stunning Colleague.

It's brilliant in its simplicity. And it's very easy to understand. So, we've taken it, run with it, and made it our own.

What does being a stunning colleague mean at Propellernet, then? It means being the person everyone wants to have on their team. Like our very own Jimmy the Glue, who earned his nickname for his innate ability to always hold it all together.

And no, this doesn't mean being everyone's best mate (let's not be too nice, remember?). It means developing a level of respect and appreciation between you and your colleagues, so you can disagree about something and deal with it, without moaning, snitching or backstabbing.

Now, we're not keen on rules; in fact, we actively try and avoid them. We think they limit creativity and, in the wrong hands, become a pedant's charter. (Look at the fiasco that occurred in 2017 when the staff of United Airlines Flight 3411 followed the rules and dragged a passenger off the plane.)[viii]

But we also know from experience that having a clear brief to work from inspires freedom and the space to play. So, we created some guidelines to support the stunning colleague behaviour we want to see:

1. Have a truly excellent work ethic. Inject **passion and enthusiasm** into everything you do and every team you work with.

2. Always strive to produce **award winning** and industry leading work.

3. Never settle for average. **Aim for remarkable**. Always think *"How can I do that better? How can I make that more amazing?"*

4 **Inspire by example**. Be prepared to get your hands dirty and muck in, and never expect anyone to do anything you won't do yourself.

5. Always be **helpful and approachable,** with a great attitude and willing to go the extra mile.

6. Always be **curious**. Never stop wanting to learn.

Ultimately, Make Life Better for yourself, your peers and your clients.

And to avoid our principles looking even slightly like a list of rules, our team members Hannah and Corryn decided to apply a little innovation and creativity to how we talk about them. The result was the *Stunning Colleague Collection* book covers, which are now displayed as a piece of art on each floor of our workspace.

The NEW
Stunning Colleague Collection
Book 1

The Remarkable
They never settle for average

The Stunning Colleague Collection

The Award Winning

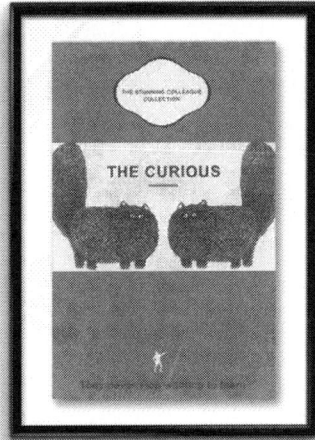

THE STUNNING COLLEAGUE
COLLECTION

THE CURIOUS

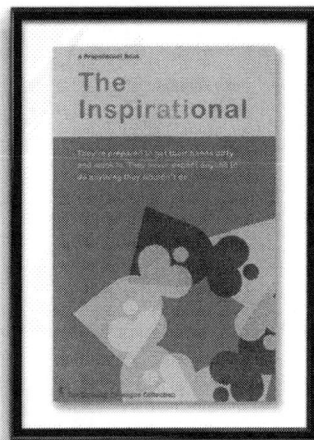

a Magnificent Book

The
Inspirational

The Stunning Colleague Collection   2

The Passionate

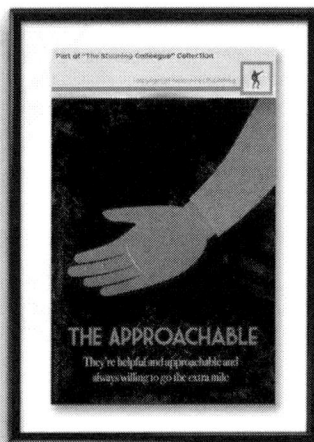

Part of "The Stunning Colleague" Collection

THE APPROACHABLE
They're helpful and approachable and
always willing to go the extra mile

Just as with the values themselves, we make sure we are upfront about our expectations right from the off. As Tom Peters, the management guru, has said, *"Recruit for attitude, train for skill."* So, we include some questions about being stunning colleagues in our interviews, and take careful note of the answers:

1. We all expect each other to be stunning colleagues. Have you got what it takes to be a stunning colleague?

    A. What makes you a stunning colleague and why?

    B. How have you helped others to be stunning colleagues?

    C. Share some examples of your stunning actions or work you've done in the past.

And from time to time, to ensure we're going on as we started, we ask our current employees to reflect on these questions too.

In a company with a positive culture, people work alongside their peers to encourage, give feedback, correct and redirect each other. Not in a bossy way, but in the spirit of collaboration. This works best when people believe in each other's intention to do great work; when it succeeds, as it does at Propellernet, it certainly makes life better.

Google is another organisation which has set out these kind of guidelines; in their case, specifically for behaviours that create high performance teams:

1. Dependability – getting things done on time and to expectations.

2. Structure and clarity – clear goals, well defined roles.

3. Meaning – work has personal significance.

4. Impact – work is purposeful.

5. Psychological safety – the standout characteristic – where everyone can take risks, voice their opinion and ask judgement-free questions. Employees can basically let their guard down.

What would yours be?

● ● ● ●

BE SUPERENGAGED

Does everyone in your organisation know what is expected of them? Can they articulate it and hold others to account? Knowing what others value and what they expect of you is much more motivating than having to second guess. The trick is to make your expectations clear, without a list of rules as long as your arm.

Do you explore your behaviours at interview stage and set your expectations even before day one? In this, as in so many things, we'd say the earlier you talk about it, the better.

YOU WIN SOME, YOU LOSE SOME

Bringing your values to life is the best way to make them stick. Our stunning colleague behaviours didn't really fly until Hannah and Corryn got busy with their book cover idea; articulating them visually has helped our team make them part of their everyday.

TL;DR

20. FOR THE SKIM READERS AMONG YOU...

If your purpose is what you're working towards, your values are how you'll get there. Chosen well, used properly and regularly given airtime, they'll help you and your colleagues ensure you're heading in the right direction, and acting in the right way.

We've chosen five core values that work with each other to help us Make Life Better, for everyone. And we invest a lot of thought, time and money in making sure they live and breathe throughout our organisation on a day-to-day basis.

We can't imagine Propellernet without them; they are the essence of us.

INNOVATION _____ *MORE IN CHAPTER 47*

CREATIVITY _____ *MORE IN CHAPTER 40*

ADVENTURE _____ *MORE IN CHAPTER 41*

FUN _____ *MORE IN CHAPTER 4*

WELLBEING _____ *MORE IN CHAPTER 30*

END NOTES

i   We've all seen the research around cab drivers' brain development. Clearly this
     is well above simply learning to drive, but the acquisition of further knowledge,
     in whatever field, changes and develops the brain. This study shows by just how
     much: www.wired.com/2011/12/london-taxi-driver-memory

ii   Lexus making the impossible, possible with the Hoverboard. Admittedly you
     need an electromagnetic skate park for it to work: https://www.youtube.com/
     watch?v=ZwSwZ2Y0Ops The Zapata racing Flyboard Air: https://www.youtube.
     com/watch?v=rNKRxsNyOho

iii www.bbc.com/capital/story/20170731-the-surprising-truths-and-myths-about-mi-
     crochip-implants

iv   www.helpguide.org/articles/emotional-health/laughter-is-the-best-medicine.htm

v   www.telegraph.co.uk/news/health/news/10143915/One-in-three-absences-at-
     work-due-to-anxiety-and-stress-official-Government-survey-finds.html

vi   hbr.org/2015/12/its-better-to-avoid-a-toxic-employee-than-hire-a-superstar

vii "Ooh! 100 PowerPoint slides to look at!" Said no one, ever. But this deck of 124
     slides from Netflix, giving a clear insight into their culture, became a viral sen-
     sation, viewed over 16 million times. They introduce the concept of the Stunning
     Colleague in slide 20. www.slideshare.net/reed2001/culture-1798664

viii hbr.org/2017/04/trust-your-employees-not-your-rulebook

ix   m.signalvnoise.com/the-calm-company-our-next-book-d0ed917cc457

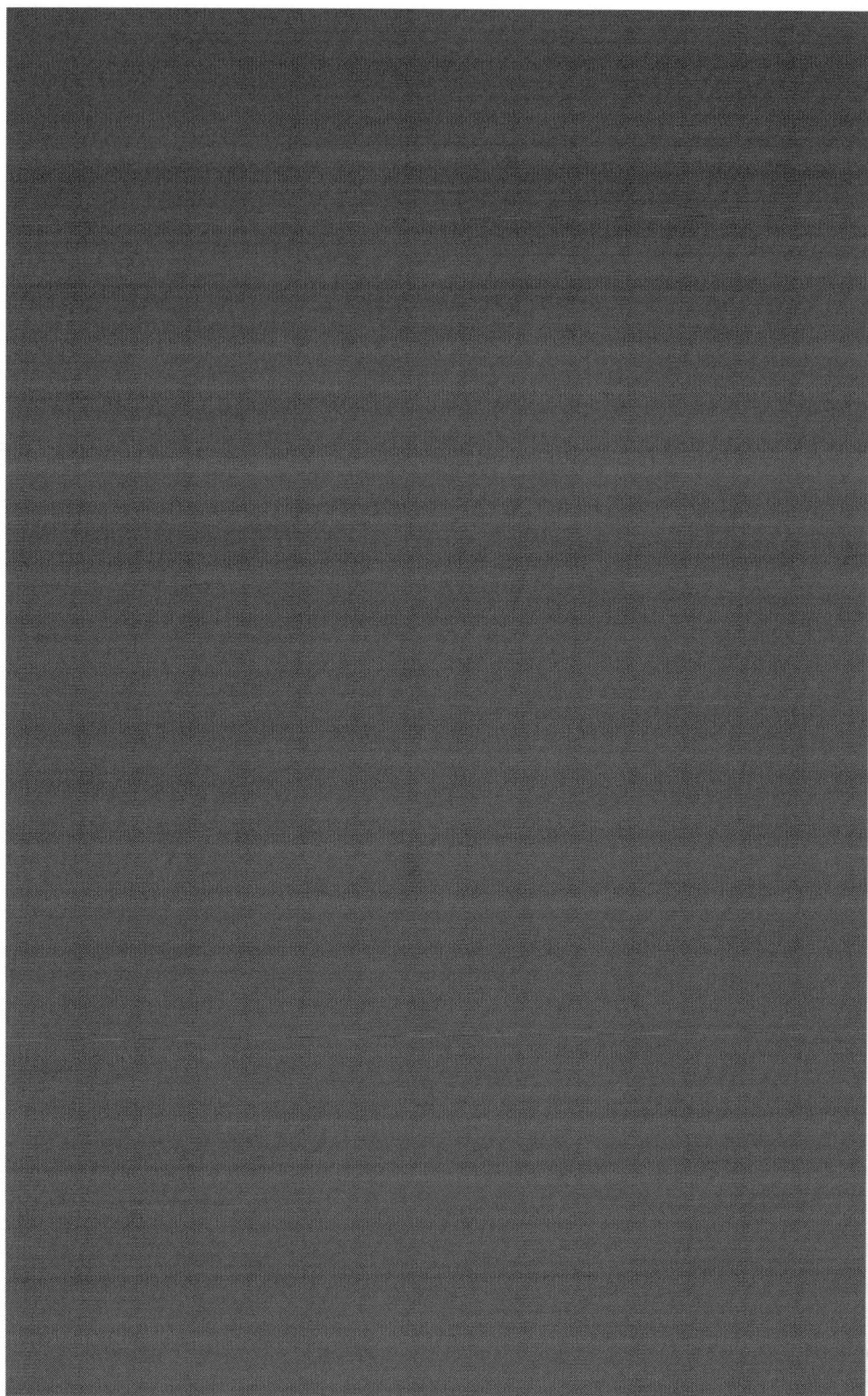

Section 4
BUILDING A BRILLIANT TEAM

21. INTRODUCTION

◀◀REWIND

To say that our early recruitment strategy wasn't commercially robust is putting it mildly. Scenario planning based on secured future revenue? Nah. Feeling quite busy and needing another pair of hands? Yep, they'll do.

We've made some stunning hiring mistakes in the past (which we won't go into, to save everyone's blushes); but it's never been the candidate's fault.

The responsibility was ours, for valuing intuition and immediacy more highly than strategy, planning and numbers. We don't do that anymore.

> *Don't hire people unless the batteries are included.*

Michael Hyatt, best-selling author and virtual mentor.

HOW TO BUILD THE TEAM YOUR BUSINESS DESERVES

When people are your business, having the right team in place can make or break you.

Hire the right person and you can see the positive ripple effect across your organisation. But if you recruit too fast, or you don't have a robust probation process in place, it can be painful, and can get pricey.

According to Randy Street and Geoff Smart, authors of *Who: The A Method for Hiring*, the average hiring mistake costs fifteen times an employee's base salary in hard costs and productivity. You don't have to be a member of Mensa to work out that hiring the wrong £35k employee could cost you £525,000. Ouch.

And it gets worse (don't worry, we'll cheer up soon). Influential business thinker Peter Drucker estimated that the typical hiring success rate is 50%. So just focusing on the £35k salary level, you could be wasting around half a million pounds every other time you recruit someone. And let's not get into the huge piles of cash you could waste if you recruit the wrong leadership team.

Aside from the financial implications, hiring clearly has an impact on team dynamics. Michael Hyatt describes people with batteries included as having their own energy source and being a force for good. The opposite is true for those who come without their own battery pack. They are a drain on their team members; gossiping, complaining and creating energy-sapping drama instead of getting involved, all of which kills momentum.

But before we sink into an un-Propellernetesque pit of despair, here's the good news: it's all preventable. Pulling in the right candidates, hiring the right people, onboarding them effectively and checking it's working out before it's too late; all of this can be done, and done well, so you can build the team your business deserves.

If you're involved in hiring, we strongly urge you to read *Who* before you write another job ad or pick up the phone to any further candidates, let alone start the time-zapping face-to-face interview process. Street and Smart have set out clear guidance, based on 1,300 hours of interviews with 20 billionaires and 300 CEOs in the largest research study of its time, talking to people whose hiring decisions have moved markets.

So, we're not going to retell their words of advice; instead, what's coming up is our take on what we've learned from the brilliant decisions and epic fails in our agency's HR history.

FURTHER READING

Living Forward, Michael Hyatt, 2016

Who: The A Method for Hiring, Geoff Smart and Randy Street, 2008

22. TALENT SEEKING

◀◀REWIND

Search marketing was relatively new when we started out. There was a land-grab to get to the top of search rankings and it felt like the Wild West of marketing, particularly as some rivals were building businesses around cheating the search engines and gaming algorithms.

So, it was hard for recruiters to get to grips with what we did, and we didn't invest the time in helping them understand. Result: they were hunting for people who didn't exist, and we were left sifting through piles of irrelevant CVs.

Eventually, we realised there was a better way.

FINDING YOUR ROUND PEGS

Here's a statistic to keep HR managers awake at night: the average staff turnover in our industry is 30%.[i]

When you consider the cost of replacing these people, let alone the money you've invested in them, you can see why our HR friends might be feeling a bit stressed. And with recruitment agency commissions sitting anywhere between 10% and a frankly ridiculous 50%, it can be an eye-watering strain on the P&L to keep bringing new people in. **We reckon we've saved around £200,000 in the last couple of years by recruiting for ourselves, freeing up money to spend on things like fulfilling dreams.** MORE IN SECTION 6

Now, we're not suggesting you ditch the headhunters completely. If you develop a close working relationship with them, and help them really understand your business, they can be a fantastic resource, particularly when you need reach.

But there's also a lot you can do to attract the right people before turning on the recruitment agency tap. Here are our top thoughts on getting on talented people's radars:

NOBODY SELLS YOU BETTER THAN YOU

- Get out there and talk about what you do. We're often found on the stage, talking enthusiastically about the way we work, as well as the work we deliver, and it pays off in terms of widening our reach. A number of our interviews start with *"I saw your MD give a talk about XYZ..."* or *"I saw someone from Propellernet sharing XYZ the other day..."*.

- Write about what you do. Other people are more interested in your opinions than you might expect. So, contribute to industry periodicals, write and share a blog, even be a bit vocal on Twitter.

- As well as encouraging the right people to want to work for you, being up front about what you stand for will discourage the wrong ones, which is better for everyone in the long run. MORE IN CHAPTER 33

APART FROM YOUR TEAM, THAT IS

- Offer a healthy referral fee and let your team do the talking. By a huge margin, most of our people have come to us after being referred by another of our colleagues. Our team tend to evangelise about the business to a degree that might feel like showing off if we included it in a job ad.

- They also tend tell the candidates EXACTLY what to expect – which makes it more likely that the people who put themselves forward will be ones who share our values.

MAKE IT EASY FOR PEOPLE TO FIND YOU

- Hang out where your audience hangs out. We've learned the hard way that a scattergun approach to recruiting doesn't pay off; you end up weeding through a lot of responses, of which very few will match your needs. Instead, we've developed a targeted approach, based on knowing who we're looking for and putting ourselves where they'll be looking.

- We're also regularly approached by people via our website and jobs@propellernet.co.uk on a speculative basis, and we take time to answer every enquiry. Even if the right opportunity isn't available now, it's never too early to start the conversation.

OR GO OUT AND GRAB THEM

- Stand out from the crowd and grab people's attention – then make sure what you're saying is worth listening to. Our Professor Elemental recruitment video got our industry talking, reached over 100,000 people and generated 786 click-throughs to our careers page, all in the first three weeks. Not bad for an investment of £700.

SEE NEXT PAGE

- You'll be all the more persuasive if you weave your values into your recruitment activity. Our video was creative, innovative and focused on how working for us could Make Life Better – ultimately, it brought our ethos to life.

CASE STUDY: PROFESSOR ELEMENTAL

Brighton is home to lots of talented people who drag themselves up to London for work each day, under the illusion that that's what you have to do to get a decent job – not knowing, perhaps, that the city is home to a growing number of great companies.

What's more, our local train franchise was doing a good job of making life worse, with regular strikes, late trains and cancelled services, often without any information at all. Hours were spent wasted on platforms, meetings missed, deadlines screwed and family life severely interrupted.

So, our creative team got to work and hooked up with Professor Elemental, a local chap-hop (think posh rap) artist, to put together three minutes of video fun which saluted our commuters and helped them plan their escape. Watch and enjoy.

www.propellernet.co.uk/careers

FURTHER YOUR EDUCATION...

- Universities and other HE institutions are a hotbed of talent, but the academic skills they have learned don't always translate successfully into the world of work. There's an opportunity here for businesses to support the transition – and find some brilliant new recruits before anyone else does.

- I have worked with the team behind Brighton University's Enterprise & Entrepreneur course, delivering the keynote speech in 2016 and talking with the course leader, Clare Griffiths, about future employability to help bridge the employment gap.

- Sam, our Insight Director, has supported Sussex Innovation Centre's Catalyst programme. It employs 6-12 masters graduates and hires them out to businesses to work on live projects, allowing them to share their expertise whilst gaining real-world experience.
Two of our most recent placement students are working on client briefs and looking at ways to use artificial intelligence to make our business more efficient.

... BUT REMEMBER, DEGREES AREN'T EVERYTHING

- A university education is brilliant, but so is the school of life. We're just as interested in what people have achieved in our industry (or out of it, for that matter) as what they learned in academia. Some of the most successful people on the planet dropped out of higher education – or didn't even make it there in the first place – so don't let the lack of a certificate lead you to overlook a great candidate.

TAKE IT SLOWLY

- Don't panic recruit. Trust us, we know. In the past, our hurry to fill a gap has meant that we've hired the wrong people, or hired the right people at the wrong level, and had to manage the consequences.

- In our experience, the best way to avoid panic recruiting is to see it as an ongoing process, rather than something you only do when you need to find someone.

  Yes, it takes time to build relationships with people who might only be a great fit in the future. But the payback comes when you have an urgent need and those people are already lined up.

IF YOU DON'T HAVE TIME TO DO IT WELL, USE A RECRUITER

- We appreciate that all this might sound like hard work – and it is, if you do it properly. So, if you need to find someone in a relatively short timeframe and you don't have anyone in mind, or the time to go out and find them, pull in the experts. At times like these, it's money well spent.

Whatever your staff turnover, however large or small your growth ambitions, your people are the lifeblood of your company, so take the time to find the right ones. As we said at the beginning, the average staff turnover in our industry is 30%. Ours is 7%, and that's partly because recruitment is always on our minds, even if we don't have a post to fill.

BE SUPERENGAGED

What's your staff turnover and where do you find most of your new people? Is this cost-effective for you?

When was the last time you, or someone from your company, stood up and told the world about what you do?

Do people join you through referrals from your current team? Could you encourage it? The amount you'd have to invest in an incentive would be minimal compared to the cost of making a poor recruitment decision.

Don't be afraid to be original to get people's attention. What could you do to stand out from the competition?

Do you hire people with batteries – and do you keep them charged up?

YOU WIN SOME, YOU LOSE SOME

Don't just call a recruitment agency and expect them to perform miracles. Brief your headhunters well – otherwise you'll just end up with a pile of CVs to wade through, few of which may be relevant.

Once you've found one that gets what you're about, treat them like part of your extended team. The right recruiter is an invaluable asset for any business.

NOT HAVING A DEGREE DIDN'T
HOLD THIS LOT BACK:

Bill Gates dropped out of Harvard and is now the world's richest man.

Deborah Meaden, formidable businesswoman and star of Dragons' Den, left school at 16 to attend Brighton Technical College before getting her first job in a fashion house.

Jon Snow, one of Britain's favourite newsreaders, was thrown out of Liverpool University for taking part in an anti-apartheid rally in 1970.

Julie Burchill left school without any A levels and went to work at the NME, the launchpad to a successful career as a journalist and best-selling author.

Mark Zuckerberg dropped out of Harvard and the rest is history, a few billion dollars and a Hollywood blockbuster later.

Richard Branson left school at 15 with just three O levels and went on to found the $5bn Virgin Group.

George Clooney dropped out of university twice before turning his hand to acting, producing, screenwriting and directing, and has picked up three Golden Globes and two Academy Awards in the process.[iv]

Just saying.

23. RECRUITING

◀◀ REWIND

Back in the day, when we started out, recruitment was all a bit chaotic. No one knew who we were, which made the talent-seeking side of things a lot harder; "Propeller-who?" was the ego-crushing reply we often got when we tried to headhunt big hitters. And when we did manage to get people to come for an interview, our lack of preparation made it all a bit vague; we didn't have a process, and it showed.

Luckily, it didn't take us too long to realise that building a few simple steps into a recruitment process would ease the chaos and release creativity, for us and our candidates.

FINDERS, KEEPERS

Our newer recruits tend not to believe us when we explain how woolly our recruitment strategy used to be. In retrospect, we were lucky to pull in the people we did. But now, having worked out exactly how badly we were doing it, and having taken steps to tackle it, recruitment is off-the-scale easier.

Sure, it helps that people now know who we are; our reputation as a brilliant place to work, combined with our talent-seeking activity, means that our jobs@ email receives CVs from all over the country. But just as importantly, the de-woollification of our interview process has ratcheted up our conversion rate, and made sure that every one of our 60 precious seats is filled by someone who's going to help us Make Life Better.

MORE IN
CHAPTER 22

MORE IN
SECTION 46

So here are the steps we now take to make sure we recruit successfully. They're easy to follow and worth the time investment, particularly if you consider the 15x salary cost of making a mistake. You probably do some of them already; do them all, and you won't go wrong.

1. **Recruit forward**

   We make a point of keeping our eyes and ears open, so we're aware of who's out there, and can keep them in mind for recruiting in the future. A coffee here or a quick pint there allows us to build up relationships and warm up potential candidates, ready for when the right opportunity comes up.

2. **Be clear about what you stand for**

   Our ambition, purpose and values underpin our whole recruitment process, from the way we design our jobs to the questions we ask at interview. As a result, all our candidates are clear about the kind of organisation they might be joining. This also allows us to recruit for attitude and values rather than skills (which can more easily be developed once someone joins us).

3. **Create and use a scorecard**

   Whilst we would never describe ourselves as a corporate kind of business, we believe you can learn a lot from the way the big firms do things, especially if you adapt them to fit with your own models. For example, the decision to use a scorecard to evaluate our interviews has been a revelation.

It's a fantastic planning tool, as it forces us to pin down what skills we're looking for and what outcomes we want from the role. And it's also a brilliant aide-memoire for the interview itself. It's surprisingly easy to forget which candidate said what; now we can benchmark how they got on and keep track of the valuable conversations we've had.

We've included an example of our scorecard at the end of this chapter; feel free to adapt it for your own business.

4. Use screening calls as a first round

Instead of booking yourself up with a series of hour-long face-to-faces, add a screening stage in which you ask a few carefully-chosen questions over the phone. We've found we can often tell quite quickly if someone isn't right for our business, and doing so before a formal interview wastes less of everyone's time, the candidate included.

5. Prepare properly

Rather than bowling up to the meeting room and winging it, take the time beforehand to work out, for example, who is going to focus on the candidate's experience and who will talk about the company's values. It shows your respect for the interviewee and we promise you, it's time well spent.

6. Ask values-based questions...

Given the strength of our values and culture, it's vital for us that anyone who joins us shares them. So, we spend a large part of each interview asking values-based questions. They are straightforward and simple, allowing room for imagination and flair, and the answers are always hugely revealing.

MORE IN CHAPTERS 18 & 19

By asking these questions, we ensure that anyone who comes on board shares our spirit of adventure, can think creatively, will embrace innovation, look after themselves and others, and be fun to have around. We believe it's played a huge part in our low turnover rate.

Whatever you do, don't fall into the trap of asking trick questions, such as: *"If you were an animal, which one would you be?"* Are you looking to employ a superengaged, highly skilled, energised person? Or are you casting for an am-dram production of The Jungle Book?

7. **... and share them in advance**

    It's only fair, if you're going to put so much emphasis on your values, to give candidates some time to reflect on them. So, we share our values and the questions we're asking around them with candidates beforehand – and get more insightful answers as a result.

8. **Ask about their private life**

    No, not THAT; but we do make a point of asking our interviewees what non-work-related secret skills or superpowers they have. A lot, as it turns out:

    *   SEO Consultant Robin is also a Twitter comedian, whose @happybirthtime account has 24,000 followers (including Matt Lucas and Dara O'Briain).

    *   Delivery Director Lucy is also a botanical expert who specialises in wreathmaking.

    *   Insight Analyst Joe is a national level Sabre fencer.
        Yep, it's a thing.

    As well as helping put candidates at ease, this line of questioning also reinforces our people-first attitude. It shows that we are interested in the complete person, not just their work persona, and that it's OK to bring your whole self into work.

    It's also reassuring for us to know that if we ever need to win a joke competition, a floral festival or a duel, we're covered.

9. Set them to work

Anyone can talk about how good they are at something; but the last thing our team needs is people who are all mouth and no trousers. Our way of getting around this is to ask candidates to do some actual work, on a live business example which we send over in advance.

We love watching them share their approach to a project or task; as well as being massively revealing, it has been known to give us that spine-tingling feeling which means we've found the perfect person.

10. Introduce the team

Once a candidate gets close to being offered a job, we introduce them to their potential team: their 'Head of' or line manager, their peers and other people who may end up working with them. It's a stop/go point that we have learned never to skip. Team dynamics are the glue that keeps a business together; people need to click at this early stage if strong working relationships are to form.

We often do this in a social setting, so we get to see the real person, not just their interview face, and so they see the real us, too.

11. Widen your reference pool

It goes without saying that all referees should be followed up, but we don't stop there. Think six degrees of separation; someone we know will know someone who knows someone who knows the candidate (LinkedIn is a great place to start). In our experience, an informal chat tells us as much (more, even) than a formal reference.

12. Feed back honestly (and kindly)

We want every candidate to have a positive experience, whether they get the job or not. So, we aim to respond to every CV personally, let those who aren't quite right go as early as possible in the process, and give detailed feedback to those who we decide not to employ. Our unsuccessful candidates have been known to recommend us to others, so we must be getting it right.

13. Never forget that interviews work both ways

This one is a biggie; that's why we've left it until last.

Sometimes, you can be so caught up in trying to decide whether someone is right for you, that you forget to explain why you might be right for them. But if they're a brilliant candidate with the potential to be a stunning colleague, they're likely to have a choice of offers, and you'll need to win them over.

So, we make candidates feel like part of the team when they walk through the door, and we keep the tone and vibe of the interview as warm as possible. We take every opportunity to demonstrate our values through our behaviour, and we answer any questions honestly and positively.

And we sell ourselves, unapologetically; we know we're a great place to work and we want them to know it too. Our interviews aren't designed to try and catch them out, but rather to invite them in.

If you follow these steps, and make sure you factor in the time to do so properly, recruitment ceases to feel like a burden and instead becomes an opportunity.

When we get it right, we get a brilliant new person who will help us Make Life Better; now we've worked out how to do it, it's one of our favourite parts of the job.

BE SUPERENGAGED

Can you recall a great interview you've had? And a bad one? What was the difference? Use your experiences from the other side of the interview table to inform how you recruit.

How did you feel about a role you didn't get? Would you recommend that company to someone else, based on the way the interviewer(s) treated you?

How successful is the recruitment approach in your company? Does the idea of starting the hiring process fill you with excited anticipation or utter dread? If you feel like you've cracked it, we'd love to hear how.

YOU WIN SOME, YOU LOSE SOME

We've learned the hard way that being handed a CV five minutes before an interview is about to start, with little time to read it, isn't the way to manage a potentially valuable conversation – and no candidate deserves to be on the receiving end of a harassed, uninformed interviewer. Prep, prep, prep.

Careful, thought-through recruitment takes time, so you'll need to manage both your candidate's and your boss's expectations. Make sure you keep candidates informed and engaged throughout the process; it'd be a shame to lose someone to a less diligent employer who got their offer in first.

ROLE: JOB TITLE	CANDIDATE 1	CANDIDATE 2	CANDIDATE 3	CANDIDATE 4
MISSION: WHAT YOU WANT THE ROLE TO ACHIEVE				
ESSENTIALS TO HAVE				
EXPERIENCE & EVIDENCE				
Track record of successful, impactful work				
<additional requirement>				
<additional requirement>				
ROLE MODEL & LEADERSHIP				
Effective team leadership experience				
<additional requirement>				
<additional requirement>				
PEOPLE FOCUS				
Aligned to our values				
<additional requirement>				
<additional requirement>				
INDUSTRY ACUMEN				
Passion for- and knowledge of- 'what's next' in industry				
<additional requirement>				
<additional requirement>				
FANTASTIC TO HAVE				
Languages, particularly French and Italian				
<additional requirement>				
<additional requirement>				

NICK THIS

SCORING

3 - exceeds expecations for the role
2 - good level of experience
1 - would need support
0 - no experience

24. ONBOARDING

◀◀REWIND

Shamefully, we used to be as chaotic when it came to onboarding as we were about recruiting. Sometimes, a new starter would arrive without anyone having been asked to arrange a welcome, a desk or a phone, or to take responsibility for what they should be doing. The first person who encountered them would have a headscratching "What the hell am I supposed to do now?" moment. #awkward

And probation? No, sorry, you've lost us. It was only when we hit a few problems with some newish team members that we realised the value of having a process for sense-checking our hiring decisions. The toe-curlingly difficult conversations we were forced to have could so easily have been avoided, if we'd just given it a bit of thought.

> *I'm still pinching myself since joining, that a company can be run in this way...I'm discovering that the challenge is more about taking every opportunity that comes along.*

Anonymous feedback from a Propellernet employee, as part of a European research study into *The Future of Work*, with Leeds University & UK Research Council, 2017.

INDUCTION: THE GIFT THAT KEEPS ON GIVING

So, you've found an industry superstar, carried out a fabulously well-prepared interview, and persuaded them to join you. Job done? No!

Sending out the offer letter isn't the end of the recruitment process. If you're doing it properly, there are several induction stages to go through before the candidate is fully on board. Skip them at your peril; as we've mentioned before, recruitment is an expensive thing to get wrong. → *MORE IN CHAPTER 21*

Here are the steps we've built in over time to make sure our new starters start, and continue, brilliantly.

1. Preboarding

The reasons why people join us vary enormously from person to person. Some are (gratefully) dropping the London commute or relocating to Brighton. Some are first jobbers who have yet to experience office life. Others have been stalking us for years until the right job came up.

But whatever their motivation, we find that most candidates need a period of time for rewiring, particularly if they've been at another agency beforehand.

Rewiring? Yep, we're not kidding. Metaphorically, of course.

Whilst we're passionate about allowing our staff to operate with a large amount of freedom and democracy, it can be hard for new recruits to get their heads around what that means. Hearing that people come before profit is one thing. Believing it, and living it, is something else.

So, while they're working out their notice, we offer them the chance to start getting to grips with the Propellernet way of doing things. We send them relevant books to read, such as Dan Pink's *A Whole New Mind*, and we invite them to company meetings, awaydays and socials. It's entirely voluntary and there are no hard feelings if they can't come along, but people tell us it's good to be asked.

As a result, when they walk through the door on their first day, they are as clued up and relaxed as any new starter could be.

Some of the great things we do that can feel a bit odd at first

- Offering total transparency and the ability to challenge.
- Giving our staff a voice (and expecting them to use it).
- Allowing them to have a say in which clients we work on and the right to veto on ethical or other grounds.
- Voting democratically on key issues, such as whether to distribute bonuses equally.
- Celebrating success stories and learning experiences, every single week.
- Expecting our staff to say if something is wrong – and to be part of fixing it.
- Asking them to share their personal dreams and then making them come true.

Even people who are joining us can be a bit sceptical about our working practices; there's an element of *"Yes, nice idea in theory, but does it really happen?"* or, more simply, *"Where's the catch?"* It can take a bit of time to realise that there isn't one, and preboarding speeds that up.

2. Onboarding

Once people have formally joined us, their in-house induction starts. We'd like to think it never really stops.

Lazslo Bock, SVP of Google's People Operations, suggests that two of the most motivational reasons for being attracted to and staying in a job are (i) being surrounded by quality people and (ii) feeling that the work you do has meaningful impact[ii].

We agree. So, we are generous with our onboarding time, surrounding the new recruit with people over the first weeks, to ensure their Propellernet batteries are fully charged up. *Get involved and drive our purpose* is the overriding theme, which is only possible if everyone understands our values, purpose and expectations in the first place.

Onboarding also gives us the chance to make our expectations completely clear. Having invested so much time and energy into hiring a dynamic individual, we'd be disappointed if they just sat around waiting to be told what to do. So, we're transparent about the fact that we involve people in decision-making, and that we expect them to have good energy and ideas, from the beginning.

As the MD, I always kick things off, sharing the agency strategy, our Make Life Better vision and our rolling plan, making sure the mission, values and behaviours are understood from day one. Other team members then pitch in to talk about their parts of the business and give the new starter a clear 360⁰ viewpoint; understanding what everyone does is a necessity, not a nice-to-have, if we're to work seamlessly as a team.

Throughout this process we're looking at attitude as much as skills (you can teach the latter, but it's tough to shift the former). We're actively trying to avoid having any bad attitudes in our team; dog-eat-dog scenarios, where people are forced to watch their backs rather than look ahead, don't Make Life Better for anyone.

We give our onboarding sessions a high profile, and our intention is that they take priority over everything else. It doesn't always happen – sometimes client work can't be put to one side – but even having the intention signals the value that we place on them. We say that we're a people-first business and this is one of the ways we walk the walk; we know from experience that it allows our newest members to hit the ground running and be superengaged right from the start.

Some of the obvious stuff we talk about

- Who's who at Propellernet
- Our work
- How we achieve results
- The way we develop our business
- How we measure client satisfaction, taking a lead from the Net Promotor Score®
- How the business is structured
- How each area integrates

Some more unusual things we mention up front

- How the agency makes money, and how much
- The fact that not everyone passes their probation
- The self-imposed cap on the size of our business to avoid stifling innovation
- The likelihood that they will choose to leave one day and how we support that
- Our philosophy around dreams, our Dreamball Machine and what it could mean for them

3. Probation

In some organisations, the probation period is more of a box-ticking exercise than a serious evaluation of someone's potential to thrive. That's not the way we do it.

Our business is complex and fast-moving. It's also conceptual and creative, driven by emotional intelligence, empathisers, insight spotters, pattern recognisers, data analysts, conversationalists, communicators and makers.

There are so many moving parts, and it only takes one jarring element to stop things running smoothly. But it also takes time to recognise that someone is getting stuck, and to work out how best to unstick them.

So, we've set our probation period at six months. It used to be three; but we found that didn't give either side long enough to get to grips with what was working and what wasn't, particularly when it came to our part-time team members.

And we don't just book a meeting for six months in and then forget about it until then. Right from the start, our new recruits have fortnightly 121s with their relevant mentor or manager. Then, three months in, we have a formal check-in session, with a follow up at six months. This is discussed on day one, so they know what to expect.

We get feedback beforehand from around the business, particularly from people that they have been working closely with over the initial weeks. It's heavily relationship-focused, and is adapted from the Net Promotor Score® question (which we also use with our clients):

MORE IN
CHAPTER 6

*On a scale of 1 – 10, with 1 being **very unlikely** and 10 being **absolutely**, how likely would you be to recommend this person to stay?*

8,9,10	= Stay, they are a high performer
6 or 7	= They have potential, but we may need to extend their probation
Under 6	= Big red flag and discussion with operations board

NICK
THIS

Some people do a virtual intake of breath at the thought of being so frank at this early stage. But the feedback we get is that these conversations are both enlightening and helpful. Mainly because they are there to support and nurture people to help them succeed, not to pick faults.

If there are already sticking points, the check-in allows us to spot them and give them the relevant time and attention, such as:

- Working closely with the new recruit on a particular issue, resetting expectations so they can address it fast and fly through their probation.

- Recognising this could be a longer-term issue, but one which can be addressed. In this case, their probation is extended, giving everyone time to explore what needs to be done for them to flourish. This happens around 30% of the time with new recruits.

- Changing something in the way we operate, or trying something new, which will help the new joiner and others. This happens regularly and helps us to continuously improve – such as changes to our office environment or our approach to coaching.

- It also gives them the chance to give us their feedback; new recruits usually have a different perspective to old timers, so we actively want to hear their thoughts about the business, and we make it clear that they can be honest with us.

After six months, we re-evaluate using the same questions, to see whether our new colleague is moving in the right direction, whether any issues have been addressed successfully, and whether the probation needs to be extended further.

But occasionally, what the probation process reveals is that we're just not right for each other. And when that happens, it's important to accept it, and work out the kindest way forward for all parties. If something hasn't clicked, and they aren't fulfilling their potential with us, it's better for everyone if we help them find somewhere where they can shine.

It's rare, but the few times it's happened so far, it's been a positive experience all round, with no hard feelings.

Our approach to induction may be unusually thorough, but experience has shown us that it's time well spent, benefitting both the inductees themselves and the company as a whole. Simon Sinek, author, motivational speaker and marketing consultant, sums it up brilliantly in *Leaders Eat Last*;

"The strength and endurance of a company does not come from its products and services, it comes from how well people pull together. Every member of the group plays a role."

This pulling together doesn't happen by chance. There's an art to it, building on the strength of our mutual relationships and the trust they engender. Our induction process is the foundation on which these relationships are built.

BE SUPERENGAGED

How did the first day at your current place of work feel? Were you fearful, cheerful or something in between? Did you feel like you already belonged? Did it live up to the expectations of your interview – or did you find a catch?

How do you onboard people? Are you cultivating attitude as well as skills? Do you actively engage in open and honest feedback from around the business, to give everyone the best possible chance of passing with flying colours?

How many people pass probation? Are you set up to spot issues early on?

YOU WIN SOME, YOU LOSE SOME

While our full-on induction process is something we now take for granted, it wasn't always that way. In our early days, we invested less time in the process, and ended up spending far more time later fixing issues that should have been caught up front.

We've also been guilty of doing things in the wrong order or rushing processes due to other pressures; you probably will too, sometimes. As we've discovered, it's still better to do things at the wrong time than not to do them at all.

Even the most intensive induction is only a starting point; our business has multiple layers, so we don't expect our new people to understand everything or join all the dots, even after a rigorous two-to-three-week process. But we do feel confident that we've set our expectations, demonstrated the importance of their input and attitude, and helped them belong.

FURTHER READING

Leaders Eat Last, Simon Sinek, 2014

Drive, Dan Pink, 2011

25. PASSING PROBATION

◀◀ REWIND

Once we eventually got round to introducing a probation period, we didn't do much when someone passed it; it was just a blink-and-you'll miss-it date in a contract. So, while the probationer might have been nervously waiting to find out whether they'd made the grade, for everyone else, it was just business as usual. What a waste of an excuse to Make Life Better.

We've flipped that around now, turning passing probation into a time for celebration, for learning and sharing, and for thinking about what the future could hold.

WHEN THE FUN REALLY STARTS

Given the huge amount of time and energy we invest in our induction process, it would be odd if we didn't make a fuss when people pass their probation. So, as well as taking them out for a celebration lunch, we mark this milestone in several different ways.

Bonuses and benefits

Fully on-board employees become eligible for full benefits; bonus, health plan and all that kind of stuff. So far, so normal. But unlike in many organisations, a new colleague also gets the same bonus as our oldest timers and biggest earners. That's just how we roll.

MORE IN CHAPTER 52

A big-up from the board

We also make a point of announcing that a new recruit has passed their probation at our next company meeting. Everyone hears it, and everyone celebrates it; there are always a few whoop whoops and, inevitably, some beers.

But there's a seriousness beneath this; we've asked all our people to invest in getting their new team member to this point, so we shouldn't let it slip under the radar.

Some fresh-eyes feedback

You know us, we do like asking questions, and the ones we ask of our new colleagues are particularly pertinent. It's easy, when you've been somewhere for a while, to take things for granted, or to do things a certain way because that's how you've always done them; a fresh pair of eyes helps us all see more clearly.

And of course, it demonstrates our willingness to engage, and cements the two-way employer-employee partnership.

The fresh-eyes sessions are run by me and Winnie, our People Manager, and cover the following areas:

- What attracted you to Propellernet?

- Have your expectations been met?

- Do you have stunning colleagues and are you being a stunning colleague?

- What's your biggest achievement so far?

- What's really working for you here?

- What could be better?

- What needs more time and attention?

- If you could change one thing, what would it be?

Without fail, these sessions bring out new ways of improving what we do, from the clients we aim to win, to making flexible working work. And they allow everyone to have an impact from the word go.

AN INVITATION TO DISCUSS THEIR DREAMS

Yes, you have read that correctly. As off-the-wall as it may sound, our Dreamball Machine is probably our most well-known, best-loved initiative, and a real highlight of passing probation. We've got loads say about it, and we'd like to do it properly, so we'll save it for a few chapters' time.

The common theme running through all these milestone markers is that they're about increasing our new employee's engagement. It doesn't break the bank to do so; it's purely an investment in time. But the return on that investment is a financial as well as an emotional one; as we've mentioned already, a people-first culture and high employee engagement creates double the business impact of those with low engagement.[iii]

And to look at it from the employee's perspective, here's Bob Chapman, CEO of global tech manufacturer Barry Wehmiller, and author of the brilliant *Everybody Matters*:

"The number one determinant of happiness is a good job; work that is meaningful and done in the company of people we care about."

Passing probation marks both the end of the recruitment programme and the beginning of a new chapter, working for a company where everybody really does matter. We want everyone who joins us to bring their whole selves to work, be happy and be superengaged; the noise we make when they pass their probation helps make it happen, right from the start.

BE SUPERENGAGED

Do you have a process for passing probation? Is the milestone recognised and celebrated or does it drift pass without a second glance? Does it matter?

What feedback would you give your MD after six months in the business? What might change as a result?

YOU WIN SOME, YOU LOSE SOME

If you don't formally tell people they've passed their probation, they might not know, and so spend agonising months wondering whether to mention it. As we've discovered along the way, that doesn't Make Life Better for anyone.

Now, people are genuinely (and pleasantly) surprised when we celebrate them passing probation; and the rest of the team enjoy it as much as they do. It's a low-cost, high impact way to bring us all together.

FURTHER READING

Everybody Matters, Bob Chapman, Raj Sisodia, 2016

TL;DR

26. FOR THE SKIM READERS AMONG YOU...

While we love working in a fast-paced industry, and enjoy trying to stay several steps ahead of the game, recruitment is one part of our business which we take as slowly as we can. Getting the right people in your team is critical, from a professional skills, personal chemistry and commercial perspective, and it shouldn't be rushed.

So, start searching informally before you need to. Build a network of brilliant people who you'd love to bring on board one day, even if you don't yet have a role for them. Interview carefully and creatively, aiming to get the best out of candidates rather than catching them out. And once you've found your round pegs, invest enough time to settle them in for success.

Or, in the words of the late, much lamented George Michael, *"If you're gonna do it, do it right."*

END NOTES

i   *Based on the IPA survey 2017* www.ipa.co.uk/news/ipa-2015-census-highlights-
    three-key-agency-employment-trends-#.WRMQ_Pnyubg

ii *Lazslow Bock noted in a Bloomberg interview in April 2017 that more than a third
    of Google's first 100 employees were still working at the company, despite making a
    lot of money from the IP. People don't stay for the money, and giving your employ-
    ees a sense of purpose has benefits beyond retention. When people can connect
    their jobs to something meaningful, their productivity increases by as much as five
    times.* www.independent.co.uk/news/business/google-hr-boss-advise-prevent-best-
    people-quitting-human-resources-tips-tricks-a7676731.html

iii www.gallup.com/services/191489/q12-meta-analysis-report-2016.aspx

iv www.oxfordcollege.ac/news/famous-university-dropouts/

Section 5
RETENTION

27. INTRODUCTION

◄◄ REWIND

As epic fails go, this is probably one of our epic-est.
In the early days, we had no idea how much of our time was being billed to clients or how many hours we needed to service the business we had. We simply did what we thought our clients wanted and got more people in when it felt a bit busy.

When we did get a handle on the numbers we realised that, based on the people we had in the building and the number of hours we were charging for, only 30% of our time – one and a half days a week – was being billed to clients. This, within an industry in which people are routinely billed out at 100% or even 120% of their time.

So sure, we didn't have a retention problem; everyone was having too much fun to want to look elsewhere. It wasn't so much retention as inertia.

These days, we make sure we bring in enough income to invest in our people; to challenge and support them as they develop their skills and experience. As a result, when they stay with us, it's for all the right reasons.

> **CFO to CEO:** *"What if we invest in our people and they leave?"*
>
> **CEO to CFO:** *"What if we don't and they stay?"*

Apocryphal.

KEEPING HOLD OF YOUR PEOPLE (UNTIL IT'S TIME FOR THEM TO GO)

Aaaaah, retention. It's so important, and yet so often not properly prioritised. How many companies fail to stick to their appraisal cycle, and don't bother to give regular feedback? How many businesses, when times get tough, cut the training and development budget first? In our experience, too many organisations put all their energy into finding people and not enough into keeping them. And that's just daft.

When people are your business, it makes sense to invest in them and help them grow. If you do it well, and the day-to-day experience of working with you lives up to your recruitment promises, the chances are they'll stay with you for as long as they can. If and when they do leave, it's more likely to be for a good reason, and on good terms.

But this kind of investment is not a quick fix, or a cheap add-on; it means offering a continual cycle of learning and development that really drives personal and professional growth. And business success too, especially if you make time for training, finding new perspectives and pausing for rest, which are all just as important.

At Propellernet, investing in our team is central to our strategy. We take it seriously and spend what some might consider to be foolhardy amounts of time and money on making it happen. We also have regular Wellbeing Check-ins to see whether our people are taking advantage of the things we've put in place.

MORE IN CHAPTER 17

So far, we haven't regretted a single moment or a single penny that we've spent: on the contrary, we're delighted with the way our people have grown and thrived, dreaming up new challenges and future directions and taking us along with them.

In this section, we've set out some of the ways we help people grow within our business; we hope you'll find them inspiring, pinch anything you think could work for you, and develop other ideas of your own. Your people will thank you, your HR manager will thank you, and your balance sheet will thank you, as your superengaged team stick around and drive your purpose and your performance forward.

28. PROPEL DAYS

◀◀ REWIND

Training and development aren't priorities for a lot of businesses – they weren't for us at the start. We were too busy trying to service the clients we had and bring in some new ones; in theory, our people could take time out to develop their skills, but in practice, we weren't freeing them up to do so.

But we've learned over time that there's a massive return to be had on investing in our people – and that it's important to ringfence the time to make it happen. Propel Days illustrate this perfectly.

> ❝ *Don't be a know-it-all.*
> *Be a learn-it-all.* ❞

Satya Nadella, CEO, Microsoft (via Justin Bariso, Inc[iv]).

THE 12 DAYS THAT PROPEL US ALL FORWARD

It's easy to see why training and development are often the last things on a to-do list, and the first to go when times get tough. When client deadlines are looming, or belts need tightening, they can feel a lot more disposable than other parts of the budget.

So, we get it. But then again, we don't. Because the thing is, investing properly in your people's development is exactly that: an investment. It's not money down the drain; it's money well spent. And in our experience, substantial investment brings substantial rewards.

Now, we're not talking enforced what-kind-of-dog-would-you-be management training, or making people do a health and safety course just to fill a tick-box. Instead, we give our team the freedom and responsibility to manage their own careers and develop themselves (with the right springboards and safety nets in place). And the most radical of the ways that we do this is through Propel Days.

TIME TO CREATE, INVENT AND LEARN

As we said back when we were talking about creativity, we have always tried to carve out time for creativity and innovation. More recently, this has developed into our system of Propel Days. These are days that every member of our team is encouraged to take on company time to 'propel themselves forward'. They can take one each month, up to 12 a year.

MORE IN CHAPTER 14

With a staff of 50, that adds up to 600 Propel Days each year. Unsurprisingly, we're often asked about the commercial impact of not having these 600 days available to charge out for client work. It's a big commitment, both practically and financially: work out 600 days multiplied by your day rate, or your average daily staff cost, and see if the number you get makes you gasp.

SOME OF THE WAYS OUR TEAM MEMBERS HAVE SPENT THEIR PROPEL DAYS

Corryn has used her Propel Days (and her weekends!) to start an online art gallery and shop selling limited edition art prints. Her love of design and illustration has led to her working with artists from all over the world to offer nine new prints by nine new artists every month. Since launching www.NineByNine.co.uk, she has collaborated with local businesses and built up a strong black book of creative contacts which we have been able to call upon for our agency campaigns and projects.

Mark has been experimenting with virtual reality and how we can bring this to life for clients. He tested this by creating a VR experience called Beyond Your Horizon for local school children, taking them to places they have never had the chance to visit in the real world (see Chapter 9). An amazing experience for them and a strong case study for us, with the new skills now being used with clients.

Sophie has written a book called *Customer Insight in the Age of Google* to share our new marketing, planning and communication strategy tool, www.answerthepublic.com, with other organisations. Their aim is to open up a new workshop revenue stream and create a new business route for the agency.

Joe has developed his knowledge of artificial intelligence and machine learning techniques to work out how he can make our repetitive technical tasks more automated.

Winnie has been mixing her time between completing her masters in pursuit of life-long learning, with applying her knowledge in a trustee role with Citizens Advice Bureau, to help the organisation innovate its services and enable it to support and empower the vulnerable and in need within our community.

Sam has used his Propel Days for a variety of activities, combining doing the stuff he loves with his passion for creativity. Highlights to date include: writing and recording a film soundtrack; running a live installation at Glastonbury; script writing; prop making; film producing; creating immersive theatre experiences and DJing at an alpine music festival. It may sound like an eclectic mix, but they've all been fed back into Propellernet in one way or another, for our benefit as well as his.

And in Sam's words, Propel Days are *"the best Research & Development lab initiative out there."* In an innovation-focused culture, that's priceless.

But it's a commitment we are willing to make, and we get it back many times over, because our team use this time to learn new skills, or develop existing ones, all of which they bring right back into our business. As a result, the returns are often many times higher than the time and money invested.

And it's more important than ever to make this investment, given the pace at which technology is changing. As reported by People Insight in *Employee Engagement Trends for 2018*:

"The half-life of a learned skill is a mere five years. This means that much of what you learned 10 years ago is obsolete, and half of what you learned five years ago is irrelevant."[1]

HELPING MAKE PERSONAL DEVELOPMENT HAPPEN...

So far, so brilliant. But just as paying through the nose for gym membership won't actually get you fit, we have also learned the hard way that creating the concept of Propel Days wasn't enough. In the first year, for example, only 146 of the 600 potential Propel Days were taken; that's less than a quarter. And while we were initially surprised, when we asked our people why, the reasons they gave made sense:

- They didn't have time or felt it wasn't a top priority for them.
- They didn't know what to do or lacked inspiration.
- They didn't feel comfortable taking a whole day out, just for themselves.

So, we tackled this up front. We realised that, if we wanted to hold people to account for their own development, *encouraging* them to take Propel Days wasn't enough. We had to *empower* them to do so, by making it clear that these days shouldn't be moved around other things, and by helping them to inspire each other and protect each other's time.

As a result, we've helped our team get more comfortable about safeguarding time for personal development. We've also started to get them thinking about how to answer the question *"If I had a whole day to myself, what would I learn?"* as early as possible, from their interview onwards.

And we've helped them understand that personal development doesn't have to be a narrow, work-defined concept; experimenting with art, sport and culture-based learning is equally valid, and can really complement the more technical and analytical work that some of us do each day. Aerial yoga, foraging, navigation and seamanship, languages and the ukulele have all since been enthusiastically tried.

... WITHOUT GETTING TOO CARRIED AWAY

Nowadays, we're so driven to commit to and protect our people's development time, that if anyone takes fewer than three Propel Days a year, we start to question whether they are serious about developing their own career, and explore with them what can be done to change their approach.

But we're not so inflexible that we start kicking off (or kicking out) if people don't take all 12 days. Reading *Work Rules!* by Google's Laszlo Bock has helped us frame Propel Days as more of an invitation than a three-line whip, which is how Google approach their legendary 20% time:

> *"Utilization varies in practice, with some individuals focusing virtually 100 percent on side projects and many others not having any side projects at all.*
>
> *"Some joke that it's really '120 percent time', where work is done after the day job rather than instead of it. More typically, a successful project starts with five or 10 percent of someone's time and as it demonstrates impact, it consumes more and more time (and attracts more and more volunteers) until it becomes a formal project.*
>
> *"The use of 20 percent time has waxed and waned over the years, humming along at about 10 percent when we last measured it. In some ways, the idea of 20 percent time is more important that the reality of it."*

Similarly, in some ways, it's the invitation to bring more of what inspires you into the business that's the most important thing. So, as long as we're facilitating and empowering our people to take their Propel Days, and most of them are being taken, we're on the right track.

BE SUPERENGAGED

What are you doing to propel yourself forward? And are you supporting your team to do the same?

Think about the priority that is placed on training and development in your business. Does it feel right to you?

What would it say about your company if people were able to do things like ukulele lessons on your time? What would the business gain from it?

YOU WIN SOME, YOU LOSE SOME

Juggling paid work with personal development will always be a challenge, and one that we didn't get right initially, with too many Propel Days being deprioritised for client work. It took a mindset shift and a long-term behavioural change to get right – with a nod to planning the right time in advance and protecting time out, in the same way that people do with their holidays.

Remember how much knowledge and experience you have within your business: use it to develop and inspire everyone else. A number of our team have designed internal learning programmes for others, such as Will's 12 Weeks of Pay Per Click for those new to paid media and Robin's 12 Weeks of SEO for those new to technical work.

FURTHER READING

Work Rules, Lazlo Bock, 2015

A New Culture of Learning, Douglas Thomas & John Seely Brown, 2011

Customer Insight in the Age of Google, Sophie Coley, 2018

29. INTEGRATION STATIONS

◀◀ REWIND

If you're expecting people to be creative and innovative, it helps to give them a creativity- and innovation-inspiring environment, away from the disruption of their desks. And we did – or at least we thought we did.

We were openly relaxed about people taking thinking time on the beach, brainstorming ideas in the Pavilion, or having a meeting in the BAi360. Yet mysteriously, it never seemed to happen; the office remained the default space for working, thinking and even eating. For whatever reason, our offer of headspace wasn't being taken up.

So, we put our heads together and came up with a better offer; one they couldn't refuse. And the rest is the stuff of legend.

> *It's rare to find a workplace that offers its employees not only excellent career development and an amazing place to work, but also the opportunity to develop themselves personally and discover new horizons. Integration Stations are a brilliant example of how Propellernet does this.*

Jenny, Paid Media specialist and Team Marmot alumni.

GETTING OUT TO GET ON

Despite all the modern kit, tools, apps and collaboration software that have been designed to improve productivity, we're in danger of getting ourselves into a bit of a techno-pickle. Why? Because the increasing amount of time we're spending interacting with technology can not only affect our personal wellbeing; it can also have an impact on our ability to think.

To paraphrase an article from the Scientific Journal, PLOS One, *Creativity in the Wild; Improving Creative Reasoning through Immersion in Natural Settings*[ii], it has been shown that:

*   Adults and children are spending more time interacting with media and technology and less time participating in activities in nature.

*   Higher order cognitive functions, including selective attention, problem-solving, inhibition and multi-tasking are all heavily utilised in a technology-rich environment and can become depleted with overuse.

*   Attention restoration theory research indicates that exposure to nature can restore these higher order cognitive functions – by 50% or more over a number of days.

In layman's terms, what this is saying is that there is a therapy that can improve your thinking and creativity, with no known side effects. It works, it's free, and you've probably heard of it, or even had a go at it yourself. It's known as BEING OUTSIDE.

Now we already knew, because our grans told us so, that a bit of fresh air will do us the world of good. But this scientific slant has encouraged us to take these wise words further; to create a shift in gear, a change of environment, a whole different physical perspective. To free ourselves up to explore new ways of doing things.

We also knew that for any exploratory work to be worth doing, it would need to be carried out across, not within, our different teams. Like many marketing agencies, we need our people to be cross-discipline experts who can pull together to deliver great work. Our insight, strategy, tech, PR, paid media, creative, content and client servicing people all need to understand the power of the alchemy of their collaboration.

And so, with these aims in mind, our alpine Integration Station was born.

DREAMING UP NEW WAYS OF WORKING IN DREAM VALLEY

Three or four times a year, we invite groups of Propellernet people to spend 48 hours at our CEO's home in the French Alps, known as Dream Valley. They take on a gentle(ish) challenge such as climbing to a summit, white-water rafting, parasailing or some other mountain activity, while focusing on this single-minded brief:

Explore the theme of integration, coming back with ideas that we can practically apply in the agency.

And it works. Being in a group in an unfamiliar environment is a great mind-opener, and a great leveller, mixing not only people from different disciplines, but people of different ages, experience and levels of authority. How successfully you contribute to navigating a series of rapids in an eight-person boat, down the white waters of the Alps, has nothing to do with expertise in your role or your position within the company, and everything to do with how you work within a team.

Different leaders emerge, and strong team bonds are formed, bonds that carry through, back to the day job, bonds that enable our people to laugh together, take on challenges and ultimately do better work.

The experience also incorporates every single one of our core values, MORE IN SECTION 3 and contributes to the off-the-scale engagement levels that our people display. Add to that the mental and physical benefits of exercise and teamwork, and you can see that it's less of a jolly to the mountains and more of a physical and emotional reset for peak performance.

THE TEAM'S VIEW

To give you an idea of how well Dream Valley goes down with our staff, here's what the first team who took part had to say about it. You can read more about their exploits on page 188.

"The whole experience gave me a new perspective on work and life. I was able to step away from the chaos of day-to-day life and just breathe. I was able to reflect on what I have accomplished, what I want to experience and achieve moving forward. Ultimately, the trip made me realise how important it is to make time for myself, because by being happy and relaxed my work has been better, my ideas stronger and my creativity restored."

Naomi

"The way the event was set up created such a relaxed, open tone that it made it easy to share our thoughts on any topic. So it's no wonder that new opportunities came out of it, for either our business, our people or Propellernet friends. New bonds were definitely formed, and I have new respect for my Team Marmot colleagues – I certainly don't look at these guys in the same way after the laughter, tears, trials and triumphs we shared!"

Jess

"We had an amazing adventure. It didn't feel like a team-building trip, but we grew closer as a team; it didn't feel like a workshop, but we shared ideas and discussed solutions as we biked, hiked and climbed. Departments and personalities mixed and united over a common goal – to challenge ourselves, to overcome and to have fun whilst doing it. I brought back a lot from our time out there, but maybe the most important to me is the desire for more adventure and more challenges."

Daniel

"My biggest takeaway was learning that none of us have to face challenges alone as there will always be a supportive team around you when you are feeling under pressure. I also learned to slow down and take things more steadily. I often try to take on too much at once, and just like racing up a mountain at top speed will cause you to burn out before you have reached the summit, so will trying to tackle too many tasks at once. Life is a marathon, not a sprint."

Jenny

"Beating a fear was a formative experience, which helped me to put work worries into perspective: stuttering in a presentation is nothing compared to falling 10m off a rock face. It also let me accept vulnerability at work, and not to be afraid of failure, because it isn't the end of the world if you stammer."

Joe

BE SUPERENGAGED

When did you or anyone in your team last get out to get on? An alpine retreat may be a stretch[iii], but what could you do to create space to innovate?

How often do you bring people from different parts of your organisation together? What might you achieve if you did?

YOU WIN SOME, YOU LOSE SOME

People outside our business often challenge us for giving every member of our team an equal voice, no matter what level they're at. And sometimes this doesn't come easily to us either. But it's foolish to think that only senior people can have an opinion or make change happen. Our trips to Dream Valley have reinforced our belief that a brilliant idea is a brilliant idea, whoever it comes from.

Case study: The mountains are calling

There's no such thing as a typical Integration Stations trip, as every team does it and discovers it their way. But here's a snapshot of how a recent alpine adventure played out.

The team (codenamed *Team Marmot*)

- Daniel – Tech SEO specialist
- Jenny – Paid Media specialist
- Jess – Client Services
- Joe – Insight specialist
- Naomi – PR specialist

The adventure

A three-day trip across grass, rocks and snow, sleeping in refuges, treehouses and chalets along the way.

- Day 1: Mountain and rock climbing (sometimes blindfolded).
- Day 2: A 17km high-altitude tough-terrain hike to a 2257m summit.
- Day 3: A 33km trip by foot and mountain bike.

The outcomes

- A plan to bring some of the clear-headedness back home by offering in-house mindfulness classes.
- A decision to offer to do PR for AlpAdventures.
- A focus on how paid media and insight teams can work more closely together to innovate and improve productivity.
- Two team catchphrases: *"Don't look down"* and *"We're all in this together"* which sum up a positive approach to taking risks.
- And an agreement that creating the life we love, and blazing trails as we go, is something we should all prioritise.

30. HOLIDAYS & SABBATICALS

TIME OFF IS TIME WELL SPENT

We're really hot on people planning and taking their time out. Here's why:

- We are humans. Not machines. We need rest to recuperate and perform.

- If you don't take your holidays, you are likely to become sick, burn out and in the most severe cases, die.

And if that all sounds a bit drama school, consider this. In Japan, there is a name for sudden death at work, through heart attack, stress or suicide: Karoshi. For something to have an actual name, it has to be a regular, recognised event. It's the stuff of nightmares.

> **" Take all your holiday. Go and unplug. Use it or lose it, because we want you to use it. Literally, just take a hike."**

Our senior management team, to everyone else, and each other.

TIME OFF: WHY HOLIDAYS MATTER

Taking the drama down a notch, it's certainly been proved that people who don't take their holidays end up having more time off sick. It makes sense: not giving yourself a break is bound to be bad for your health. That's why full-time employees in the UK are legally entitled to a minimum of 28 days off a year (including bank holidays).

Now of course, everyone is entitled to be ill, and have time off as a result, but it's better all-round if that can be avoided. From a team perspective, a planned absence is way easier to navigate than an unplanned absence. And from an individual one, if it's a choice between a week feeling rubbish, lying under a blanket watching *Loose Women*, and a week somewhere fun doing something fun, we know which one we'd choose.

At Propellernet, our sick rate is five times less than the national average (1.1 days vs 5.7 days a year), which clearly means less unplanned absence for everyone to navigate, including our clients. And we achieve that, in part, by actively encouraging people to take their holidays – and throughout the year, not just in a panic at the end of it. We check in with them half-way through the year to see whether they're on track; it's astonishing, even within a people-first culture like ours, how much encouragement some people need to take a break.

And as a *Harvard Business Review* study showed, taking time off is as profitable for the business as it is good for the individual, leading, as it does, to lower sick rates and higher staff retention. Plus there's the knock-on effect of fewer people anywhere near burnout (and its associated impact on both work and personal relationships).

RESEARCH STUDY: *Harvard Business Review*

The amount of time off people take in the USA has been consistently eroded over the last 15 years, from an average of three weeks a year to two today. With this in mind, the *Harvard Business Review* teamed up with the US Travel Association[v] in 2017 to understand the relationship between wellbeing and taking time off from work, asking:

"Is work getting in the way of success?"

Here's what they discovered: the answer is yes. Why? Well, there are multiple reasons, but two main culprits:

- The fact that the technology that is supposed to give us more freedom actively ties us into working more.
- The myth that the only route to success is working harder, for longer.

As the study concluded:

"If you take all your vacation days and plan ahead for trips, you will increase your happiness, success rate, and likelihood of promotion, and you'll lower your stress level to boot."

Which sounds a lot like making life better to us.

TIME OUT: WHY SABBATICALS RULE

Sabbaticals can be taken after five years at Propellernet. And 10.
And 15. At the time of writing, we've only been going for 15 years
but we're open to them being taken at 20, 25 and 30 years if anyone
sticks around that long.

A concrete example of how we strive to Make Life Better, a sabbatical
is the ultimate rejuvenation point, giving the individual the freedom to
go off and do something amazing for a month, whilst being paid,
knowing they can come back fired up and ready to make a big impact
on their return.

So, on a personal level, a sabbatical is clearly a massive treat. But from a
company perspective, it also allows our people to find inspiration from
outside of the office, as well as within it. As we're in a creative industry,
that's critical; getting out and about, talking to different people, seeing
new countries and experiencing new things, all adds richness to our
creative colour palette.

Some of the unforgettable experiences our staff have had on sabbatical

- Stef took his son to California for a once-in-a-lifetime trip to learn to
  surf, check out the LA Dodgers baseball team and drive the Pacific
  Coast Highway, covering more than three thousand miles over a
  month.

- Sophie went to Namibia, taking in the elephants of Etosha, Skeleton
  Coast, Red Dunes, Fish River Canyon, Waterberg Plateau, Victoria
  Falls – bringing back a whole new business venture for Propellernet.

  MORE IN CHAPTER 36

- James took off to Argentina with his wife and three children, to visit
  their ancestral home and soak up their heritage.

- Eshé went to Thailand to discover the wonders of the East, returning
  with a heightened desire to follow her passion for photography and
  gastronomy, which led to a whole new career.

  MORE IN CHAPTER 32

Some people have already celebrated their second sabbatical, and a handful are approaching their third. We're looking forward to hearing their stories too.

Sabbaticals are particularly important when you consider the rampant short-termism that exists in the marketing industry:

- *Marketing Society* figures from 2016 showed that Chief Marketing Officers in the UK only stayed in post for an average of 18 months.

- This was echoed in the US, with marketers in brand companies lasting an average of 42 months in 2016 (down from 48 months in 2014).

- According to *The Drum* (a global media platform for the marketing industry), the industry average for the length of client-agency relationships is just 38 months.

With this kind of turnover, and the ever-present risk of burnout, it's healthy for us to encourage our people to take an extended break, to properly unplug from the mainframe, and take proper time to consider their future with purpose and conviction.

Life isn't a rehearsal and we want everyone to be able to bring the best version of themselves into the agency every day. Checking out to check in on this, every five years, feels good.

And talking of turnover, our rate is less than a quarter of the industry average, at 7% versus 30%. We're convinced that the way we approach both holidays and sabbaticals might just have something to do with it.

BE SUPERENGAGED

Do your people take their holidays, or are they often 'too busy'? What could you do to change that?

When was the last time you took a break and spent time doing very little? How does the thought of doing nothing make you feel? What could it do for your imagination?

Do you offer sabbaticals for long service? What might you gain if you did?

YOU WIN SOME, YOU LOSE SOME

We don't mean to be rude, but if you take one action from this chapter it's this: go away, take a hike. It's definitely a win some.

31. POSITIVE PARTINGS

◀◀ REWIND

For a while, hardly anyone left. That wasn't as good for our business or our people as it might sound.

Every team, company or organisation needs new blood to bring in new energy and ideas. When football manager legend Sir Alex Ferguson shared his formula for assembling five trophy-winning squads,[vi] *"Dare to rebuild your team"* was one of his top three priorities. And helping people to leave positively is all part of the building and rebuilding process.

> *I say to all my team that no one will retire at Goodman Masson; you will all leave me at some point. And that's a good thing, providing that when you go, you don't leave as good recruiters, you leave as a great business people.*

Guy Hayward, CEO of recruitment agency Goodman Masson, founder of MyLondonWorks and Great Place to Work® awards regular.

WHY WE CELEBRATE WHEN PEOPLE LEAVE

Imagine for a moment that you've landed a brilliant new job that's going to take you in a new direction, make the most of your skills and help you pick up some new ones. You're excited about the move, but first you need to hand in your notice.

How does that conversation with your bosses go? Is it toe-curlingly awkward, peppered with fake smiles which fail to disguise their true feelings? Or do they show genuine excitement on your behalf, encouraging you to talk about where you're going and the adventures that lie ahead, wishing you well and hoping you'll succeed?

You can probably guess where we're going with this one.

The fact is, when you have a culture that encourages your people to think outside their everyday roles, develop new skills and embrace their dreams, some of them may leave to pursue them – and that's OK.

PLANNING TO LOSE YOUR TALENT: MADNESS OR MASTERSTROKE?

At Propellernet, we believe that it's more than OK. It's part of our strategy: we actively plan for the fact that our culture can empower our people to leave us. This allows us to put systems in place to manage the leaving process as successfully as possible, all round.

Rather than getting all Eeyore about it, we choose to take the view that every business needs new blood, new ideas and new thinking to replenish its energy. And we're generally pretty chuffed for the leavers too. So, whatever their reason for deciding to go, we believe that by helping them find their next step, make that move and leave on a high, the chances are they'll take us into their new futures and continue to be part of our strategic network going forward.

This all seems logical to us; but when we talk outside the agency about how we approach people leaving to pursue their dreams – dreams we've actively engaged in with them – we're often met with:

"Are you MAD? Why would you plan to lose your best talent?"

"Well, look in the mirror", we reply (though rarely out loud), *"it's going to happen someday, so it would be madder not to plan for it."* Particularly given the free-range perspective on employment that is becoming the norm; it's been a long time since the job-for-life has been seen as something to aim for. People will leave; let's make sure they do so positively.

Of course, people leave for other reasons than to pursue a dream and, very occasionally, it doesn't happen as amicably as we'd like. But generally speaking, people leaving should be an opportunity to seize, not a threat to fear; you just need to make sure you handle their departure well.

MORE / CHAPTER

Here's how we make our partings as positive as possible.

Plan for the 'what happens next'

There's no point hoping that everything will just sort itself out. Hope is not a strategy. Instead:

- We work out the impact of this person leaving – every high performer will be missed by their team and their clients alike, so it's best to think this through in advance.

- We think about the best way to approach replacing them. Could this be an internal opportunity for one of our team, opening up a space elsewhere, or an external route for someone new to come in?

- We talk to the rest of the team about how they think the role should be defined going forwards. As industries grow and develop, job requirements can change to match, so recruiting for the exact same role may not make sense. It's a great time to check in on what we and our clients actually need.

- The leaver might have some brilliant ideas about how the role could be developed, so we talk to them too.

Share the news, and the plans, with everyone

Neither colleagues nor clients like to find out at the last minute that people they've been working with are leaving. It's just rude. So:

- We encourage the person who is leaving to tell those closest to them and discuss the potential impact as early as possible.

- Once we have an idea of the impact, and have started making our plans, we let the rest of the agency know, and invite them to contribute.

- We also tell our clients, giving them plenty of notice to get used to the idea, and helping them feel confident that we are planning for a smooth transition. We invite them to feed into our discussions about next steps, as their external viewpoint can be valuable.

Start taking the next steps

Having worked out what the next steps are, it's important to crack on with them; replacing people, done properly, takes time. So:

MORE IN CHAPTER 23

- If we're recruiting externally, we start the process as early as we can. Sometimes we might already have someone in mind; other times we need to look further afield.

- We also involve the leaver in recruiting their successor if we possibly can. This can sometimes feel weird for them, but in our view, they are the experts about their role and can help us find exactly what we're looking for.

- We also make time for a proper exit interview, so we can find out whether there's any way we can support them in the future, and hear any last thoughts on how we could improve the role they're leaving behind. It's all good feedback for the business, and helps us part friends.

Celebrate – and mean it

If you're planning on staying in touch (and you should), the way you say goodbye matters. So:

- Partly to thank them for everything they've done for us, partly to show them that we share their excitement, and partly because we just love any excuse for a knees-up, we always give our leavers a good send-off.

- As well as celebrating the strong relationships that have been formed, helping them leave on a high also helps leave the door open for the future.

In short, people will leave. The world will keep turning, life will go on, so you might as well make it as positive as possible. The good ones never really leave you anyway.

BE SUPERENGAGED

What would your boss say if you handed in your notice? What would you say to someone who handed theirs in to you?

Can you imagine leaving your job to pursue a dream? What support and encouragement would help make that happen?

Are you still in touch with former members of your team? Do you still work with them, or support them in some way? How could you all benefit if you did?

YOU WIN SOME, YOU LOSE SOME

Sometimes, even the best laid plans go awry. Keep reading to see how we've tackled that scenario.

MORE IN CHAPTER 33

32. THEY CAME, THEY LEFT, THEY CONQUERED

When great people leave to start a new adventure, we send them off with our blessing, and do whatever we can to help them with their next step. It's our way of saying thank you for all the brilliant work they did when they were with us (and a lot more use than a gold watch).

Here, in their own words, are the stories of three of our heroes who left Propellernet to take on the world.

GAVIN: SEARCH SEVEN

Working at Propellernet was great fun. I always felt like part of the family and involved in the direction of the company. And they also helped me develop the direction of mine.

I always felt challenged, in a good way: I can't imagine another agency letting me take the unplanned, fast-track route from PPC Executive to Account Director in less than two years, going from a delivery role with no experience to a client-facing, team leader one. Learning from Jack, James and Rachel how to manage teams and clients was invaluable, and I really enjoyed the steep learning curve and the extra responsibility that came with it.

And Jack and the team were equally supportive when I came up with a challenge of my own. As the agency grew, and the client entry threshold grew with it, I realised that some of the clients I was working with might end up being too small for Propellernet. I had also been nurturing an idea about developing an agency of my own, one with an ethical edge and the community at heart.

So, I presented my plan to the team; I would take a few of my clients and set up on my own. This would allow Propellernet to focus on bigger clients which could support their growth, and give me a client base from which to launch my own agency. What did they think?

They thought yes, and that's how Search Seven was born; a specialist SEO & PPC agency with a pledge to give up to 7% of our profits to charity and community projects every year. We work in partnership with many agencies, locally, nationally and globally, as well as with direct clients. We're doing really well, and getting off to a flying start certainly helped.

And I didn't just take clients with me when I left. I also took a mixture of culture and team philosophy techniques, in terms of making sure the team is happy, motivated and feeling loved, as well as some key client service and admin strategies to ensure I could put in place processes for things like new business pipelines, client delivery and invoicing. And I almost feel like I've taken Jim with me too; he has remained a superb mentor to me throughout.

It's so unusual to get this kind of support to build your own start-up, and that's the thing about Propellernet. Even though the size has almost quadrupled since I first joined, the people-first culture has remained intact. That is incredibly important, and they nail it.

www.searchseven.co.uk

ESHÉ: FOODIE ESHÉ

My life completely changed when my name was pulled out of the Dreamball Machine. This was the push I needed to follow my dream: to build my own mobile kitchen and take it around Europe, cooking and making videos with the foodies I met along the way.

I'm really lucky, because most employers wouldn't help you realise a dream that means you might leave them, but that's what makes Propellernet so brilliant. Jack, the founder, has this way of making you think absolutely anything you want is possible, and everyone at the company brings something unique to the table, which makes it a magical place to be. Being around so many of those kinds of people was really inspiring and it elevated my ambitions.

I also gained so many skills that will be useful in my new career. For example, knowing how to make a compelling business proposal has come in handy when negotiating a collaboration for my blog or a freelance gig for my photography and design work. I also learned the value of building and maintaining meaningful relationships through my work in the PR department, which has helped me create links with a range of people who I hope to work with in future.

Talking of opportunities, I've recently been featured on The Hairy Bikers – Home for Christmas TV series. Before I got the gig, I had to create a proposal for what I could contribute. I turned it around ahead of schedule, in a very short timeframe, and with a more professional finish than they were expecting. This showed them that I could be relied upon to deliver and that I would go the extra mile. That's very much the Propellernet way of working, and it will stay with me, wherever I go.

Propellernet have not just inspired me to follow my dreams; they've helped them become reality. They were happy for me to use my Propel Days to develop skills like food photography, and they supported me financially to go on relevant courses. I used the Dreamball win (plus my own savings) to buy and renovate a vintage caravan on eBay. Now, a year later, the kitchen is finished and I am ready to go.

My next step involves a few different paths. I'm setting up as a freelance brand stylist (with a focus on the food industry) which involves helping businesses market themselves with graphic design, photography and web design, plus a bit of digital marketing advice if they need it. The other half of my time will be spent focusing on my food blog and Eshé's Kitchen. I can't wait.

foodieeshe.com/foodie-eshe-the-next-step

RIK: WE ARE HAPS

Propellernet has helped me live the life of my dreams.

Like many graduates during the 2008 crash, I was unemployed, depressed and was starting to have no belief in myself. Being offered an internship at Propellernet changed everything.

I loved my time there and worked with some awesome people; they were (and still are) genuine friends, not just colleagues, united by a shared goal of making life better. I was chuffed to be elected as the first Fun Minister, in charge of the new health and wellbeing fund. And that's when I became interested in the science of happiness and wellbeing at work.

It was also around this time that I hit a real low point. I always get the winter blues, but that January was particularly dark. My mum had a spinal stroke, and in the same month, my grandad passed away. I really hit rock bottom. Initially, I tried to distract myself by keeping busy, working all hours during the week and partying all weekend. But that just made things worse. My work suffered. My health suffered.

Thankfully, I had incredible support. I used a Propel Day to go to Dream Valley where I got some excellent advice from Jack: "Stop working so hard and focus on your wellbeing." Unusual advice from an employer, maybe, but not from a friend.

So, I slowed down, and life got better. I started focusing on my wellbeing, particularly mindfulness and nutrition. I did a nutrition course (paid for by the Health and Wellbeing Fund) and discovered how to naturally boost serotonin and support my mental health. The quality of my work got better. My health got better. My relationships got better. I got better.

But it was killing me to see other people, and lots of them, feeling low like I had been. I began helping close friends who were going through tough times and my purpose became clear: empower people to slow down and create their own happiness.

So, after seven awesome years at Propellernet, I made the difficult decision to take this purpose further. I quit (with the full support of the team) to create WE ARE HAPS, a SuperFruits powder to feed your happy.

Since then, I've fallen in love. I've travelled the world, exploring different ways to live and work. And now, I'm in Portugal, setting up Europe's first slo-working place. I've learned to love my life and all the emotional highs and lows it entails.

None of this would have been possible without Propellernet, and the support hasn't stopped since I left. I still use the beautiful shared office space when I'm in Brighton. I still chat to the team when I need advice. I still create parties with fellow Red Stars. I'm still part of the family. I'm still overwhelmed with gratitude. Thanks.

www.wearehaps.com

33. FACING PROBLEMS HEAD-ON

◀◀ REWIND

We were utterly rubbish at having difficult conversations in the early days. We had such a positive outlook, such confidence about the future, that if something went wrong we tended to ignore it. Sure, there was some uncomfortable shifting in seats, the odd snatched glance or raised eyebrow, but very little in the way of action-taking.

It took us a while, but we now know that it's far more productive to get hold of an issue and tackle it, than to let it rumble on. And it's probably kinder to everyone involved.

WHAT TO DO WHEN THINGS DON'T GO ACCORDING TO PLAN

Keen as we are to focus on the positives, our leavers don't always skip off into the distance to follow their dreams. We've had to have some difficult conversations, and have had people leave us for negative reasons, too.

Here are some of the experiences we've had to learn from.

GROSS MISCONDUCT

Even in an organisation that aims to put people first, things can go wrong. No matter how much we strive for high engagement, and encourage feedback and positive change, we're just not right for everyone. And very occasionally, this means we need to ask people to leave.

When these exceptions happen, it's important that HR procedure kicks in. You can't play at things like breach of contract or other legal issues, and although it's not very us to be all policy heavy and procedural, the process is there for a reason; to make sure everyone gets a fair hearing and the right decisions are taken.

In a company where people are proper friends as well as colleagues, the need for dismissal can cut particularly deep: loyalties can be torn and there can be a real sense of loss. However, we are running a business and we need everyone to keep to their side of the bargain. When people don't, we have to take action – and these days, we don't shy away from it.

LOSS OF BUSINESS

However focused you are on making life better for your clients, they won't all stay with you for ever. There many different reasons why client/agency relationships come to an end; some are within your control, and others far outside it. Which is why every agency sets out to create a healthy pipeline of prospects, as well as building strong, enduring relationships with the clients they have.

In June 2016 we lost a significant client, because they went bust. The business evaporated, with them owing us a few thousand pounds in invoiced fees. They were within their 30-day payment terms, but the fees never arrived; we received a phone call to share the news one Tuesday morning, and that was it.

Unfortunately for us, that client accounted for 10% of our predicted revenue. We didn't have prospects who could replace that revenue in the short term. And some of the expected growth from our other clients didn't materialise either. Oh, and did we mention Brexit? Yes, *that* June, *that* year.

In other words, we hit a commercial challenge and a half.

Now, in many agencies, the automatic response would be to make some people redundant; a case of *"your client goes, so you go"*. But we've always refused to be a hire-and-fire business. So instead of jumping to pull the redundancy trigger, we aimed in a different direction, by owning the problem, naming it and sharing it, to try and fix it.

The *Commercial Challenge*, as we called it, was communicated to the whole team. We set out our approach, which was to try and keep everyone employed, holding our nerve until new business landed. And we set out a clear plan for how we could all help make that happen:

- We shared the agency revenue forecast (which is already an open document) in the company meeting, to give context to the problem, highlighting the revenue drop and the direct hit to our short-term profitability.

- We discussed new business and client growth opportunities and asked everyone to play their part in bringing them about – backed up by the six months' salary cover we had in the bank.

- We adapted our Monday morning check-ins to include specific opportunity-spotting for clients, individually or in teams, to help replace the lost revenue.

- We limited our discretionary spend to what was necessary for us to function well, postponing significant spending on things like events and conferences.

- We agreed that the company bonus we had accrued would not be paid out, to give us an extra buffer – although no one was delighted, they felt it made sense.

- And, as a team, we stepped up our efforts on product innovation.

Admittedly, this was a little scary for some of our newer team members, who hadn't been in the world of work for long. But the majority took it as a positive, embraced the transparency and even enjoyed the camaraderie involved. There's nothing like a challenge to get you all to pull together.

And guess what? In three months, we had turned the situation around. Everyone kept their jobs; a handful were even promoted as a result of their exceptional performance under pressure. Sharing the problem made it easier to solve; and the need to innovate also brought some new product ideas to light.

There's no doubt that, if we had had more bad news, or lost another client, or the Brexit decision had had a greater immediate impact, we might have had to make different decisions. But as we proved, there are many other levers you can pull before the redundancy trigger.

REDUNDANCY

Some businesses see redundancy as business as usual. For us, as a people-focused business, it's a last resort.

For those that lead by the numbers, not their people, redundancy can become a way of balancing the books. A way to cut headcount (and so ensure shareholder return) or to meet short-term performance goals, rather than safeguard the future security of the business. A way to make a small number of people outside the business rich, at the expense of those within it.

This may be usual, but it's not right, and it's not the Propellernet way. Very occasionally though, it is something we have to consider. In fifteen years, it's happened twice. And what makes it all the harder is that transparency becomes redundant in this situation too.

We're unusually open about various parts of our business, from strategic decisions right down to our P&L accounts. But legally, in a redundancy process, we cannot share information in the way we would normally, to protect those people whose roles are affected. And that has an impact of its own.

MORE IN
CHAPTER 52

For example, in 2012, we developed a new division of the agency, innovating with a product offer which, on paper, had the potential to fly. But it didn't take off as we'd hoped. The work dried up, and unfortunately, we were unable to redeploy the excellent people we'd hired for this project into our core business. And so, reluctantly, we had to go through the redundancy process.

Not only was this hard on the people whose roles had become redundant, it also had a negative impact on the rest of the team. Our regular feedback sessions highlighted that the lack of transparency and communication around this issue had made people feel like they weren't trusted.

And we'll be honest, that was a tricky one for us. We're proud to have built an open and collaborative culture, with a high degree of engagement built through transparency and trust. Our people are used to knowing almost everything that goes on, which makes it all the more unsettling when we simply cannot share.

Now, clearly, it was the right decision; it was more important to safeguard the rights of the people who were directly affected than it was to be open with the rest of the team. But the way our people reacted to this extreme situation only reinforced our feeling that working to engender trust, rather than maintaining secrecy in everything we do, is critical to our success.

BE SUPERENGAGED

What's the ratio of positive departures to negative ones in your business? Is there anything you could do to increase the former? It's not a quick fix, but it's one worth investing your energy in.

What happens in your business if there is a downturn? Could you try setting your team a commercial challenge – and would they take it on? It's worth thinking about these things in advance; planning to improvise is always time well spent.

Are redundancies a routine approach or a last resort for your business? What could you change to make it the latter?

YOU WIN SOME, YOU LOSE SOME

We wholeheartedly believe in being transparent, but sharing the bad stuff can freak people out, so ongoing communication is critical. The Commercial Challenge was a real success, both in terms of business outcome and rumour-avoidance, but for some of our team it was all a bit too much and led to them panicking in private.

Our advice is to keep your bosses' doors and your lines of communication wide open. Repeat yourself, constantly. And keep the conversation going until everyone is comfortable.

TL;DR

34. FOR THE SKIM READERS AMONG YOU...

In an organisation that puts its people first, retention should be a cinch. And if you plan for it, and make sure you deliver on your plans, it will be. But it has to be built into your strategy and your budget, and kept in even when things get tough.

Investing in your people's personal and professional development, looking after their wellbeing and empowering them to take time away from the office, will all improve their concentration, motivation and productivity. And it will make them more likely to stick around, or ensure they only leave for a totally brilliant reason.

We believe our wide and varied approach to looking after our people is what keeps them, and our business, thriving. It's like giving everyone a metaphorical hug throughout their journey with us.

Or, perhaps more eloquently, from literary master, writer and activist, Maya Angelou:

"I've learned that people will forget what you said, people will forget what you did, but people will never forget how you made them feel."

END NOTES

i   *A New Culture of Learning, Douglas Thomas & John Seely Brown, 2011*

ii *journals.plos.org/plosone/article?id=10.1371/journal.pone.0051474*

iii *If you're not in a position to create your own alpine retreat, you're welcome to come and borrow ours. Start the ball rolling via superengaged@propellernet.co.uk.*

iv *www-inc-com.cdn.ampproject.org/c/s/www.inc.com/amp/135536.html*

v *hbr.org/2016/07/the-data-driven-case-for-vacation*

vi *hbr.org/2013/10/fergusons-formula*

Section 6
DREAMS

SOME OF THE DREAMS WE'VE CAPTURED SO FAR

- *Experiencing weightlessness*
- *Writing and recording an album*
- *Helping homeless people in our community*
- *Going on safari*
- *Learning to cope with pain, and eventually becoming pain free*
- *Getting into property development*
- *Jumping off a helicopter over the Grand Canyon*
- *Developing scriptwriting skills and bringing them to life on film*
- *Running a summer camp in Brighton for children in poverty*
- *Going to Japan during the cherry blossom season*

- *Using AI to solve problems*
- *Experiencing La Tomatina*
- *Seeing orangutans in Borneo*
- *Learning to sail*
- *Going to Coachella*
- *Having a song played on the radio*
- *Travelling to Cambodia, Vietnam and Laos with my children to do charity work helping other children*
- *Renewing wedding vows*
- *Starting a microbrewery*
- *Doing the Mongol Rally from London to Ulaanbaatar (for charity)*
- *Owning a home*
- *Ragging round the Nurbergring in a supercar*
- *Motorbiking across Africa*
- *Going to Burning Man*
- *Learning to fly*
- *Playing on stage at Glastonbury*

IN THE LAST FIVE YEARS, WE'VE MANAGED TO MAKE A SURPRISING AMOUNT OF THEM COME TRUE.

35. INTRODUCTION

◀◀ REWIND

Profit gives you freedom – and what you choose to do with it says a lot about the kind of organisation you are. What we choose to do is reinvest our profits into our people and our business in unusual ways, rather than hand it over to a faceless bunch of shareholders.

But being this ambitious requires a healthy profit and a high level of commitment. It's not something we could have taken on if our business wasn't sustainable, and it's taken years of hard work to get right.

It's also required us to stick to our guns in the face of scepticism; when you stray this far from accepted business norms, that's an occupational hazard. We're always happy to be challenged, but so far, our passion for dreams remains undented.

> *The temptation is to convince yourself that your employees' dreams are not relevant to your business. That is only true if your employees are not relevant to your business – and if that were true, why would you employ them?*
>
> *Most employees feel like they are being used. But if you can genuinely convince them that you have their best interests at heart, then you will reverse that belief and, in the process, create a spirit of teamwork and loyalty rarely unleashed in the corporate world before now."*

Matthew Kelly, author of *The Dream Manager*.[ix]

PROPELLERNET DREAMS: OUR NOT-SO-SECRET WEAPON

No, we're not in a Disney film. And no, we're not trying to get on the X Factor. But as you may have gathered, dreams are part of everyday life for everyone who works here; they're our not-so-secret weapon.

For those of you who might have been wondering what on earth we've been going on about, it's finally time for us to explain how and why dreams make sense in a 21st century, profit-making business. So, suspend your disbelief, open your mind and buckle up for the core of our approach, the fire fuelling our business, and the heart of this book: Propellernet Dreams.

THE BUSINESS CASE FOR DREAMING

Many of us never get the chance to realise our dreams. They can seem invisible; unreachable. But what if they weren't?

What would happen if your place of work actively encouraged you to think about your life dreams, both professional and personal? How would you react if they openly asked you what your dreams were, and invited you to share them? And what would be the outcome of including dreams in the company's strategy?

That's our reality. We're making our bucket list our business plan. And we reap the benefits of it every single day.

It all starts when someone passes their probation. They have a Dream Consultation with me, during which I ask them two questions:

1. What can you do to Make Life Better in the agency, so we are more successful?
2. And if we are more successful, what can we do to make one of your dreams come true?

We've captured around 300 dreams so far, and we're constantly thinking about how to deliver on them. What people are dreaming of, what's driving them, can often be surprising; equally surprising is how often we are able to incorporate them into our business plan:

- Sometimes we help them pursue their dreams, in parallel with their work.
- We can sometimes find ways to weave their dreams into how we work as a business.
- We've targeted clients whose strategies or products align with people's passions.
- We've helped people make their dreams bigger and involve more of us in making them happen.
- Some have even become start-up businesses in their own right.
- Others have led people to leave us and pursue their dreams, with us backing them every step of the way.

So, encouraging our staff to share their dreams doesn't just put a smile on their faces. It opens the door to new business acquisition, new product ideas, personal skills development, operational improvements and investment opportunities.

STAYING AHEAD OF THE ROBOTS

Our passion for dreams also allows us to take advance action against the looming challenges of the future workplace. In the face of seemingly constant threats and Nostradamus-like predictions of how automation will DESTROY ALL OUR JOBS[i], this creative approach to business development and different ways of working could help us develop new, unautomatable ones.

We're not trying to pretend that this will be easy; but it does play to our strengths. We'll need to be adaptable (which we are), with a positive attitude to risk (which we have). And we'll need to keep exploring, and keep seeking innovation, creativity and adventure, with ingenuity and enthusiasm (which we do).

By embracing these new challenges with purpose, we should be in a position to treat the machines as colleagues, not rivals.[ii] The future belongs to creative minds working alongside AI; in an ideal world, we'll automate the ball-ache out of work, and make the parts we do more enjoyable and more productive.

As Garry Kasparov, the (potentially bitter) chess grandmaster who was beaten by AI chess machine Deep Blue, said, *"Machines have no curiosity, no passion and most importantly, machines don't have purpose."*

SUPERENGAGING THROUGH DREAMS

We, on the other hand, have curiosity, passion and purpose in spades, and our pursuit of dreams is central to how we bring that to life. It unleashes a powerful spirit of teamwork and loyalty; it's a huge part of how we Make Life Better and keep our employees superengaged.

A brilliant example of this comes via our Product Director Andy, who talked about his love of cycling in his Dream Consultation. He cycles most days and is a regular long-distance challenge rider; he took part in the Boundless Brighton to Amsterdam bike ride with five colleagues[iii] to raise money for Brighton Housing Trust.

We find that kind of passion inspiring, so when the universe threw up the chance to pitch for a cycling client, we leapt on it. Evans Cycles is now on our roster and Andy is pretty pumped.

Having won the account, we developed a remake of the famous Hovis advert from 1973, in which the original Hovis boy, Carl Barlow, cycled up the same Gold Hill. But this time, he was on an Evans electric bike (he is in his 60s now, after all). The national press, cycling industry and our marketing colleagues were all wowed by it, and our client, like Andy, is pretty pumped too.[iv]

BRINGING DREAMS TO LIFE: THE DREAMBALL MACHINE

Although building people's dreams into our business plan is somewhat radical – dare we say it, unheard of – we don't stop there. From time to time, we also set a ball rolling and make someone's dream come true. Just like that.

As a symbol of our commitment to dreams, as well as a practical way of dispensing them, we have a Dreamball Machine. It's a giant, old-fashioned sweet dispenser, about 5ft high, which has pride of place next to our waltzer reception desk, for all to see.

Everyone who passes their probation gets to have their name in a Dreamball capsule. Then, whenever we hit a target, or win an award, or just because we feel like it – because there are no rules around dreams – we release a Dreamball. And the person whose name pops out gets to have their dream brought to life.

Really? Yes, really.

We used to say the dream had to be possible; going to the moon, for example, isn't something we felt we could deliver.[v] But the longer we've been imagining dreams, the more we're making the impossible, possible.

For some, it's been a simple case of paying for a ticket:

- Jim and Steve fulfilled a childhood dream by going to the football World Cup in Rio.
- Alan learned how to ride a motorbike and then biked across Africa.
- Helen went to Las Vegas with her husband to renew their wedding vows.
- Andy is planning a trip to Japan to experience the wonder of Tokyo in cherry blossom season.

In other cases, we have had to spend more than just money, working with our contacts and investing our time to pull them off:

- Carla wanted to celebrate her dad's 60th birthday in style by taking him on a skiing holiday. We have strong connections in the Samoens region, and our CEO lives there. So we struck a deal with a local chalet owner, which meant Carla could take her entire family along and really make the dream big.
- Flo's dream was to go on a Cuban adventure. A few conversations with our travel client who has a speciality in the Caribbean meant that Flo and her sister got the trip of a lifetime, which would otherwise have bust our budget.

And some of the dreams we've fulfilled so far didn't even come out of the Dreamball Machine, or need money at all, just time and commitment to see them through:

- Richard wanted to get involved in scriptwriting, and has now done so, for our clients and for Brighton Housing Trust.
- One of our team wanted us to help him find his dad. Amazingly, we did.

Even though each of these people knew about our focus on dreams, our philosophy around Make Life Better and our ambition to be the best place to work in the world, it was still a massive shock to see their Dreamball released. But a brilliant one.

One that stayed with them, one they talked about to their family and friends, one that made them evangelise about their workplace.

And clearly, Dreamballs couldn't happen in the way they do without a successful business behind them. It's a virtuous circle: taking care of the business makes it possible to have dreams on the agenda; but having dreams on the agenda, and the engagement that creates, is also part of what makes our business a success.

It's an experiment; an experiment in the motivation of hearts and minds. The result fuels our commercial engine and gives us the freedom to experiment more.

Or, as Matthew Kelly concludes, *"Dreams are invisible, but powerful. You cannot see them, but they keep everything going."*

BE SUPERENGAGED

How radical are you feeling? Could you make dreams part of your company business plan? You don't have to have a Dreamball Machine to make it work: finding out what your people are dreaming of doing, and then trying to bring their dreams to life through the business, is a great way to start.

How future-focused are you? Have you started thinking about how your company might be affected by growing automation? Could dreaming play a part in staying ahead of the robots?

Be honest. What could be more fulfilling than knowing you've helped your team achieve their dreams?

YOU WIN SOME, YOU LOSE SOME

So far, there's been no 'lose some' in our dream journey, unless you count the fact that people don't always believe us when we first mention it. A typical response is "Run that past me again?" or even "You are kidding, right?"

We're also frequently asked: "What's the catch?" Guess what – there isn't one.

FURTHER READING

The Dream Manager, Matthew Kelly, 2007

Insanely Gifted, Jamie Catto, 2016

The Magician's Way, William Whitecloud, 2009

Deep Thinking: Where Machine Intelligence Ends and Human Creativity Begins, Garry Kasparov, 2017

36. FROM DREAM TO BUSINESS PLAN

> *As a big animal lover, six weeks on safari was my dream – and those six weeks were absolutely incredible. But my involvement with Wild Dog Safaris has snowballed into something much bigger, which takes incredible to another level. We've developed such a strong bond with Liz and her team, and seeing the impact our work has had on her business has been amazing.*

Sophie, Audience Strategy Director and co-founder of our latest start-up.

HOW SOPHIE'S SAFARI DREAM LED TO A DREAM PARTNERSHIP

One of the most brilliant things about dreaming is, it can turn a passion into an innovation.

Director James Cameron has never successfully answered why *Titanic*'s heroine Rose didn't just budge up on the door-raft and let Jack climb on (spoiler alert: it didn't end well). But he did very successfully turn his love of diving and passion for the ship's history into a technically-innovative, multi-million-dollar box-office smash. As a way of transforming a hobby into a profit-making project, that's hard to beat.

Similarly, we've found that planning to improvise, and giving people permission to dream on company time, means we often benefit from the innovations they dream up. And because our business plan is fluid, we're able to snap up these dream-inspired opportunities when they arise – and to approach them from an unusual angle.

Our reaction to the dreams of Sophie, one of our talented strategists, illustrates both these advantages perfectly. Here's how it unfolded.

- Sophie loves animals, and she spoke passionately at her Dream Consultation about her dream of going on safari.

- Realising how motivated she was by this, we didn't just wait for her Dreamball to come up, but instead started putting out feelers in the travel industry.

- This led us to connect with Wild Dog Safaris, a safari company in Namibia, run by Liz Kirby.

- Wild Dog Safaris needed marketing help, so Sophie began to steer their online marketing strategy.

- As a thank you, Liz arranged a six-week sabbatical for Sophie – a visit to see the elephants of Etosha, Skeleton Coast, Red Dunes, Fish River Canyon, Waterberg Plateau, Victoria Falls... which was the start of something much bigger.

During her time in Namibia, Sophie discovered that Liz has the same philosophy as Propellernet. She is driven to Make Life Better for her people: protecting those who work with Wild Dog Safaris; supporting the education of their children; breaking the cycle of poverty and developing the communities around them. Wellbeing is important to Liz and she has a strong spirit of adventure.

This struck a deep chord with us. So, we decided to investigate how we could use our skills and knowledge to drum up business, grow Wild Dog Safaris and help Liz support families in Namibia.

THE VALUE OF MOTIVATION FOR A PEOPLE-FIRST BUSINESS

Wild Dog Safaris is a much smaller client than we would normally take on, and we couldn't make the sums add up using a traditional business model. But we felt that the motivational richness this relationship could create for our team outweighed everything else. So instead, we came up with a whole new approach: offering our time and expertise to develop marketing strategy and execution for Wild Dog Safaris, in exchange for free safaris for the team.

Now clearly, in a 21st century economy, the concept of bartering services is unusual, to say the least. It breaks the mould of how any marketing agency makes money. But that's only if you believe money is the only thing that drives value.

In our people-first environment, our commercial value is driven by the motivation of our team. Our partnership with Wild Dog Safaris gives them the opportunity to combine the trip of a lifetime with generating business for a like-minded organisation. The sense of motivation that this gives our people is off the scale.

So far, five members of our team have spent time in Namibia, with their other halves in tow: sharing their skills and developing new ones; widening their understanding of eco-tourism; experimenting with VR to bring the safari experience to life, whilst enjoying a terrific experience.

All of which has helped put Namibia on the map, with coverage from *Huffington Post* through to the *Mirror*, *Radio Times* and everything in between. And all of which is helping us widen our offering to current clients and drive our new business pipeline by demonstrating creative flair.

We're aware that this might all sound a bit self-indulgent. How lovely, you may be thinking, to have the luxury of being so philanthropical. And you'd be right that this kind of investment takes money. But it's money that we've put aside to invest in our beliefs, rather than taking it out of the business as dividends or bonus schemes. We've quite literally put our money where our mouths are.

And as exciting as our work with Wild Dog Safaris is, it's not the end of the matter. At the time of writing, we're about to embark on a start-up business, with Sophie at the helm, to develop more interest in Namibia, using everything we've learned, and our commercial savvy, to continue the work Liz has helped us to start. It's Sophie's dream writ huge, and it's coming to life right before our eyes. Watch this space.

The last word here goes to Liz herself:

"What Sophie has done for us is beyond my wildest dreams. How can we ever repay you?"

BE SUPERENGAGED

What passions are burning within you and your team, and what could they lead to? How could you build on them to create innovative opportunities for your business?

Would you be prepared to approach a business arrangement in a non-traditional way? What would stop you?

What drives your organisation's commercial value?

YOU WIN SOME, YOU LOSE SOME

Client business can come in all shapes and sizes. Our relationship with Liz is based on mutual trust and shared values, and we make agreements on a handshake; the social equity of our relationship is just as important as any commercial agreement.

Partnerships like this rely on a clear alignment of both your business priorities and your personal ones. It's not possible with everyone. But it is possible – and it is game-changing.

37. FROM DREAM TO A NEW PRODUCT

> *Being given the time and support to learn new skills and explore a new area was brilliant. Seeing the product go from a handful of visitors to thousands of daily users has been really exciting, and it hardly felt like work!*

Dan, Ruby Developer and app-building legend.

HOW DAN'S DREAM LED HIM TO BUILD US A KILLER APP, FROM SCRATCH

Like most businesses, Propellernet is made up of a whole range of different kinds of people. As we've said before, we're a powerful mix of empathisers, insight spotters, pattern recognisers, data analysts, conversationalists, communicators and makers – and some of us have other, hidden qualities that just need to be set free.

Our colleague Dan is one of the best technical SEO people in the country, but he is also a maker at heart. He told us that he loved building stuff (something he wasn't doing on a day-to-day basis) and that his dream was to develop a product from scratch.

So, knowing that Dan was both motivated and talented, we took a leap of faith, moved him off client work, and gave him the time and space to play at what he enjoys doing most. He's taught himself to code, and now uses that skill to make new tools and apps that Make Life Better for people.

Chief amongst these is www.answerthepublic.com, an online tool built by Dan that helps businesses do a bit of market mindreading. In simple terms, it uses the queries people type into in search engines to help marketers understand what their target audience is looking for online. This allows them to work out what's happening in their customers' worlds and so develop content and SEO solutions that answer their queries. It's brilliant, it's useful, and it's free.

Now 140,000 people a month are using it, and it's making life better for people in marketing, content, PR and beyond. We know this, because people like Steve Rayson (founder of tech company Buzzsumo), Darrel Evans, (founder of Yokel Local, Las Vegas) and SEM Rush (a tech tool based in Philadelphia) tweet about it daily and share it with their networks.

AnswerThePublic is creating brand awareness and positive vibes about Propellernet, which is helping us grow the rest of our business around the world. It's an idea that became a project that became a new business stream. It's also fulfilled Dan's dreams of building stuff – including his dream job.

BE SUPERENGAGED

What unknown talents might your team be hiding? What might happen if you gave them the time and space to set them free?

Can you imagine being given permission to turn a passion into a new product? How would that make you feel about your organisation?

YOU WIN SOME, YOU LOSE SOME

www.answerthepublic.com is a brilliant example of how, if you give people creative freedom, they feel free to create. No one asked Dan to develop this app; he just took something he'd observed from his everyday job (the limitations of the Google Suggest tool) and decided to try and build something better.

He enjoyed the process so much, and it was so successful, that he's done it again, this time building an app to help PR people understand search analytics: www.answertheclient.com

We can't wait to see what he comes up with next.

38. FROM DREAM TO CHARITY PARTNERSHIP

"" *Working with colleagues at Propellernet has provided a massive boost for Brighton Housing Trust. They have personified compassion for those sleeping rough, and have offered practical help, such as releasing staff to undertake specific pieces of research through our Rapid Research programme, which has led to us directly securing funding to enhance our services to rough sleepers.* ""

Andy Winter, CEO, Brighton Housing Trust.

HOW OUR COMMUNITY GOT TO SHARE IN DAN'S DREAM

While we're pretty proud of our *Culture Catalyst* survey responses as a rule (have we mentioned that? We have? Several times? Oh) we don't always get top scores for everything. For example, in 2015, only 60% of our team said they felt good about the ways we contribute to the community.

That was a real wake-up call for us, especially since we were involved with various local initiatives at the time. But for whatever reason, they weren't resonating with the team, or they weren't having enough impact.

So just as we were trying to work out what to do about it, along came Dan (not AnswerThePublic Dan, we're lucky enough to have two) for his Dream Consultation with me. The first part highlighted an exciting new project plan that he could develop as part of his day job. But when he switched to talking about his wider dreams, I was really moved by what he had to say:

"You know, there are places I want to go, people I want to meet, things I want to achieve. But what's really killing me is walking to work each day and seeing more and more homeless people on our streets, feeling helpless to help them.

"Can we help them? Can they come and use our facilities, our equipment, can we help them get back into work, can we do something about this problem that is getting worse? More people are suffering. There are plenty of people here who want to help and do more in our community... can we do something?"

Err, yes, Dan. Yes, we can.

That very same day, a friend of the agency, Vicki Hughes from Fugu PR, sent round the Brighton Housing Trust Christmas fundraising video (created by BEAST[vi]), in which an advent calendar motif brought to life that it can only take a month to become homeless[vii]:

- 1st December – The rent is overdue
- 2nd December – Council Tax penalty
- 3rd December – Dad loses his job
- 4th December – No more ballet lessons
- 13th December – No presents this Christmas
- 15th December – Credit cards rejected
- 17th December – Car towed away
- 19th December – Utilities cut off
- 23rd December – Eviction notice served

As always, we whizzed it round the agency, asking for support in sharing and donations. And 15 of the team came back and asked if there was anything more practical they could do.

So just like that, there they were; 15 people plus Dan, all ready to engage their time and energy supporting local homeless people. Coincidence? We like to think of it as dreams moving in mysterious ways.

Needless to say, we didn't hang about. It turned out that Stef, our Deputy MD, knew the CEO of Brighton Housing Trust, Andy Winter. So we set up some initial working sessions with him and have been dedicating our time and effort to raising awareness and funds for BHT ever since (bringing in over £30,000 in the first year alone). Their vision is that no one should be street homeless in Brighton by 2020 – that's less than two years away. We're on it, doing everything we can to help them achieve this.

Now, this partnership didn't come about by wanting to tick a box on a CSR checklist, or be seen to be doing good deeds. It came directly from the team, a dream and a desire to have a wider impact on the world outside our window.

But as an aside, our latest *Culture Catalyst* survey showed that 94% of our team now feel good about the ways we contribute to the community. That's the power of a culture that seeks to Make Life Better, even when it happens more by dream than by design. It's impactful, it's engaging and we're inviting more of it in every day.

BE SUPERENGAGED

Could your team be as engaged by something outside your organisation as inside it? Don't be afraid to look further afield for inspiration.

Is the culture in your organisation one that would embrace this kind of opportunity, and run with it? If not, how could you change it?

YOU WIN SOME, YOU LOSE SOME

Always remember that passions are personal. Just because the leadership team might love a project, it doesn't mean that everyone else will. In our case, the community initiatives we were involved in at first just didn't inspire our team. With BHT, it's a different story.

39. FROM DREAM TO HOUSING DEVELOPMENT

> *I've always wanted to get into property development, but I never thought talking about renovating a house would make people cry in a company meeting. That's never happened before. Who knew construction was such an emotional subject?!*

Jim, Propellernet founder and aspiring property mogul.

HOW INVESTING OUR PROFITS IN PROPERTY FULFILLED A TEAM DREAM

Sometimes, if you're lucky (or you make yourself lucky, by having an open mind) one person's dream can make others' come true.

Jim is one of the founders of Propellernet, and a man with a highly commercial brain. But lurking beneath his business persona is a Kevin McCloud wannabe, with a passion for property development.

So, when Jim was thinking about how to get a better return on our cashflow than the zero percent that the bank was so generously giving us, he had a brainwave; to invest the money into buying a property and converting it into flats. This would allow him to pursue his renovation dream, while feeding the profit back into the business.

Brilliant! But there's more.

We know (because we ask) that for many of our team, owning a property is a dream that feels out of reach. Getting the money for a deposit together is hard enough. But in Brighton, there's often a queue of fifteen people at every open day, of which five might be cash buyers and another five down from London, looking to snap up a second home. As a result, offers often end up going above asking prices; the competition is beyond fierce.

And that's when we had a second brainwave: to offer first refusal on the renovated flats to the Propellernet team. They would have to fund the purchase in the normal way, and pay a fair market value, but they wouldn't have to battle it out with the rest of the world – and could also choose how the place was decorated and fitted out.

Now, making people cry isn't part of our business plan, but when we announced this idea at a company meeting, there were quite a few tears (as well as a fair bit of beaming). We haven't hung about; at the time of writing, we've already bought our first property and turned it into three flats. Our PR Director Hannah has moved into one with her husband Tom; their first owned home.

And as well as making dreams of property ownership come true, Jim's dream has engaged others in our team who are interested in property development, whilst delivering a commercial return 180 times higher than that of the bank. You may think we're making this up; we can promise you, it's true.

We don't see this as a one-hit wonder either. It's now become part of our business plan and, given the success of this first project, will stay that way. Jim already has the next property in his sights and the paperwork is all underway... we'll keep you posted.

Probably the best person to sum up the impact of this is Hannah herself:

"Ever since I was a child I've always dreamed of designing my own home, but after saving every penny we could pinch, even a rundown property that we could make our own was still way out of reach.

"Then this incredible opportunity came along, and as it was a project for Propellernet too, it meant we could get involved and make it into the home we've always wanted. We absolutely love what we have created, and we wouldn't have been able to do it alone. I'm so fortunate to have found Propellernet, and to be part something so special. It has truly made my life better."

Yep, we're feeling a bit tearful about this one too.

BE SUPERENGAGED

How open are you to pursuing unusual business opportunities? It took a lateral-thinking leap for Jim to come up with his property development plan, but it's really paying off; as well as helping our staff realise their dreams, we're getting a direct financial benefit.

YOU WIN SOME, YOU LOSE SOME

It's important not to get too carried away with your own enthusiasm. We were so excited about this project that we decided to throw a party in the house we bought before we started the build, to raise money for our favourite charity.

So, we did a recce and worked out we had capacity for 300 people. We lined up KraftyKuts and J Felix (Tru Thoughts) to perform, planned themes for different rooms and checked out sound systems for each area. We briefed designers to create high-end screen-printed invites that could also be turned into prints to sell, set up fundraising pages, and were close, so close, to printing tickets.

Then one of our friendly local council contacts explained that if we went ahead, we were going to get arrested for putting on an illegal rave, disturbing the peace, breaching health and safety laws... take your pick. And one of us might even have gone down for a bit. Ooops. Luckily, we managed to pull this potential stinker just in time.

40. DREAM EXPLODERS

SO...

What would you say if we told you we'd fulfilled a dream of creating an immersive music and theatrical collective of renegade creative freedom fighters called the Red Stars[x], an antidote to the aggressive and soulless cultural gentrification and over-manufactured corporate suffocation of the underground music scene?

What would you say if we added that they subsequently starred in a festival in the Alps, a radio show, a (fake) sponsorship campaign, a closing party take-over, a (spoof) kidnapping, a pop-up club, a digital festival invasion and a thirteen-part web mini-series? And then took to the stage at Glastonbury 2017?

Would you think we were off our (alt) rockers?
You might be right. But oh, the fun we have had – and the engagement we've built. Here's the full story.

WHEN DREAMS BECOME EXTREME (AND THE FUN THAT CAN BRING)

ENTER THE RED STARS

Mark is a talented member of our creative team who is also a musician and showman, and a brilliant storyteller to boot. Based on his experiences of playing at festivals, he had started to dream up a tale about some people called Jake Sniper and the Coverts, who go by the code name of the Red Stars, living in a futuristic world as a creative freedom-fighting force.

For a long while, this was all in Mark's head. Until our CEO Jack asked him, almost in passing, *"What's your dream?"* And his answer was the longest and the bonkersest one we've ever heard.

"So, I've been dreaming about this claustrophobic society, right, where every citizen is monitored, tracked and given a social score, their last remaining freedoms of music and performance completely regulated. It's being taken over by an evil corporation, OneCor, a dastardly media and entertainment goliath which is sponsoring entertainment and buying up all the independent festivals.

"Imagine it, it's like Simon Cowell and Orwell's 1984 Big Brother coming together and stamping out all creative freedoms, creating a vision that unsponsored entertainers are bad and a risk to the 'social harmony charter', treating them like criminals. And the Red Stars are freedom fighters who are society's only hope of creative survival."

Errrm, OK Mark, we thought. You sure you don't just want to swim with dolphins or something?

But the more he talked about it, the more engaged we all got in bringing Mark's nightmarish dream to life. Every person Mark shared it with added a layer, a character, a possibility. No one more so than Sam, our Insight Director (and sometime musician, creative and producer) who was bowled over by Mark's vision from the moment he heard about it, and has become, in Mark's words, *"the brains behind the operation"*.

And yes, it was unusual; crazy, even. But that wasn't enough to stop us; when has it ever been? So, after a few conversations, ideas sessions and general excitement, we decided to see how big this could go.

OPERATION SOUR MILK

MORE IN
CHAPTER 41

In 2015, we held a festival out in the Alps, in Dream Valley. Codenamed SlopeOff, it brought together 200 people from Propellernet, our families and friends, as well as a number of people from other agencies. We spent a week enjoying mountaintop DJs, sunrise adventures, secret forest fondues in yurts and raves in old cinemas. It was the perfect platform to launch the Red Stars on an unsuspecting world.

Mark was in his element. He masterminded Operation Sour Milk from scratch, working with Propellernet people, friends, family and connections to create a raft of immersive experiences, all of which would play back into our client work in one way or another.

- It started with a radio show, hosted by a mouthy giraffe that had fallen in with a bad crowd, SnowyG. So far, so normal. Kind of.

- Half-way through the festival, a fake sponsor turned up: Gordon Romance, CEO of OneCor (played by a local improv student). He wandered around telling everyone how bad it was and that he'd probably buy it and do something else with it. He was pretty convincing.

- There was also a fake product, Alpine Milk: *"17 life-enhancing flavours, designed to help you thrillax to the max"*. Everyone got a sample in their welcome packs.

Then, as the week went on, things got even weirder.

- The Red Stars put a transmission over the radio show: *"We must save the music. We must save the music"*. Red star symbols appeared in the snow and were projected onto the mountains; there were posters on lampposts saying, *"Wanted: Red Stars"*. Gordon Romance offered a reward.

- At the closing party, Gordon's sponsorship presentation was interrupted by him being kidnapped by two Red Stars and bundled into a Land Rover, which sped off out of the canyon.
- Meanwhile, out of the forest, five other Red Stars appeared with red flares, slowly moving toward the staging area. They jumped on stage: one of them playing a sonic riff on his bass guitar; another on the visuals; one on the beats and one on the decks. Then they blasted out a two-hour DJ dance set.
- I played one of the sets in character as Madame Duart, a double agent who could be working for the corporation or could be a genuine Red Star. Even now, no one is sure which.

You might think Mark couldn't top that for craziness – but it was just the start. After Operation Sour Milk, came:

OPERATION HOLY MOLY

A headline hijack of the Brighton Digital Festival, surrounded by an installation of dancing spheres, in association with our friends at guineapig[viii].

OPERATION RED DAWN

An alpine planning summit, during which we pitched plans for a web series to an award-winning director, came up with more outrageous ideas for festivals, and dreamt up a new (real) beer brand.

W.A.R.S (WE ARE RED STARS) – A WEB SERIES

As pitched to the director in Operation Red Dawn, and now in production, a 13-part hard-hitting serialised sci-fi film, with an original script and score, about to be released at the time of writing.

OPERATION "HELLO CLEVELAND"

As pitched to Simon Vaughn, the art curator of Glastonbury (who just happened to be in our offices one day), a three-day role as hosts of MORE IN CHAPTER 48 a stage in the Shangri-La area at the 2017 festival. At which we also launched W.A.R.S, to 70,000 like-minded musical fanatics who were up for an experience and something slightly off the wall.

As Simon describes it:

"The Red Stars came from another time, and yet it felt as if they had always been a part of Shangri-La. Seamlessly integrating with our narrative, as well as taking it to another level, a nano-installation that almost took over the whole field. One of the most outstanding small venues at Glastonbury 2017."

And slightly less eloquently, but none the worse for it, here's how members of the audience described it:

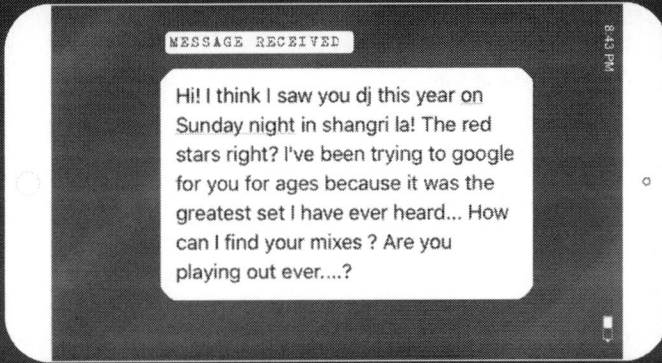

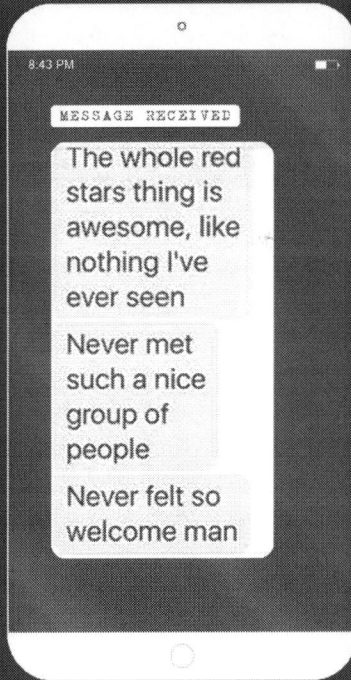

8:43 PM

Hi! I think I saw you dj this year on Sunday night in shangri la! The red stars right? I've been trying to google for you for ages because it was the greatest set I have ever heard... How can I find your mixes ? Are you playing out ever....?

8:43 PM

Yea I was there... you were playing sort of like.... future garage squelchy resonant uk bass drops in-between indie tunes(!) and other mad stuff... me and my mates were head down skanking it was amazing.
Im from Yorkshire dude. we go to glastonbury every year and shangri la is always ace, but that was one show I'll remember for sure. It made me want to dj man! and im 37

Id love to hear something....!

8:43 PM

The whole red stars thing is awesome, like nothing I've ever seen

Never met such a nice group of people

Never felt so welcome man

BUT DID IT MAKE LIFE BETTER?

Clearly, this is something we've had a lot of fun with. But fun aside, we're sure you're wondering what this has to do with creating a purposeful, profitable, sustainable business that puts its people first. And the answer is, everything.

Since Mark first voiced his dream in 2014, it's made waves across our business, touching almost everyone in some way, shape or form. It's galvanised our team, encouraging seamless collaboration as more of us become Red Stars. And in the process, it's created space and freedom for us to experiment with and develop valuable new skills for our clients:

*Content creation * Storytelling * Scriptwriting * Animation*
*Music production * Filmmaking * Installation building*
*New product development * Creative mastery * Audience building **
*Boundary destroying **

And of course, we've made a bit of a name for ourselves as radical innovators along the way.

If we'd never have tried, we'd never have known, and we'd never have had so much fun. Or advanced the creative skills and sense of adventure of our team and the spirit of innovation that runs through it.

The Red Stars and all that has followed has taken Make Life Better in a new direction, in a compelling and unusual way. We've embraced it as if our lives depended on it, because our business actually does.

- -

TOP SECRET

RS01   UNKNOWN MARTYR / Origin Unknown
RS02   KIM SLADE Musician / Adventurer, Unknown Epic
RS03   NIKKI GATENBY / DJ, Writer, Propellernet
RS04   KRIS TURVEY / Musician, Concept Artist, Kuato Studios
RS05   SAM ZINDEL / Musician, Producer, Propellernet
RS06   MARK SLADE / Originator, Musician, Propellernet
RS07   RIK TURNER / DJ, HAPS, Slo-Working
RS08   PAUL WILLIAMS / DJ, Sound Lecturer, BIMM
RS09   JACK HUBBARD / TroubleMaker, Propellernet
RS10   JAKE DENHAM / 3D Designer, Adventurer, Unknown Epic
RS11   TOM HARRIS / Event Producer, Dream Explorers, Teacher
RS13   GEORGE YOUNG / Writer, Musician, General in the Field
RS16   ROBIN FRY / Actor, SEO, Happy Birthtime
RS18   ANGUS WILSON / DJ, Producer, Eames
RS20   NICOLA MOORE / Designer, Festival Artworker
RS23   ANTONY PRIOR / Music Agent, Ultra Runner, Bagelman
RS24   ANNABELLE WILSON / Special Ops
RS27   SIMON VAUGHN / Art Curator, Shangri-La, Glastonbury
RS36   NEIL WHITTEN / Tech Wizard, StoryStream
RS45   KELTON TURVEY / Inventor, Robotics, Maker
RS55   ALAN STOCKDALE / Drummer, Filmmaker, Foundlight Productions
RS69   JAMIE PATTERSON / Director, Jump Start Productions
RS89   BEN LETTIE / Mindful Guru, Slo-Working
RS127 MIKE WOOLDRIDGE / Inventor, Engineer, Maker

transmission ends

BE SUPERENGAGED

What if you felt able to say yes to the craziest idea you'd ever heard? What might you have to do to get into that mindset?

Where could that take you? What might you and your team learn, and what could your clients gain as a result?

YOU WIN SOME, YOU LOSE SOME

If someone on your team is engaged, passionate, and energetic enough to come up with something totally radical, embrace it. Be brave, go with their ideas and let them see where they could take you.

Not everyone will get what you're doing. And that's ok. Dreams are personal; one person's dream could be someone else's nightmare. Not everyone has to be involved – but that shouldn't stop you from grabbing hold of a dream with both hands and seeing what's possible.

Oh, and don't explode things at Glastonbury. It makes the production people very nervous.

41. DREAM VALLEY

" *I once read that the best way for a company to build personality and culture is for the CEO to commit time and resources to activities which are not linked to generating profits.*

Dream Valley shows without any doubt that Propellernet stands for something beyond money. It's become a beacon for who we are. "

Jack Hubbard, CEO, Propellernet.

LEADING FROM THE FRONT: HOW OUR CEO LIVES HIS DREAM

Our Dreamball Machine sits in our reception as a symbol of our commitment to dreams. But it's not the only one we have. Over in France, in the middle of the Alps, is the biggest, most souped-up symbol of what our dream focus is all about: Dream Valley.

Dream Valley was born when Jack, our CEO, decided it was time he fulfilled a few dreams of his own. He wanted to meet and connect with as many brilliant people and ideas as possible, and to inspire a forward vision for our growing portfolio of companies, without having to travel the world and miss out on his children growing up. And to spend more time outdoors, exploring the mountains, while he was at it.

So, being someone who takes everyone's dreams seriously, including his own, he went ahead and did it. He moved his family to the mountains and built an alpine playground for business innovation. A place where people with ideas for positive change can share adventures and dream up visions for better ways of living, working and being.

Hundreds have made the trip, many keep returning and a few have even bought homes there. You may already have read about the SlopeOff Festival at which the Red Stars were launched (www.slope-off.com) and the way we use Dream Valley as an Integration Station to bring different parts of our team together. Here are just a few of our other alpine highlights.

MORE IN CHAPTER 40

MORE IN CHAPTER 29

THE PROPELLERNET 10 YEAR PARTY

One of the earliest, and still talked about, trips to Dream Valley was to celebrate our first 10 years as a company. We flew out the whole team and their loved ones for a weekend of skiing by day and celebrating by night, including a hip-hop show with Jack, co-founder Jim and four other team members on the decks.

A jolly, for sure, but one that the team had absolutely earned, and a great opportunity for some high-altitude team bonding.

⛰ WALKSHOPS

Jack regularly invites aspiring entrepreneurs and seasoned leaders to Dream Valley for mentoring and collaboration sessions, sharing thoughts and dreams while hiking the alpine hills.

The key thinking and decisions behind many important projects took place in Dream Valley, shaping such wonders as: The Happy StartUp School; Unknown Epic; wearehaps.com; Foodie Eshé; flux.am; thebiglemon.com; coglode.com; Bagelman; Holiday Extras; Acumen Business Law and Maptio.

⛰ ALPTITUDE

Now in its third year, Alptitude is a collaboration with the aforementioned Happy StartUp School, which brings 25 entrepreneurs from all over the world together for a week-long adventure camp.

The mornings are spent on talks and workshops; in the afternoons, the conversations continue out in the mountains (while hiking, paragliding, foraging for wild mushrooms or other heart-rate boosting activities).

Alptitude has helped us grow a network of like-minded, hyper-connected entrepreneurs who share our values, as far afield as Cape Town, Mumbai, Sydney and New York. We now run the event twice a year, once in Dream Valley and once in Mount Hood, Oregon.

⛰ MAN VS MOUNTAIN AND MOUNTAIN DIVAS

Troubled by the concept that men only hang out in groups in pubs or on stag nights, we came up with an alcohol-free plan to get them together and encourage meaningful conversations, whilst tackling a peak or two.

In May 2015, all the male employees at Propellernet, as well as the husbands, boyfriends or best mates of our female ones, were invited to come and take part. We carried out a challenging 15km hike up and over a mountain, and raised £1,545 for ActionAid into the bargain.

Two months later, 24 Propellernet women went on a similarly adventurous experience, hiking, biking and white-water rafting their way through a 24-hour laughathon.

In both cases, we all left as a different team, having deepened our working and personal relationships in a way we could never have done in the Lion & Lobster.

KIDSKI

Jack's passion for snow is so strong that he considers the opportunity to ski as one of the essential human rights. So, at the time of writing, we're planning a pilot project in which three parents come for three days skiing with one of their children. If it's successful (and we can't for the life of us see why it won't be) we'll build it into the Propellernet calendar and make sure every family has a chance to have their turn.

We're losing count of all the amazing things that have happened at Dream Valley. We certainly don't have space to tell you about them all here, but feel free to sneak a peek at www.dreamvalleyprojects.co.uk and consider yourself invited to pop in and meet Jack for a chat about it if you're ever in the area.

Dream Valley is our most ambitious articulation to date of the fact that dreams are part of our business, that we will put time, energy and money into making them a reality, and that we all benefit as a result.

Or as Jack describes it,

" *Dream Valley is about living our company values of fun, adventure, innovation, creativity and wellbeing, and living them large. Seeking to Make Life Better for everyone, every day, in every way, without compromise, has put deep, strong roots down in our company culture; Dream Valley extends that culture way beyond the people on the company payroll.*

We didn't copy a blueprint; we stayed true to what we stand for and took it to extreme levels.

And it's awesome. "

BE SUPERENGAGED

What does your CEO dream of? Are they willing to follow their dreams in ways that breathe life into your company values? The dreams don't need to be as ambitious as an alpine playground; they just need to combine their passion, their people, and their purpose.

YOU WIN SOME, YOU LOSE SOME

The Dream Valley experience has been a total win. We've had breakthroughs that couldn't have happened back home. We've developed a deep sense of team spirit, the kind that only happens in a tree house gazing over a Mont Blanc sunrise. We've brought Dream Valley principles (such as WalkShops and mindfulness) back to Brighton, to improve the way we work every day. Most of all, we are proud that our work in Dream Valley is inspiring a global community of business people to follow their dreams.

If there's a lose some, it's the way outsiders view it. Some still see time away from a desk or meeting room as time away from work. In these kind of workplaces, it's easy to get your boss to sign off a conference trip where you spend three days snoring through PowerPoint overload, but it's not OK to get to know your fellow humans on a deeper level while nourishing your soul with fresh air and nature vibes.

Old-school thinking like this is both a human health hazard and a business killjoy. We believe that sharing time, engaged in physical adventure, in nature, with likeminded collaborators, is the most generative business context that exists. And in Dream Valley we've proved that to be true, hundreds of times over.

42. DREAM BEERS

AMBITION + EXPERIMENTATION = INNOVATIVE GROWTH

Growth. It's seen by many as the holy grail of business: getting bigger, earning more, showing off a bit. And the most obvious way to do so is to take on more clients, and hire more and more employees to service them.

However, as we explain in more detail a bit later on, we're not up for that kind of growth. We think the risk to our people and our values is too great. Instead, we choose to grow these values, as well as our culture, purpose and performance, through innovation.

MORE IN
CHAPTERS
46 & 47

And often, Dream Valley is where it all starts. It has been a springboard for so many ideas, start-ups and established businesses that we get a bit tired just thinking about it. We're not exaggerating when we say that hundreds of entrepreneurs have come through the Dream Valley turnstiles; making connections, taking part in adventures and being mentored by our founder Jack as they follow their dreams and create better futures.

But that's not all. From time to time, our alpine incubator delivers an idea or start-up that needs our financial backing as well as our motivational support; something so exciting that we invest in it ourselves. Enter Chris Drummond.

TURNING BEER INTO BUSINESS

Jack had heard about Chris, and his plans for a craft beer subscription service, Crafted Crate. And a number of our people had mentioned that they would love to get involved with craft beer in their Dream Consultations. So, we invited Chris to Dream Valley to see how we could help, and find out where it could lead.

Snowboarding in the mornings, discussing ideas on the chairlift, then back to Jack's Dream Lab (a converted barn) for afternoons on the laptop...

So far, so typical. Dream Valley worked its magic and the plans became reality; Crafted Crate won 200 new subscribers and started shipping beer. In exchange for equity, we paid Chris a year's salary, so he could quit his hated day job and focus on his dream venture.

But although the business got off to a good start, we quickly spotted some warning signs:

- We were one of many craft beer subscription services and had no real point of difference.
- The business model lacked purpose and creativity, and didn't play to our strengths.

Once again, a trip to Dream Valley allowed us the time and space to have a rethink and dream up a new idea. Or two ideas, in fact.

INSIGHT 1: Industrial beer production is wasteful and places a high demand on our planet's resources.

COMPETENCE: Chris has a background in sustainability engineering and is deeply passionate about waste reduction.

IDEA: Build the world's first off-grid zero-impact craft brewery.

INSIGHT 2: Craft beer cans are a work of art. The artists, illustrators, designers and copywriter we spoke to aspired to create their own.

COMPETENCE: Propellernet is a creative agency with a strong network of artists, illustrators, designers and copywriters.

IDEA: Inspire the world to design and drink their very own craft beer brand.

The more we dug into it, the clearer it became that our dreams were pulling us in different directions. Chris had his heart set on a sustainable brewery; we wanted to present a craft beer canvas for the world to sketch their ideas onto.

So, we decided to disband the joint venture and set up two new companies. Chris founded Good Things Brewing, and we founded CraftedCans (www.craftedcans.com).

UNCONVENTIONAL STEPS ON THE PATHWAY TO DREAMS

The route we took to get to that point was unconventional to say the least: from dream consultations, mountain adventures and start-up launches, via a search for purpose, insight gathering, storytelling, artwork, sustainability, intuition and analysis, to separation, reconciliation, deliberation and action. But who needs convention when there's innovation to be had?

At the time of writing, our second longest-serving employee, Rachel, has moved within our business to become a founder in CraftedCans. A seasoned entrepreneur with a passion for food, drink and hospitality, who cut her teeth on our core business and sharpened them on CoverageBook, she's loving every minute of her third Propellernet career.

And while we're no longer business partners, we're right behind Chris and his new venture, cheering him on. Dream Valley (with a little help from us) has inspired him to leave an industry he hates, discover his true passion, follow his dream and lead the charge towards zero impact in the world of craft brewing. We think that's pretty cool.

BE SUPERENGAGED

How good are you at spotting opportunities for investment? Would you be prepared to put your company's money into a start-up?

How good are you at spotting warning signs? Do you have the confidence to step back from a plan that you have been excited about, and acknowledge that there might be a better way?

YOU WIN SOME, YOU LOSE SOME

You could argue that our craft beer experience was more of a lose some than a win some; we invested in something which didn't work out and had to pull out. That's one way of looking at it, but we (unsurprisingly) prefer to take a different view.

Yes, we tried something new, and it didn't turn out the way we'd originally planned. But instead of just cutting our losses and walking away, we invested the time in finding a different path, and this time it was the right one, for both parties. Crafted Crate is a great reminder that straight ahead isn't always the best way forward.

43. THE BOTTOM LINE

Never interrupt someone doing what you said could never be done.

Amelia Earhart, flying pioneer.

PAYING YOUR FUN TAXES

We're all about full disclosure, so we do feel the need to let you know that dreams are taxable.

Yes, really.

As we have learned, the good people at HMRC assume that work is meant to be miserable, and don't understand that you might be inspired to create something of value whilst cycling across the countryside, walking in Japanese cherry blossom, dancing in a forest or gazing across the African plains.

Their view, essentially, is that something this enjoyable can't possibly be work, and is therefore a benefit in kind. That means the Dreamball Machine is fully taxable; quite literally, a tax on fun. But we haven't let that stop us, and neither should you.

Our experience has shown us that it's worth going to these great lengths to maximise fun levels, and to pay the fun taxes we incur. Without any fun in their working day, employees eventually become miserable. Then they leave, and profits start looking miserable too.

Whereas, by focusing on dreams, we build in a sense of fun and inspiration from the start. This allows us to encourage our people to learn new skills, develop new products and become better business people. It also allows us to boost the economy, attract and retain the very best people and do world-class work in a warm, open environment.

Or, as one team member puts it:

"Truly anything is possible here – I feel driven to do more every day. Plus, I get to hang out with excellent people and laugh lots."

That's got to be worth paying for.

TL;DR

44. FOR THE SKIM READERS AMONG YOU...

Our commitment to dreams is a big topic, a massive adventure and a huge part of our business – but it is really simple to sum up.

We believe that building dreams into our business plan is the best thing we have ever done, and is worth every penny we've invested in it. It's allowed us to inspire and support our fabulous people to do brilliant things, both on a personal and a business level, and helped us to keep them as part of our wider team, one way or another. It has made us who we are.

So the big question is, are you ready to dream?

There tend to be two distinct reactions when we tell people about our commitment to dreams. Some people think we're mad, or lying, or both. Others are inspired to give it a go for themselves, even if on a smaller scale.

If you're one of the former: no offence taken. We get that it's not everyone's cup of tea; we hope you've enjoyed hearing about what we've got up to nonetheless. But if you're one of the latter, we'd be happy to help you incorporate some of our thinking into your own business. Get in touch for a chat by all means; it's one of our favourite topics (in case you hadn't guessed). In the meantime, here are a few key pointers to get you started:

- Allow dreams to become part of your everyday conversations.
- Hold Dream Consultations with your team and encourage them to be frank and ambitious.
- Be open to new thoughts, ideas and suggestions. You never know where they might take you.

We'd love to hear how you get on.

END NOTES

i www.theguardian.com/technology/2017/jan/11/robots-jobs-employees-artifi-cial-intelligence

ii Debate is raging about this; even Facebook's Mark Zuckerberg and Tesla's Elon Musk can't agree. Musk warns that AI may potentially be an existential threat to the human race, whereas Zuckerberg, quoted in July 2017, was very optimistic about the technology.

iii Andy was joined by Steve, Vinesh, Dan, Will and Jim. You can read their exploits here: www.propellernet.co.uk/amsterdam-or-bust/

iv To see the advert, search for Return to Gold Hill on YouTube.

v A couple of people have actually joked about going to the moon. It probably won't happen in our lifetime, but you never know; if it becomes feasible, we'll consider it.

vi beast.agency

vii You can watch the video here: www.facebook.com/FirstBaseCentre/vid-eos/1021904781205099/

viii guineapig.global/dancing-spheres

ix Matthew Kelly's books have sold over one million copies and appeared on numer-ous best seller lists, helping companies think about their employees and tackle the problems of high turnover and low morale, by investigating what really drives their people.

x www.weareredstars.com

Section 7
HOW WE MAKE IT MAKE IT WORK

45. INTRODUCTION

> " *Every business person, employee, entrepreneur or creator... understands that we are all operating on borrowed time and money. We need to make a choice. We can continue to run this growth-driven, extractive, self-defeating programme until one corporation is left standing and the impoverished revolt. Or we can seize the opportunity to reprogram our economy – and our businesses – from the inside out.* "

Douglas Rushkoff,
author, *Throwing Rocks at the Google Bus.*

THE ART OF THINKING DIFFERENTLY

We've found that flipping normal business convention on its head creates space for doing better business:

By having an ambition to be the best place to work in the world, we question whether our actions will help us Make Life Better for our clients and each other. Our record engagement levels show that we're succeeding. (More in Chapter 4)

By having no exit strategy, no plans to sell and no end date, we run our business in a way that brings freedom and fun forward to now, rather than waiting until retirement to be able to enjoy them. (More in Chapter 10)

By asking about dreams and bringing more of our life into the office, we add more fuel to our growth path than we would ever have done by simply doing more work. (More in Section 6)

By embracing positive leavers, we're building up an alumni who are going on to blaze a trail in the world, and staying connected to support them in their success. (More in Chapters 31 & 32)

In short, by broadening our thinking, we're letting new light in. And the same goes for our workspace, too.

DESIGNING OUR BUSINESS AROUND A NEW KIND OF GROWTH

In 2015, I was the keynote speaker at a Chamber of Commerce event entitled *A day for growing your business,* and I talked about how our decision to cap the size of our team at 60 had forced us to innovate to grow. This was met with some trepidation and one direct challenge of *"You're not ambitious enough."*

But we beg to differ; and we're not alone. More and more people are recognising that 21st century growth isn't just about more bums on seats. If you're running a future-fit, innovation-focused, people-first business, you should be able to come up with other, better solutions. As Douglas Rushkoff continues:

"Plants grow, people grow, even whole forests, jungles and coral reefs grow – but eventually they stop. This doesn't mean they're dead. They've simply reached a level of maturity where health is no longer about getting bigger but about sustaining vitality... Companies deserve to work this way as well... but in the current business landscape, that's just not permitted."

We believe that, when it comes to ambition, it's not the size of your business that matters, it's what you do with it. We're plotting our own route, based on our belief that being small in number does not mean being small in ambition – or positive global impact.

The route we've plotted, and the way that leads us to run our business, is clearly working. We outshine much larger companies on key metrics such as high engagement, strong margins, low sickness, low turnover, no reliance on external funding (instead reinvesting our own profit to grow our ambitions). This hasn't happened by chance; it's a direct result of the choices we've made, which you can read about in the following chapters.

Of course, one size doesn't fit all and there are many other approaches to growth out there. But for us, people are our strategy. So our business is all about growing our people, both personally and professionally, so we can have a bigger positive impact on the world.

BE SUPERENGAGED

What does growth mean for you? Is it just about size or are there other ways that you could create it?

How does the way your organisation is set up affect your plans for growth? Are they working together, or at odds with each other?

YOU WIN SOME, YOU LOSE SOME

People have suggested to us that what we're doing isn't scaleable; that our mission to Make Life Better through a people-first culture can only be achieved within a smallish business. But we just don't see growth as a two-dimensional concept.

For us, one of the ways of growing is to share our philosophy; spreading the word and encouraging other businesses to challenge convention and reap rewards as we have done. And no, we won't profit directly from that. But we will have contributed to making the world of work a better place.

FURTHER READING

Throwing Rocks at the Google Bus, Douglas Rushkoff, 2016

46. SIZE

> **"** We all know spending time with children is invaluable compared to buying their love. It's the same in our business, time is more precious than a bonus – although that's nice as an addition, it can't be seen as a replacement. We are in the business of people, we must behave like it. **"**

Simon Sinek, author, Leaders Eat Last.

WHY WE'RE STICKING WITH 60 PRECIOUS SEATS

If you've ever worked in a huge company, you may have experienced a *"Who's that?"* moment, when you see someone wandering happily around the building, and think *"Is that a client? An intern? ... A burglar?"* It rarely is a burglar, but it's disconcerting nonetheless to be sharing your office space with people you couldn't place in a line-up.

At Propellernet, we work in communications, so being able to communicate well with each other is important – and knowing who everyone is tends to help. We believe that being relatively small (but perfectly formed) gives us the space to have time for each other and builds trust and engagement – the foundations of doing great work.

So how did we decide what the right size is for us?

In his bestselling book, *The Tipping Point*, Malcolm Gladwell explores social structures and cites the importance of small groups for the distribution of messages. He argues that the maximum number of members that can reasonably exist in a human group is 150.[i]

This is based on Dunbar's Number[ii], from research suggesting that, due to biological limitations in our brain, any group larger than 150 will automatically split into factions and become less efficient; whereas in small groups where everyone knows each other, it's easier to spread messages.

W.L. Gore Tex Associates (makers of GoreTex and lots of other stuff too) share Gladwell's view, choosing to split off new divisions as the company grows beyond units of 150 staff.

IN A WORLD TRAPPED IN BIGNESS, SMALL IS BEAUTIFUL

However, others take a much smaller-scale view of the magic number. For Howard Gossage, Creative Director and owner of advertising agency Weiner & Gossage, the limit was just 15:

"The aim was never to grow beyond 15 people. To this day, that remains the antithesis of pretty much every business plan any agency has ever written itself."

And Bill Bernbach, another advertising genius, articulately pointed out the problem with getting too big in his resignation letter from Grey back in 1947. Seventy years on, his words still make a lot of sense:

"Our agency is getting big. That's something to be happy about. But it's something to worry about too, and I don't mind telling you I'm damned worried. I'm worried we're going to fall into the trap of bigness; we're going to worship techniques instead of substance, we're going to follow history instead of making it... I'm worried lest hardening of the creative arteries begins to set in."

We couldn't agree more, Bill. We don't want the hardening of our creative arteries to set in, just as we don't want to wonder who the people in our building are, or struggle to communicate with each other because we feel like strangers. So we've chosen to avoid the trap of bigness, and set ourselves the magic number of 60.

THE EVERYDAY IMPACT OF OUR MAGIC NUMBER

Limiting our size in this way brings a whole new level of accountability into the business. It's a strategic principle that drives us in a number of ways.

For example, with only 60 seats in the house, we have to be extremely careful about recruitment. So when someone leaves, we don't automatically replace that role; instead, we review our overall business, work out what skills we need going forwards and design the role and recruitment plan accordingly.

← MORE IN CHAPTER 31

Similarly, at this size, we can't afford passengers. Everyone in our company knows there are only 60 seats and that they need to earn their place.

We've set a clear expectation that everyone will take responsibility for their personal impact, and should be able to demonstrate what they are doing to propel our business forward and Make Life Better.

Our size also means we can make engagement part of everyday life. A great example of this is the full company meeting (known as New News), a laid-back occasion with an informal agenda that takes place without fail every Friday at 4pm.

Anyone can take the floor, and we all pitch in to share the latest news and events in our company, our industry and our lives. It's also a time for celebration, as we stop and congratulate those who have achieved something remarkable that week.

In larger organisations, these moments can get missed in the flurry of activity or the race for the next deadline. Instead we take time out to pause, reflect and applaud each other. With growth as a mindset, not a competition, this is the freedom of smallness.

BE SUPERENGAGED

Are you clear about the impact each of your people are having on the business, and how they're driving future growth? Do you have regular conversations about this with your team?

How often do you get together as a company to share and swap stories? Is that feasible, based on the size of your organisation? If it isn't, how about on a smaller scale, within a department or team?

How often does your team come together to celebrate recent achievements? When was the last time you gave someone a round of applause for something they'd done? What might be the result if you did?

YOU WIN SOME, YOU LOSE SOME

If you're not careful, a capped headcount might feel like a cap on progression. If there aren't any roles above yours, and no possibility of creating any, where do you go next?

Our answer is that this is only true if your structure is ladder-shaped. We approach progression through an abundance of futures, as you'll discover later on.

MORE IN ← CHAPTER 49

FURTHER READING

Throwing Rocks at the Google Bus, Douglas Rushkoff, 2016

Leaders Eat Last, Simon Sinek, 2014
The Tipping Point, Malcolm Gladwell, 2000

Changing the World is the Only Fit Work for a Grown Man, Steve Harrison, 2009

47. INNOVATION IN GROWTH

◀◀ REWIND

It's our firm belief that our limit of 60 precious seats, as well as helping us communicate and celebrate better, forces us to innovate in order to grow. But while that's easy to say, it's hard to do – and we didn't get it right first time.

Before landing on our strategy of creating technology products, we went through various different ideas, at some cost to the agency. We made some rookie errors – like underestimating the time and investment required to successfully launch a new product. And we bust some myths along the way, such as: *"You just got lucky."* To which we'd reply: *"Yeah, sure, but the 30,000 hours of graft might also have played a part."*

It has been one of the hardest parts of our journey, much harder than if we'd just gone ahead and doubled our size by doing more of the same. But it's also been one of the most rewarding things we have ever done, from which we have learnt more than we could ever have known, about our industry, our abilities and each other.

> **Genius is 99% perspiration and 1% inspiration.**

Thomas Edison. Genius.

> **I am a great believer in luck. The harder I work, the more of it I seem to have.**

Coleman Cox. Wit.

THE SECRET TO GROWING WITHOUT GETTING BIGGER

Some people just don't believe that growth within a limited headcount is feasible. And you can see why: to look at it at a GCSE Business Studies level, if you fix the number of people in your team, the only ways to increase your revenue are to either charge your clients more (no thanks) or work your team harder (no thanks squared).

Our answer is that you have to work smarter; change the revenue game and look for opportunities to do things differently.

Back in 2014, when we reached 50 people and £4million revenue, growing to 100 people and £8million seemed the obvious path to take. But it doesn't take Carol Vorderman to work out that, whether you divide £4million by 50 or £8million by 100, you end up with the same revenue per person (RPP): £80,000.

Aside from the finances, we liked being a team of 50; there was a good vibe, and we knew we didn't want to dilute it down by getting much bigger. We felt that adding another 50 would just lead to less space, more management, more process and cultural cliques.

MORE IN CHAPTER 46

So, on the basis that RPP is the best measure of the financial resources available to Make Life Better for everyone in a company (rather than just the major shareholders), we concluded that we needed to step off the obvious, but ultimately unfulfilling, path towards doubling our revenue growth. A smarter move, we felt, would be to focus on doubling our RPP growth to £160,000.

And to do that, all we needed to do was develop a product that we could sell a million times over, without hiring more people. Well, we do like a challenge.

BUILDING A TEAM TO HELP US CHANGE COURSE

As our team and business plan had evolved, we had become experts in both Search Engine Marketing and Public Relations. We had spent Malcolm Gladwell's 10,000 hours in the relatively uncharted space where algorithmic analytics meets creative communications, and the time we'd invested had paid off.

Along the way Gary, our Strategy Director, had become particularly excellent in both fields, and so was becoming a human bottleneck. If you wanted a great idea you went to Gary; if you wanted to win a pitch, you took Gary along. His reward was to work longer hours than everyone else, while other rising stars were being overlooked and underdeveloped. So, setting him free to pursue new product development seemed to make sense, for everyone.

We knew that Gary had dreams of starting a technology product business that built on our PR expertise, so that's where we began. We read a few books and ran a few experiments on the side. We found an intern who could build our ideas (Alan) and a software coding and product start-up veteran (Jonathan). And we worked out that we also needed a product manager, two coders, a designer with an appreciation of code and a couple of PR experts to bring the alchemy of what we do in the agency to life in our new product.

The good news was, we already had the right team in house: Gary, Alan, Dan, Stefan, Stella and Rachel. In theory, we could start working on new product ideas without investing in new people. But we soon worked out that if it was going to succeed, they needed to be able to give it proper attention.

PROTECTING TIME TO INVEST IN THE FUTURE

All of which led to one of the bravest decisions we have taken to date. We knew it was going to hurt but we were pretty sure it was the only way to do it. So, we took a deep breath, took the team out of the agency, brought Jonathan in as a consultant and ring-fenced their time to focus on technology for a three-month trial period.

And hurt it did. A lot. These people were all core parts of our day-to-day business. Pitching to clients, tackling new challenges and running the main agency was tougher than tough without them.

But as people who wear Lycra like to say, no pain, no gain – and in this case, the pain was well worth enduring. Once we gave the team the time to focus on technology and technology alone, things started to take off; so much so, that at the end of the three-month trial, we green-lit the project and agreed to commit 50% of our annual profit to future development.

And that's when the hard work really started.

GETTING OUR GRAFT ON

We quickly learned that Edison was right about the amount of graft required to hit on a winning idea. Forget about overnight success; this was definitely more of a marathon than a sprint.

For two years the team toiled away exploring technology products, without writing a single line of code for the global selling product we have now. And even after we released the first beta version of our starter for ten, PerfectFit, it took months before we were confident that it was going to be our primary technology product.

Jonathan had urged us to design something our agency Propellernet would use; if we could Make Life Better for ourselves, he suggested, other agencies would be interested in buying it too.

One of our big problems at the time was using shared Excel spreadsheets to manage influencer outreach campaigns; not only were they clunky, they crashed when people were updating at the same time. The solution we created was PerfectFit.

We built a prototype and the agency started using it, even raving about it a little. We called a few friends in PR and found they too were frustrated with their Excel spreadsheets – and they leapt at the chance of trying our new, smart solution. Word spread fast and our diaries filled up with demos. We signed up customers who paid us actual money.

Validation. Valuation. Champagne all round?

Sadly not. Not yet, anyway.

During the year that followed, it became clear that we had overcooked the complexity of the product. People were buying it, but not using it. We needed to make it simpler if it was going to take on the world.

So, after taking a few hundred more decisions, based on customer feedback and first-hand observation, we took one feature of PerfectFit and turned it into a new, single-minded product – the ability to create coverage reports.

The result was CoverageBook, the first of our software as a service (SaaS) products for the PR industry (www.coveragebook.com). It may have taken a few years, but it was worth the wait.

COVERAGEBOOK: GROWTH THROUGH INNOVATION

To give you the background, coverage reports are the reports that PR people generate for their clients, to demonstrate the impact, reach and engagement that the coverage has had. They are made by manually finding and cutting web pages from coverage found on the internet and pasting them into PowerPoint. Although the end report is valued by clients, putting them together is time-consuming and frankly tedious work.

We estimated that automating the production of coverage reports, including all the metrics generated by the coverage, would allow people to complete the task in 10% of the time. We were confident that getting the other 90% back to spend on other things would Make Life Better all round. And so it has proved.

Our SaaS team have reimagined PR reporting for the 21st century and are selling the product on a licence basis, in more than 3,000 cities around the world and counting. They've subsequently added www.answerthepublic.com and www.answertheclient.com to our portfolio, which are also inspiring and supporting the marketing industry worldwide.

——➤ MORE IN CHAPTER 37

> " *Fantastic product. I love the ease of making coverage books and the fact I don't have to learn a system. Just cut and paste URLs. I like how the product is continually evolving.*
>
> Heather Hansen,
> Assistant Director of Communications, Stanford

> " *I am so happy I found this tool! I could not live without it now. Clients are extremely happy with the layout and how easy it is to make sense of each placement. It is FANTASTIC. I cannot sing the praises of CoverageBook enough.*
>
> Jessica McCafferty Brennan, Vice President, Janice
> McCafferty Communications
> (New York, LA, Chicago PR Consultancy)

> " *Just use CoverageBook. Works for videos, online or offline coverage, social media, custom sections, anything you like. Calculated metrics are exceptionally useful. PDF exporting and online sharing are easy to use and look great.*
>
> Senior Digital Communications & Design Specialist,
> The Genome Analysis Centre, UK

SOME OF THE WAYS PEOPLE RAVE ABOUT COVERAGEBOOK

All of which is pretty exciting. But the fact that we've done all this without recruiting any significant numbers of people (just two more awesome folk in Dave and Andy), and that we've boosted our own revenue far more than we could have done by growing in a more traditional, headcount-based way, is what excites us the most.

By asking the right questions, and by being prepared to ringfence the time and team to answer them, we have turned innovation into growth. By setting out to develop a product that makes our own lives better, we have come up with something that is now a must-have for the global PR industry. All without any external funding, and all created through reinvestment of our own profit, hitting breakeven in good time to deliver a new revenue stream into our business.

And the real kicker? It was staring us in the face all the time.

Five years ago, when we first started exploring the power of dreams, we asked people to answer these two questions:

1. What can you do to Make Life Better in the agency, so we are more successful?
2. And if we are more successful, what can we do to make one of your dreams come true?

We should have realised the potential for CoverageBook when pretty much the whole PR team came up with the same answer for making life better across the team:

Dan	Coveragebooks - automating these & charging for them
Eshe	Coverage reporting to be more automated, not manually screengrabbing
Isa	Automating coverage and charging project fees
James M	Creating a plug in to make coverage books more effective
Rik	Automation of coveragebooks
Sophie T	Automation of coverage reports
Gemma	Reporting and coverage automation & consistency

Taken from Propellernet's bucket list business plan

But we weren't ready, or flexible enough, or open-minded enough to use this insight to answer the need. Hindsight is a wonderful thing.

SO, WHAT DID DEVELOPING COVERAGEBOOK TEACH US?

Looking back, what we've learned is that our strength lies in our culture of learning by doing. We've realised the first two years weren't wasted; during that time of exploration, the team developed new skills and experiences that made them far better placed to succeed when they hit on the right solution.

We've also realised that Coleman Cox was right, way back in 1922, when he equated luck with hard work; and we'd add that having the right mindset is equally critical. Yes, you could argue that we were fortunate to come up with a brilliant product at the right time. But it was a combination of experience, passion and our culture of innovation and open-mindedness that generated the idea, not luck. And it was tenacity, not luck, that meant we saw it through.

Too many people believe that ideas are the most valuable things in business. In reality, it's the execution of them that deserves the credit. Derek Sivers[iii], writer, entrepreneur and founder of CD Baby (an online store for independent musicians) has a powerful take on this:

*"To me, ideas are worth nothing unless executed.
They are just a multiplier. Execution is worth millions."*

There are an infinite number of ways we could have executed our ideas that would have resulted in failure. Being open-minded, leaving egos out of the work, treating everything we did as research, spending a huge amount of time observing and listening to each other and our potential audience, all paid off.

It was the sum of thousands of small decisions that led us out of trouble and towards success.

Derek Sivers isn't just pulling his multiplier argument out of thin air; it's calculated based on years of experience. Here's how he came to his conclusion:

Awful idea	=	-1
Weak idea	=	1
So-so idea	=	5
Good idea	=	10
Great idea	=	15
Brilliant idea	=	20

No execution	=	$1
Weak execution	=	$1,000
So-so execution	=	$10,000
Good execution	=	$100,000
Great execution	=	$1,000,000
Brilliant execution	=	$10,000,000

" To make a business you need to multiply the two.

The most brilliant idea, with no execution, is worth $20.

The most brilliant idea takes great execution to be worth $20,000,000.

That's why I don't want to hear people's ideas. I'm not interested until I see their execution. "

BE SUPERENGAGED

Are you trying to grow by doing more of the same? What might happen if you diversified?

Is there a business problem you could solve for yourself that could become a new product opportunity? Would you be prepared to take some of your staff out of the day-to-day business to give it a try?

If you're thinking about getting into a new area, who could you call on for help? Experience and support are priceless when you're in start-up territory. We were lucky to cross paths with Jonathan Markwell, a local tech wizard, data expert and all-round great bloke, who shared his wisdom with us on a consultancy basis.

It's also worth thinking about where you would get your investment from. We've been clear from the start that we never wanted to rely on external funding for growth; instead, we keep the investment amongst ourselves, where we know we can continue to put our people first, whilst still in the pursuit of profit.

YOU WIN SOME, YOU LOSE SOME

When it comes to CoverageBook, the win-somes and lose-somes really are two sides of the same coin. Every mistake we made taught us something invaluable:

- *At the start we placed too much value on ideas, rather than execution. New ideas would distract us from finishing the ones we'd already started; by mid-2013 we had over 20 product ideas. We only needed one: the one that was going to make the difference to our revenue.*

- *We jumped on the 20% Google bandwagon, but realised that this wasn't enough freedom to deliver on our high expectations. In the end, it took over 30,000 people-hours to get from the first "Hey, I've got an idea" to the launch of CoverageBook; but in revenue terms, that was time well spent.*

- *We hired a talented developer straight out of a Masters programme, but failed to give him the support he needed. After a year he had created a huge code base and learned lots for himself, but the business had gained nothing of tangible value. Even our own team couldn't use the tech he had built. Once he was properly supported, the work really took off.*

It took us months to recognise that the 'simple', 'technically trivial' tool we'd developed on the side was what our customers actually needed and was worthy of our complete focus – but wasn't as simple as we had thought.

If we had to sum up what we've learned in one sentence, it's this: there is no such thing as an overnight success.

FURTHER READING

Public Relations' Digital Resolution, (eBook), Stella Bayles, 2015

How to sense-check your progress

NICK THIS

If we've convinced you of the value of doing some new product development, that's brilliant; we'd love to hear about it. Email superengaged@propellernet.co.uk to let us know how you're getting on.

As a ball-park, we'd recommend allowing at least 18 months of full-time work for a great idea, executed by a great team, to become profitable. You're likely to be on the right track if:

- You can get your first version live on the internet in a day.
- You get at least one external paying customer (who actually uses the product) within three months of starting work.
- You get at least ten paying customers over the following three months, and it gets progressively easier to sell and get them to use it.

PerfectFit was far slower than CoverageBook on all these fronts; it took two weeks to go live, six months to find a paying customer and only generated one new customer a month. When CoverageBook pulled in 100 active customers in just three months, we knew we were on to a winner.

48. SPACE TO THINK DIFFERENTLY

CREATING ROOM FOR IDEAS AND INNOVATION TO FLOW

As we've said before, we're not big fans of the word no. When people tell us that you can't please all of the people all of the time, we tend to see it as a challenge, not a threat.

But our desire to Make Life Better for our team does sometimes butt up against the fact that different people want different things. For example, whenever we do a *Happier Habitat* survey, and ask for feedback on our working environment, we get some contradictory responses.

For every *"I don't like silence in the office"*, there's a *"Noise levels can hamper concentration"*. And for every *"When it comes to pitching to journalists, I think quiet rooms would help"*, there's a *"We could do with more of a buzz – people find it too quiet sometimes to pick up the phone"*.

All of which is fair enough, and in need of being taken seriously. So we've responded by designing a workplace in which there's room for interaction and collaboration, as well as for quiet, focused work. Space is important, so we've made sure there's enough of it; personal space, collective space and room to breathe. The fact that we've capped our headcount at 60 has certainly helped.

HOW THE FOUNDRY HELPS US THINK DIFFERENTLY

We've also taken the idea of free-thinking and collaboration and run wild with it, turning one of our floors into a hip-hotel-style lobby, called the Foundry.

It has no desks, or pods, or anything typically businessy; instead it has flexible seating, a stand-up section, lounging areas, a coffee station, a fully stocked bar, turntables and mixer and a big screen. And it has fundamentally changed the way we work.

Being tied to a desk and the same four walls isn't the way to supercharge creativity; having different spaces, open working and the freedom to move around creates better connections and lets more ideas flow.

Team members often come to the Foundry to work, to meet, to bounce ideas off whoever happens to be there, or just to hang out in their breaks. It's a place where sparks fly.

LETTING SERENDIPITY IN

Now, if you're in marketing, the concept of the Foundry might not sound all that radical. A bar area in the office, where people can bring their laptops? So what? Well, as ever, it's what we do with it that counts. And it goes way beyond just us.

Howard Gossage, Creative Director and owner of Weiner & Gossage, has described his business as less of an agency and more a mix of social club and symposium – where people are free to drop in and engage in animated discussion (and, yes, have a beer or two).

We totally buy into the idea that exchanging ideas and experiences with a wide range of people can fuel creativity. So, inspired by Howard, and by Dutch company Seats2Meet, who launched the Serendipity Machine app[iv], we're also using the Foundry as a co-working space; to let the outside in, to try and engineer happy accidents, and to bring about chance connections that lead to valuable relationships.

How does that work? Well, so far, like this.

- We invite creative mavericks and other like-minded individuals to come and work in the Foundry. *"Why not pop in and use our co-working space, next time you're in town?"* is as formal as it gets.
- Authors, journalists, entrepreneurs, designers, builders, storytellers and start-ups have all come and spent time as part of our working community.
- We don't charge them for it; the value of this exchange transcends money.
- The real value comes from the connections that happen within our willingness to work as a community; we're trading ideas, inspiration and social currency.

And once again, it's a win win. From the visitors' perspective, they get to come and work for free in a cool, creative environment in the heart of Brighton, with coffee, beer and flying sparks on tap. But it's paid off for us too, in a variety of ways.

- It's created a pipeline of potential staff and clients who have come in, seen what we're all about, and wanted to get involved in one way or another.
- It's provided us with a source of inspirational guest speakers to come in and share their stories, through our regular *Found* nights[v].
- It's enabled us to supercharge our projects – by offering collaborative space for clients to use, and by creating an extended collective of skilled people who we can pull in if needed.
- And, in one particular case, it helped one of our dreams take off.

HOW THE FOUNDRY HELPED THE RED STARS GET TO GLASTO

In 2017, a friend of a friend called Simon, who was Art Curator of Shangri-La (Glastonbury's naughty corner), came to meet Mark and Sam in the Foundry and discuss their mad-cap idea of getting the Red Stars to perform there.

During the conversation, Simon mentioned that he was struggling to work at home since the birth of his daughter. Mark and Sam, both dads themselves, immediately sympathised and invited him to come and work in the Foundry whenever he needed some headspace.

So, that's what he did, on a regular basis. Which meant he was on the spot when Mark and Sam were brainstorming, planning and building their ideas; happy to listen and join in, getting more and more enthusiastic as the conversations progressed.

And that's how something that started off as a crazy idea, and a conversation with a friend of a friend that was little more than a favour, became the event of a lifetime. The Red Stars did indeed take over an area of Shangri-La that summer; their dream brought explosively to life, through the value of social currency and a desire to work differently.

MORE IN CHAPTER 40 →

This wasn't a deal made with hard cash. It was a handshake over creative ideas that were able to collide because of circumstance. It's not growth or profit that enables this kind of magic to happen; it's creating the space to let serendipity in.

BE SUPERENGAGED

How happy is your habitat? Do you take the time to ask your team how they feel about it? You never know; the insights you get could inspire you to change the way you all work, for the better.

Do you have the space and the inclination to open up your workplace to like-minded individuals? Who would you ask, and what do you think you could gain from it?

YOU WIN SOME, YOU LOSE SOME

We've been lucky so far in that we haven't had to turn anyone away from our co-working space due to too much demand, though we have had to say no to a few meeting room requests because we needed them for agency work.

The one rule we have introduced is asking whoever has invited the visitor to share their name and photo on Slack. It's partly so we don't get sucked back into the "Is it a burglar?" cycle, and partly so everyone can go and say a proper hello.

FURTHER READING

The Serendipity Machine, Sebastian Olma, 2012

THE TYRANNY OF HIERARCHY: INCHING UP THE AGENCY LADDER

A typical client services department has a rigid hierarchy which has to be painstakingly climbed, one rung at a time:

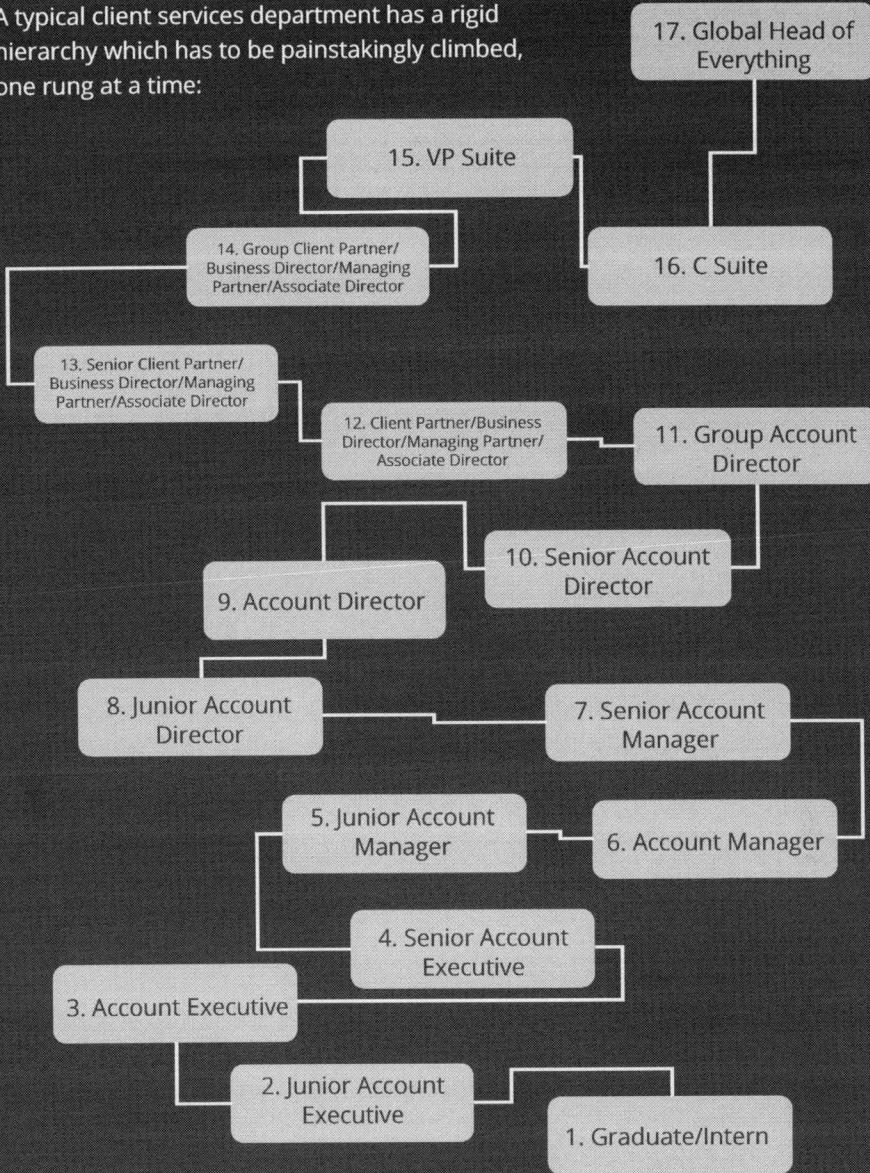

17. Global Head of Everything

15. VP Suite

16. C Suite

14. Group Client Partner/ Business Director/Managing Partner/Associate Director

13. Senior Client Partner/ Business Director/Managing Partner/Associate Director

12. Client Partner/Business Director/Managing Partner/ Associate Director

11. Group Account Director

10. Senior Account Director

9. Account Director

8. Junior Account Director

7. Senior Account Manager

5. Junior Account Manager

6. Account Manager

4. Senior Account Executive

3. Account Executive

2. Junior Account Executive

1. Graduate/Intern

WE BELIEVE IT'S WHAT YOU DO, NOT WHAT YOU'RE CALLED, THAT MATTERS.

49. STRUCTURE AND PROGRESSION

> *I love the lack of hierarchy here. I can talk to anyone, everyone is accessible, no one is worried about getting involved and supporting a new idea. I've not heard 'No' yet.*

Propellernet employee in our anonymous Culture Catalyst Survey.[xvi]

THE ONLY WAY ISN'T UP

In our ever-changing, fast-moving world, we need to be able to respond accordingly; to grab opportunities as they come up and deliver on them. That's why, instead of having a fixed five-year plan, we've developed a rolling one, through which we plan to improvise on a regular basis.

But it's impossible to be this responsive if you're working within a rigid framework. And anyway, as Propellernet favourites The Corporate Rebels[vi] assert, *"The command and control model is outdated; even the military says so."*

What you need instead is a structure that flows, under the guidance of freedom and democracy, with more open communication and fewer structural barriers. Which all sounds lovely in theory, but how does it work in practice? Here's how we do it.

WE DON'T HAVE RUNGS FOR RUNGS' SAKE

At the heart of the way we work is our lack of a strict hierarchy. We're not a flat structure – that leads to chaos – but we're hierarchy-light, and we aim to keep the rungs on our ladder to a minimum.

As a result, our team has a say in much of our company decision-making, from whether we should take on a new client to what the Fun and Wellbeing Fund should be spent on. And the same goes for client work too. We believe that the people who are closest to the information are the ones best placed to make the decisions, and so we empower them to do so, whilst giving them all the support they need.

MORE IN CHAPTER 57

MORE IN CHAPTER 16

This not only makes us more efficient, it's also central to wellbeing; people who are given autonomy rather than having wait for approval have been shown to suffer less stress.[vii] It's not just business logic, it's biology.

WE MAKE EVERYONE CLIENT FACING

Traditionally, the role of client services is to be the link between the people who do the actual work (the creatives/tech specialists/engineers) and the people who pay the bills. They manage the relationships, agree the deadlines, take and deliver good and bad news and occasionally get treated as a punchbag by both sides. Which not only makes their job spec a bit rubbish, it's also a shockingly inefficient way to do business.

So, just as we encourage the people closest to the information to make the decisions, we also empower them to explain those decisions to our clients. And we get the right people to speak directly to each other – our tech people speaking to the client's tech people, for example – which can save a whole heap of misunderstanding down the line.

This way of working means that no-one hides behind the client services people and everyone is accountable to each other. As Group Senior Global Client Account Director types love to say, there's no I in team.

WE WORK IN INTEGRATED TEAMS

Our teams are fluid and change on a project-by-project basis, depending on what the client needs. So instead of having all the tech types in a fixed team and the PR pros in another, we have a cross-skilled team working on project X, another working on project Y and so on.

It's possible to be working on more than one project and so be part of more than one team; it's another reason why our internal communications are so strong (and it's also great fun). And from time to time, we do pull all the people who work in the same discipline together as a group. But in the main, everyone works with anyone and that's the way we like it.

WE DON'T PUT OUR STRIKERS IN GOAL

Another reason why we avoid rigid hierarchies is because we don't buy into the concept of prescriptive job specs; specific roles at specific levels involving specific skills and experience. We'd rather build roles around what people excel at, and enjoy.

We're clear about this from the beginning; in fact, it's a question we actively ask at interview:

"We don't want to put our strikers in goal. By that, we mean we don't want to put you in a position in which you can't excel, doing things you don't enjoy or simply can't do really well. So, tell us, what aren't you good at?"

Some of the answers we've been given have surprised us; but we've not regretted asking the question yet.

THE FREEDOM OF EXPLORING: CAREER ADVENTURES

" *Why choose a career ladder when there is a climbing frame?* "

Kara Melchers, Managing Editor of *BITE* at Creativebrief, and peripheral path expert.

LEADERSHIP WITHOUT LAYERS

Our lack of a career ladder is therefore a deliberate choice, and one we're happy with. But we're also happy to be open about the fact that this could, if not addressed, lead to confusion for our people about where their careers are heading. It's one of the knottier challenges we have had to wrestle with; how do we answer when our people ask, *"Where do I go next? What's my path?"*

These are great questions, and our answer is this:

"It's up to you. The joy of our lack of ladder is that it puts you in charge of your career, and allows you to develop a skill set far broader than you would within a narrow job description. You can ask for as much support and guidance as you need; we're here to help you grow what you're great at.

"The only thing we ask is that when you leave, you're not only a better specialist in your field, but also a better business person. Other than that, it's your career adventure, and you're in the driving seat."

So instead of a hierarchy, in which roles become scarcer as you get to the top, we offer an abundance of opportunities through lateral growth. That doesn't mean there is no leadership, but we see the leadership role as one of inspiration rather than micro-management.

We encourage every person to do the best work they can, exploring new avenues and being rewarded for their impact. We aim to give continual in-the-moment feedback, and carve out time for personal development, whilst supporting ongoing growth through learning on the job and our monthly Propel Days. We've also employed a resident coach, whose role is to work thorough any issues, challenges or decisions that our people are grappling with.

MORE IN CHAPTER 28

The result is that, instead of forcing our people to fit into a linear structure, we help them create their own paths through the business, embracing all different types of skills and abilities along the way. These paths tend to fall into one of four categories:

1. **Specialist progression**. The closest we get to a typical route up through the business.
2. **A bit of a wiggle**. Throwing themselves into the bends of what they are best at, which may mean changing specialism, or even creating a new one.
3. **Going off piste**. Being part of the agency *and* a founder of a new start-up business within our business.
4. **Taking a leap of faith**. Leaving to pursue a new business and/ or dream, with our support and blessing.

As these aren't the kind of examples you'll find in the Ladybird Book of Career Paths, we've explained them a bit more below.

SPECIALIST PROGRESSION

In some cases, for some people, the route upwards *is* the best route forwards. But if we're not careful, this could lead to adding in more levels, and creating the hierarchy we're so keen to avoid.

So we're experimenting with different ways of recognition and reward. We haven't solved it completely; for those of our people who are motivated by a strong hierarchy, the accessibility and empowerment of our flatter structure isn't enough of a trade-off. We're exploring with them how to get the best of both worlds, so they can continue to progress with us. Watch this space.

A BIT OF A WIGGLE

It may not be a technical term, but it's the perfect way to describe the path that many of our people take through the agency.

Sophie joined us as an intern, with a journalistic background and strong spirit of curiosity. Her first posting was in the PR team where she crafted ideas, stories and communication strategies for key brands.

Her creative flair led her to the Creative team, driving ideas and insights as a springboard for PR. And from there, her nose for insight and ability to sniff out new opportunities saw her leap into the Strategy and Insight team – leading the charge on qualitative insight across client business.

Today, Sophie is our Audience Strategy Director, bringing strategy to life, speaking at events and hugely in demand. We didn't have an Audience Strategy Director role when she started; Sophie carved the role out for herself, playing to her strengths via PR, Creative and Insight along the way.

GOING OFF PISTE

For others, the route to success is to get involved in one of our start-up businesses (which often start life as someone's dream).

CoverageBook, our technology business and tech start-up, was created by a Propellernet team. It allowed them the freedom of founding a new business, with the security of being in full employment; light on risk, heavy on opportunity. This way of working felt unusual at the time but is now very much part of our new business development plans.

MORE IN CHAPTER 47

Similarly, we're following up our work with Wild Dog Safaris by developing a specific marketing venture of our own. The original WDS team will be the founding members of this new business, again with the backup of a secure job and working environment.

TAKING A LEAP OF FAITH

Sometimes, in an organisation that prioritises dreams, people's desire to follow theirs is so strong, it becomes their future. And when great people leave in this way, we help them in every way possible, to thank them for all the work they did when they were with us.

MORE IN CHAPTERS 31 & 32

Progression at Propellernet, then, means something different for everyone. Our people don't inch up a rigid ladder, or collect a series of over-defined job titles. They develop their leadership and learning abilities, and trail-blaze in whatever path they decide to tread, inspiring others along the way.

Being given permission to create your own career adventure can be scary; it's certainly a lot more effort than being told what to do. But it's a critical part of developing future-fit careers in a time of great change – and the results speak for themselves.

MORE IN CHAPTER 59

BE SUPERENGAGED

How formal is your organisational structure? Do your people have the freedom to design their own career paths? Could they?

How responsive are you to people who want to change direction? Is your organisation supportive, are you happy to invest in any training or mentoring they might need to move successfully?

YOU WIN SOME, YOU LOSE SOME

Getting to grips with freedom around career development takes time, and we've not cracked it yet. It can be hard for employees to break free from the traditional promotion mindset, and managers and mentors need to develop strong coaching, leadership and inspiration skills to support them.

Succession planning in this environment takes a different path too. It's not a question of 'find and replace'; instead, we create roles that play to people's strengths. It helps us keep our culture alive, and to continue our planning to improvise.

There is no blueprint, no roadmap to fall back on; and that doesn't make it easy. But it does open up endless possibilities of "Where next?"

FURTHER READING

Superbosses, Sydney Finkelstein, 2016

Reinventing Organisations, Frederic Laloux, 2014

50. FLEXBLE WORKING

◀◀ REWIND

We were late to the party on this one. Flexible working has been transforming business outcomes for years, enabling people to work at their best and allowing those who can't be based in an office full-time to stay in the workforce and progress their careers.

So, what held us back? Fear, mainly. A fear that it might disrupt our client relationships; a fear of what might go wrong. Which is unusual for us, but understandable, given the importance of our clients to our business.

Finally, though, we got with the programme. We saw how successfully it was working elsewhere, and realised how well it fitted in with our determination to Make Life Better. It was time to ask ourselves, *"What would you do if you weren't afraid?"* and then get on and do it.

> *We have ended up in an always-on digital landscape, constantly pinged by updates and enduring a state of perpetual emergency interruption, or 'present shock'... previously known only to 911 operators and air traffic controllers.*

Douglas Rushkoff, American writer and zeitgeist-capturer.

LET'S TALK ABOUT FLEX, BABY

As you may have gathered, we really REALLY love our office. We've taken a lot of time and care over it, creating a space in which the noise-lovers and the undercover librarians can all work in peace and harmony and where there is always beer in the fridge.

→ MORE IN CHAPTER 48

However, as delicious as it is, our office isn't always the right working environment for the job in hand. It's brilliant for collaboration and teamwork, for people to bounce off each other and connect face-to-face, for serendipitous meetings of minds and ideas in free flow, for maintaining our culture and celebrating together.

But it can also make productive deep thinking and meaningful work challenging, in all the wrong ways. It can become an interruption factory, fuelling our addiction to distraction and getting in the way of getting work done. And the lure of digital technology only adds to the problem. In the words of Bruce Daisley, EMEA VP of Twitter and the brains behind the *Eat Sleep Work Repeat* podcast[viii]:

"We operate on a cortisol-drenched adrenalised attempt to check our emails all the time. The consequence of cortisol and adrenaline in the system is that you end the day feeling exhausted."

In fact, according to Bruce, 50% of the working population reports feeling exhausted at work. That's half of us, permanently knackered. Blimey.

TODAY, EVERYONE WANTS SOME FLEXIBILITY

In the past, when our people needed to focus intensely on a piece of work, they tended to navigate around it by coming in early before anyone else, staying til most people had gone home or logging on in the evening. Booooo!! Hiiiiisssssssss!! So, it's not surprising that, in a recent *Culture Catalyst* survey, they suggested that more flexibility around when and where they worked would make them more productive.

And they're not alone; the demand for flexible working is growing, in all industries and across all ages and genders. A recent survey by flex experts Timewise[ix] revealed that 87% of the UK's full-timers either work flexibly in some way already, or wish they could, with 92% of millennials, 88% of Generation X and even 72% of the baby boomers preferring this way of working.

So, as a forward-looking business, we need to create a workplace that's future fit. And as a people-first one, we need to help our people work in the right place at the right time for them. That doesn't mean more hours, it means better hours, which is why we've introduced flexi-hours for all.

WHAT THE FLEXI-HOURS PLAN MEANS AT PROPELLERNET...

We've always had standard hours of 9am to 5.30pm, in line with our clients' typical working days. But our new flexi-hours plan sets 10am to 4pm as the core work hours, leaving our people to decide for themselves when and where they spend the other two and a half.

If people want to finish at 4pm, they tend to start early; if they want to start at 10am, they stop a little later. It's up to them. Either way, the plan provides us with six hours of collaboration time during the day, with other hours for focusing on individual thinking and deep learning.

It also means our team members never have to miss a sports day or the first day of school, and can choose to go running before work, or simply walk into the office, rather than jumping in the car – better for everyone in the long run.

And it ensures that there's a defined window for face-to-face work with clients. They, and we, enjoy it when they come in to work with us, and it's an important part of creating strong working relationships.

... AND WHAT IT DOESN'T

Flexibility works best when it works both ways, so there has to be a bit of give and take. Our flexi-hours aren't a sneaky way to accrue extra holiday, nor an unbreachable human right; if we need to get in front of clients outside our core hours, then we do so.

So even if someone prefers to work, say, 7.30am to 4pm, that doesn't mean those hours are fixed and guaranteed; that's hardly flexibility in action. Instead, we ask people to take their team's and clients' needs into account, and flex around them.

At the same time, we're always happy to respond to specific circumstances. If someone is writing a business plan and needs three solid uninterrupted days to do it, we'll send them off home with a laptop and our blessing. The core hours aren't a ball and chain.

To date, four key ingredients have helped make flexi-hours a success:

- **Everyone having the right tools**
  Remote work needs the right kit – laptops, mobiles and collaboration tools such as Slack.

- **Everyone having the right attitude**
  In or out of the office, whatever the time of day, our mission remains to Make Life Better for clients and colleagues. If working flexi-hours, or remotely, supports this, we're generally comfortable with it.

- **Everyone respecting each other**
  There's a danger that flexi-hours can reinforce the always-on culture, by tying people to their phones instead of their desks. Being able to switch off when the working day is done – and that switch-off being respected by the rest of the team – is critical.

- **Everyone trusting each other**

  Just because you can't see someone, doesn't mean they aren't working. Trusting people to be grown-ups and get on with their work rather than sit watching *Homes Under the Hammer*, and focusing on outputs rather than inputs, tends to bring out the best in them.

Since we introduced flexi-hours, none of our major business goals have come under pressure. In fact, our productivity has gone up, we've hit more of our targets, and our people are happier as a result. Gone are the days when you had to work 9-5 to pour yourself a cup of ambition; we love you Dolly, but life has moved on.

Some of the things our team say about flexi-hours

"I feel like I have much more space to accomplish everything I want to, both at work and personally. In fact I feel like I can get more done! It's brilliant."

"The biggest drivers for me are wellbeing and being there when I need to for my family. It's definitely reduced stress in my life."

"I feel more productive since flexi-hours have been introduced, both in and out of work."

"Taking the pressure out of mornings (and the chaos of parenting/school runs!) has been such a massive deal."

"I'm less stressed and more rested, which lends itself to increased creativity and productivity."

"Flexible working has definitely made my life better (thank you)."

BE SUPERENGAGED

Do you think you could be more productive by working fewer, but better, hours?

When do you work best? And where? Does it depend on the day, the project or your mood?

How easy would it be for you to introduce flexibility around when or where your people work? Do you have the right technology, and the right levels of trust?

YOU WIN SOME, YOU LOSE SOME

In true Propellernet style, we didn't just impose flexi-hours on our team. While we were pretty sure they'd be up for it, we checked it out with them first (and weren't surprised to discover that they all wanted to give it a try).

So, we had a ten-week trial period, after which we checked back in with the team to see whether it was working and what could be improved. For example, we'd originally said that everyone had to keep everyone else informed about their movements; as you can imagine, that created an information overload and nearly broke Slack (our internal comms channel). We've relaxed that requirement now, and it's working a treat.

FURTHER READING

Deep Work, Cal Newport, 2016

51. STOPPING THE BRAIN DRAIN

◀◀ REWIND

None of us were parents when we first started the business; now, 15 years on, we have over 40 children between us... and counting. In the intervening years, we have slowly but surely become aware that we need to think about how to support the people who have other people to care for – or risk losing some of the most amazing talent in our team.

PARENTS NEED JOBS (AND LIVES) TOO

Unusually in our industry, our business is made up of 50% women and 50% men. And it's important that it stays that way. Why? Here's why.

Margaret Heffernan, entrepreneur, author, international businesswomen, speaker and interviewer encourages us to think about team dynamics at work in her highly popular TedTalk, *Why it's Time to Forget the Pecking Order at Work*[x]. Her research finds that successful teams exhibit three traits:

- They have high degrees of empathy and social sensitivity to each other.
- They give each member of the team roughly equal time, so no one's voice dominates, and there are no passengers.
- They have women in them.

The targets for more women in the boardroom are backed up by sound business sense. For example, according to a report by McKinsey, gender-diverse companies are 15% more likely to achieve financial returns above their industry average.[xi] And an article in *Forbes Magazine* quotes several studies which have come to similar conclusions.[xii]

The lack of women in senior roles is a complex issue, and one we don't have space to debate fully here. But it's certainly true that, in many industries, women step out of, or back from, their careers to raise their families. And a key factor is the lack of good quality flexible jobs for them to come back to.

When flexible experts Timewise carried out a survey in 2016 focusing on women returners,[xiii] asking about the kinds of jobs they would consider, 93% said they would be prepared to work part-time, whereas only 6% would consider a full-time job with no flexibility. But with less than one in 10 quality jobs[xiv] being advertised as flexible in some way, there is clearly a massive gap between flexible job supply and demand, which employers need to fill.

MAKING IT POSSIBLE FOR PARENTS TO RETURN TO WORK

We're not going to let our people fall into that gap. All the women (and men) who work with us are incredibly talented, and we want to hang on to them. We also want to encourage them to lead full lives; that includes spending time with their growing families as well as being engaged in their jobs, which we know can be a hell of a juggling act.

And it's not only because we care – from a hardnosed business perspective, it would be stupid to suffer this talent brain-drain without trying to do something about it.

So, how do we tackle it? Well, on a personal level, we've been known to slip new parents a copy of *Mothers Work!* by Jessica Chivers, a cracking read which discusses the issues playing on these mothers' minds, nudges them to be proactive and gently draws them away from the pressure of perfection.

More strategically, our flexi-hours approach helps, but it's not enough on its own. 45% of us are parents (split evenly between men and women) who might prefer to work fewer hours than the standard week. So we take the time to find out what they need, and help them come up with a solution that works for everyone.

As a result, 25% of our team now work a mixture of part-time hours. The patterns include: three or four days a week; shorter working days over the full week; four longer days over a five-day week; variable mornings or afternoons at home, or a mixture of all of the above.

And it's not just a mum thing or even a parent thing; this kind of flexibility is open to everyone, and it's up to all of us to make it work.

We've found it's helped us to hang on to our talented team members, and to support them in managing their work-life balance; and we're not the only ones. According to research by flexible recruitment company Ten2Two:

- 83% of employers agree that flexible working has benefitted their business, with 56% agreeing strongly and none disagreeing.
- Benefits of flexible working quoted by employers include greater retention of valuable staff, employee wellbeing and satisfaction, and access to a broader talent pool when recruiting.

However much you love your job, sometimes the way to Make Life Better is to work a little less. And that's OK with us.

BE SUPERENGAGED

What's the gender split of your business? Is it different at a junior level to a senior one? How does the split affect your team dynamic?

Do any of your team work part-time or flexibly? Is it something that you offer proactively, at the point of hire, or is it simply a response to employee requests?

What's your brain drain like? Do you tend to lose people when they become parents, or do you make it possible for them to come back and succeed?

YOU WIN SOME, YOU LOSE SOME

A good example of how flexibility allowed us to hang on to a great person is Simon, who freelanced with us on a project for two days a week. We thought he was brilliant and wanted to keep him, but he wasn't up for working full-time, so we compromised on four days a week. If we hadn't been prepared to be flexible, we couldn't have persuaded him to join our team.

Too many part-time roles are created by lopping a day off the individual's working week and expecting them to produce the same amount of work, but more quickly, and for less money. That way disaster lies, for everyone involved. Successful flexible jobs are properly designed, with flexibility built in. Basing the job description on outputs not inputs, and thinking through the principles of where, when and how much work needs to be done, are two good starting points.

FURTHER READING

Women on Top, Margaret Heffernan, 2007

Mothers Work! How to Get a Grip on Guilt and Make a Smooth Return to Work, Jessica Chivers, 2011

52. TRANSPARENCY

◀◀ REWIND

Back at the beginning of the Propellernet journey, we were a bit too disorganised to be transparent. We were so determined to avoid being hemmed in by process that we failed to get a proper handle on the numbers; we couldn't share things like revenue forecasts or KPIs with the rest of the team, because we weren't confident about them ourselves.

Clarity on vision, purpose, values and commercials all took time to reach. Once we sorted ourselves out and got a grasp of the facts and figures, we were able to start sharing.

WHY HONESTY REALLY IS THE BEST POLICY

We're in the business of communication, so it would be pretty rubbish if we didn't carry this through by communicating clearly and openly with our clients and our team.

But transparency in business is astonishingly unusual. Many businesses today are managed almost entirely for short-term results, with quarterly profits being considered more important than sustainability of employment, and redundancies being used to balance the books. These tactics are rarely talked about[xv], which can encourage gossip and fear among staff – and fear flies in the face of innovation and creativity.

Guess what? That's not the way we do things. We believe a lack of clarity and direction holds people back; you can't win the race if you don't know which way to run. Plus, if we want to Make Life Better, communicating our strategy and goals clearly, simply and truthfully has to be more productive than fibbing about them or hiding them away.

Here are some examples of how open and honest we are about the way we work.

STRATEGIC PILLARS

Our approach to our business is anchored in nine strategic pillars which, cunningly enough, are all Ps (well, we are in marketing):

1. **Performance**
   The impact of our work for clients

2. **Profitability**
   How performance drives commercial success

3. **Purpose and Proposition**
   How to Make Life Better and Be Found

4. **Promotion and Publicity**
   New business and marketing

5. **Product**
   Developing our product

6. **Paid**
   Developing our Paid Media trading desk

7. **People (Agency)**
   Maintaining 60 precious seats

8. **People (Clients)**
   Engaged client relationships

9. **Pricing**
   Confidence for safety, innovation and reward

We report on each of these to the team every quarter, sharing the status of our strategic approach, goals and progress. As a result, there's a real sense of ownership of the strategic momentum of the agency.

KPIs

Five numbers make up our headline KPIs, and everyone across the agency knows them: 100, 90, 80, 70, 60. But what do they mean?

£100k: Revenue per person
The average for our industry is usually between £80k and £120k.

*MORE IN
CHAPTER 47*

90%: Recommendation level
Taken from our regular client satisfaction surveys and internal employee engagement surveys.

80%: Client revenue retention
We would love this to be 100%, but we're realists, and know that clients can leave for many reasons, some outside of our control.

70%: Amount of our time we aim to bill to clients

60: Precious seats for people in our business

*MORE IN
CHAPTER 46*

Clearly, it's more complex than this list might suggest; there are spreadsheets-a-go-go sitting behind these numbers. But the point is, everyone in the business knows what the headlines are. And we update the whole team on our progress on a quarterly basis, as well as sharing our commercial achievements, growth projects and dreams.

COMMERCIALS

Agency life can be precarious at times. As we know from experience, you can be one phone call away from a client terminating your contract, through no fault of your own. What matters is that you plan for it, respond to it and keep the business and your people safe.

→ MORE IN CHAPTER 33

One of the ways we manage this is by sharing the business numbers with our team. So, our agency revenue forecast is open to everyone to view, as are our P&L accounts. We share them regularly and encourage feedback, so people can ask questions and probe their understanding around our decisions.

This means, of course, that we're committed to sharing the tough stuff as well as the good news. And while that can be daunting for some, it can also open people's eyes to how complex running a business can be, which is great for developing their commercial nous beyond their everyday role.

It also means we're opening ourselves up to challenging questions, such as:

"Why do we need to make a profit?"

"How can I take my Propel Days when client work needs to be prioritised?"

"If our prices are going up by inflation this year, why aren't our salaries?"

And while some might question the wisdom of being put on the spot by this kind of enquiry, we say, *"Bring it on"*. From a management perspective, it keeps us on our toes; there hasn't been a question we couldn't answer (yet) and having everything out in the open means there is nowhere to hide.

Similarly, from a team perspective, it helps people focus on their work and avoid getting bogged down in office gossip and scaremongering. It also gives our team a deeper insight into the business, whilst at the same time building their trust.

HOW WE APPROACH TRANSPARENCY AROUND REMUNERATION

We're a people-first business, and fairness is at the heart of this approach. So, in the spirit of democracy, we aim to give everyone an equal voice and the same:

Bonus | Healthcare plans | Contributory pension rates | Dreamball chances | Health and wellbeing activities | Ministry of Fun initiatives | Access to Propel Days | Options for flexible working

And so it goes on.

However, we don't give everyone the same salary. The amount that someone is paid is reflective of their experience, ability and impact, and we have chosen to keep that private. Why?

Well, there is a lot of debate within the industry about whether salaries should be open for all to see, and a wide range of views on how salaries should be calculated.

One view is that each role should have a set salary, which everyone at that level earns. It's what happens in many public-sector businesses, where roles are clearly defined, though it would be more difficult to apply to a low-on-hierarchy business like ours, even if we wanted to.

The other end of the spectrum, as explained by Laszlo Bock in *Work Rules*, is how Google operate. They have a 'pay unfairly' policy, based on the following;

- They focus on output, rather than job title, because no two people are the same, or create the same value.
- They think it's OK to pay two people in the same job completely different amounts.

- Their view is that great engineers are worth many times more to them than average engineers (and they have the evidence to prove it).
- They believe that if everyone with the same title is given the same amount of money, it encourages the best current and potential performers to quit, whilst overpaying the worst performers.

So for Google, fairness does not mean attaching a salary to a job title. Fairness is when pay is commensurate with contribution. Their system does have its critics, particularly given the wrangle over gender equality and pay, which has been a publicly awkward challenge for them.

At Propellernet, we've developed our own approach, which is based on a banding system and allocated by role and impact. It's not an exact science and we know it's an emotive issue, but ultimately it comes back to our principles around engagement and trust. We trust everyone in the business to do the right thing, and we expect them to trust us to do the same.

Our belief is that, if they trust us to do right by them, there is no need to reveal the numbers involved. But in the spirit of transparency, we're happy to debate the way that pay and rations work.

For example, in answer to the question *"If our prices are going up by inflation this year, why aren't our salaries?"* we had a full and frank discussion in one of our weekly company get-togethers. And our answer was, *"You don't get a pay rise for turning up. You get one for doing great work, having positive relationships with those around you, getting fantastic client feedback and creating a profitable impact on the business. Inflation has nothing to do with it. Impact is everything."*

At the end of the session, one of our team said, *"That's what I love about working at Propellernet, we can openly have a difficult conversation".* We relish this kind of feedback, as it reinforces our belief that it's never worth crossing your fingers and hoping that tricky things will go away. If one person mentions something, others are likely to be thinking it, so it's best to get it out in the open.

Looking ahead, we're considering whether we should push transparency to the limit, by becoming an employee-owned company. It's not a straightforward decision; there are multiple layers to this one, but the principle certainly floats our collective boat. We'll keep you posted.

In the meantime, our commitment to transparency demonstrates the trust we place in ourselves and each other, and acts as a catalyst for invaluable feedback. It's also a springboard for developing a sense of personal responsibility.

It's a subject on which we're often asked, *"Where's the catch?"*

There isn't one. You can't hide a catch in transparency.

Like many businesses, we used to allocate our bonuses on a percentage-of-salary basis. So, while everyone got the same percentage, the actual pile of cash that each individual received varied wildly, with higher-paid team members getting a bigger share of the pot than their lower-paid colleagues.

Then, in 2011, we questioned whether this was fair. Whilst we saw the logic in linking salary to experience, we concluded that bonuses are different; if they are a reward for hard work, then they should be equally shared among our equally hard-working people.

We knew that introducing something like this could be contentious; clearly, for the highest earners, it would mean a drop, not a raise. But we've never let trickiness get in the way of making a decision, so we asked the team what they thought.

While it wasn't unanimous, the team were overwhelmingly behind making it fairer, and giving everyone the same. And even the ones who hadn't voted for the change felt that it was a democratic decision and were happy to go along with it. So that's what we do now; and we're proud of what it stands for.

BE SUPERENGAGED

What are the strategic pillars driving your business? Is it something you have thought through, agreed and shared? If not, feel free to start with ours, see which could work for you and what else might be missing.

How honest are you about your company finances? Do you think transparency is a possibility; if not, what's holding you back? What might you be prepared to share and what might you keep private?

YOU WIN SOME, YOU LOSE SOME

If you're planning on being open about your finances, having a brilliant FD is beyond essential. And if your business is purpose driven, having an FD who lives your values to the full is mission critical.

Our self-confessed 'canary down the mine' FD, Simon, can see danger from miles off. He's continually scenario-planning to work out where we might need to improvise next. He has a wonderful way of interpreting numbers so that everyone in the agency can understand them. And his belief in the value of our people-first approach means he would never seek to sacrifice staff for short-term gain.

In Simon's hands, quarterly company updates of the full P&L can come down to less than 10 numbers, which he delivers by telling the stories behind them, innovating how the data is displayed for ultimate simplicity, and making the accounts feel like part of our adventure.

FURTHER READING

Where is the Money? A Guide to Agency Finances, Simon Collard, 2014

Likeonomics, Rohit Bhargava, 2012
Rework, Jason Fried & David Heinemeier, 2010

TL;DR

53. FOR THE SKIM READERS AMONG YOU...

Our people-first focus, and determination to Make Life Better, are principles that we're proud of, and we talk about them a lot. But, they're not just words; they're built into everything we do, from the way we structure our business to the way we plan for growth.

That means taking seemingly radical decisions, like capping our size at 60. It means giving our people choices about how, when and where they work. And it means being open; open to discussion, open to new opportunities and different ways of doing things. It also means literally opening up our space to like-minded individuals, and opening our doors to let people leave.

So yes, we talk the talk, but we totally walk the walk. Every day, in everything we do.

END NOTES

i   *Malcolm Gladwell* web.stanford.edu/class/symbsys205/tipping_point.html; www.aupc.info/
     wp-content/uploads/2015/07/V8I1-13.pdf

ii   en.wikipedia.org/wiki/Dunbar%27s_number

iii sivers.org/multiply

iv   www.seats2meet.com/downloads/The_Serendipity_Machine.pdf

v   *Found is a range of Propellernet-hosted events at which speakers come to inspire. Highlights to
     date include: Keiver Harvey from http://guineapig.global/, makers of one-off creative installations;
     Dr Stephen Spencer FRGS and Toby Nowlan FRGS, BBC production team from Planet Earth 2;
     Tom Nixon, Co-founder of Nixon McInnes, front runners of agency culture; Kim Slade, Founder of
     Unknown Epic adventure company; Adam Buckingham, Director of The Real Junk Food Project,
     with a mission to feed bellies, not bins.*

vi   *Joost Minnaar, Pim de Morree and Freek Ronner, known as The Corporate Rebels, are on a mis-
     sion to make work more fun. They quit their frustrating, corporate jobs and set out to travel the
     globe to visit the world's most inspiring organisations. While checking off their renowned Bucket
     List, they share everything they learn.* corporate-rebels.com/david-marquet/

vii *According to 2004 UCL Public Health Research, jobs that gave workers less control were linked to
     higher rates of mental illness. Workers in the lowest hierarchy had an early death rate four times
     higher than those at the top.*

viii dots.brilliantnoise.com/bruce-daisley/

ix   timewise.co.uk/article/flexible-working-for-everyone/

x   www.ted.com/talks/margaret_heffernan_why_it_s_time_to_forget_the_pecking_order_at_
     work#t-929426

xi   www.mckinsey.com/business-functions/organization/our-insights/why-diversity-matters

xii www.forbes.com/sites/karstenstrauss/2016/04/06/why-women-on-company-boards-boost-perfor-
     mance/#ff02c3d45d31

xiii *What Do Women Returners Want? A Timewise survey commissioned by the Government Equalities
     Office, 2015* timewise.co.uk/wp-content/uploads/2014/02/What_women_returners_want.pdf

xiv *The Timewise Flexible Jobs Index 2017* timewise.co.uk/article/flexible-jobs-index-2017/

xv   *Rohit Bhargava, in Likeonomics, tells us: "The first and most basic reason for distrust is because
     there are so many companies and people who choose to lie to us, either by making misleading
     claims or simply by hiding the truth."*

xvi *Anonymous feedback from a Propellernet employee, given as part of a European research study
     into The Future of Work, with Leeds University & UK Research Council, 2017.*

COMPUTER SAYS NO

Unconventional thinking can make others feel uncomfortable, so it's not surprising that people sometimes challenge us about the way we do things. Often in public, occasionally quite rudely. Once, comically, by a potential supplier, who was trying to flog us his services (we didn't bite).

Rather than be offended, we actually enjoy the banter.

We're also aware that, if one person has raised something, a load of other, less bolshie types may well be thinking it too. So, we're happy to put our thinking to the test and see whether it stands up in the face of other people's opinions.

Here are some of the things we've had thrown at us over the years, and how we've (politely) responded:

"You're not ambitious enough."
That depends on your definition of ambition. Scaling your business is one thing, scaling your purpose is something else. Our ambition is to be the best place to work in the world; it doesn't get much bigger than that.

"Are you MAD? Why would you plan to lose your best talent?"
People will leave, so we may as well plan for it, keep them involved in one way or another, and make sure we part friends. It would be madder not to.

"It's not about people, it's about profit."
Who says we have to choose? We've proved that we can do both. Putting our people and purpose first drives both our performance and our profits; and they're pretty healthy, thanks all the same.

"Why would you let everyone in the agency see the all the revenue coming into the business?! Surely that's a risk?"

If you're making people responsible for delivering profit, you should trust them with knowing where it comes from and the part they need to play in generating it. Surely it's more of a risk to keep it under wraps?

"I'm not interested in your freedom. I don't want you walking down on the beach on my money."

We're not robots (yet) and all the evidence shows that people who regularly take time out perform better. Do you want a robot attached to a computer churning out commoditised work, or an inspired colleague, who may just light up your world? We know which one we'd choose.

(This comment came from a potential client; unsurprisingly, we didn't work with them.)

"It's easy to keep your staff happy and win awards if you take them all skiing."

As it happens, we won the Great Place to Work® award BEFORE deciding to take the company to Chamonix to celebrate our first decade. And we make no apology for going the extra downhill kilometre to keep our staff happy.

We appreciate that some companies may choose to reward their shareholders when the business overperforms, rather than the people who made it happen. Guess what? That's not how we do things.

"Are you a cult?"

Yes, we are.

OK, we lied. But take a step back here, questioner. Should it really be so shocking to see people raving about their place of work on social media? Is your view of the working world so jaded that you can't imagine people enjoying their jobs?

The reason people love working for us is because we have made it our business to put people first. While that may not be the norm, it's our norm. And the numbers on our P&L show us that it's working.

"I had a look at your website, this place seems more like a playpen in a kindergarten than a serious business!"

Oh, how we loved this one, which came from a financial chap who we were considering signing up to source and support our company pension plan.

Maybe if financial institutions focused more on health and wellbeing, and less on chasing high risk profit, the UK wouldn't have had to bail out the industry in 2008. Just saying.

We understand that things like including dreams as part of the business plan would make questioners like these feel a bit on the uneasy side. And that's OK; one person's dream can be another's nightmare. But we reserve the right to keep doing it our way.

Section 8

WHAT WE DO FOR CLIENTS

54. INTRODUCTION

HOW TO BE FOUND IN A WORLD OF NOISE

This isn't a book about search marketing, or SEO, or how to keep one step ahead of those fiendishly clever people at Google. One thing at a time, eh?

But the way we work with our clients is clearly a big part of the way we deliver on our purpose and Make Life Better all round. And unless you're someone who knows us already (in which case, hello again!), that won't mean much without some context. So here's the Brodie's Notes version of what we do.

MAKING OUR CLIENTS THE ANSWER TO THE QUESTIONS PEOPLE ASK

There are already more than one billion websites online. ONE BILLION. That's a lot of haystacks getting in the way of your needle. And if that hasn't made you feel dizzy, these stats on the world's daily internet activity probably will:

- 500 million tweets

- 150 billion emails

- Four-and-a-half billion videos uploaded to YouTube

- 3.5 billion Google searches

Yes, at least that many of these things happen every day. Every. Single. Day – and the numbers are growing all the time.[i]

With all this digital noise going on, it's increasingly difficult for businesses to make their brands stand out, and to get their products and services in front of the right people at the right time and in the right place.

Our roots as a business are in search engine optimisation (SEO), which is based around the fact that the best time and the best place to get in front of consumers is when they are actively searching. And with 1.2 trillion searches happening every year, there are lots of opportunities to be the answer when someone googles a question.

So how do you take advantage of these opportunities? Well, as a result of all this searching, there's a huge (anonymised) data set out there, which marketers can use to work out what people are looking for, what emotions they are experiencing, and what trends are emerging.

It's this data that we use to help our clients provide the answers that people genuinely want and need; to Make Life Better for those searching, whilst helping our clients to be found. We like to think of it as mind-reading marketing.

That's what we do, in simple terms; we help our clients to Be Found. But how?

MORE IN CHAPTER 56

- We gather data to create insight around human behaviour.

- This helps us understand what motivates people, how they behave and what their goals are.

- We use this to work out the best ways to get our clients in front of people.

- This could be anything from dreaming up impactful PR stories to creating zeitgeisty shareable content to paying for awareness via online advertising.

It's not a one-dimensional discipline; it requires an unusual blend of technical know-how, data science skills, creative ingenuity and PR savvy. Luckily, we have a multi-skilled team of people who are not only really good at their particular bit of the job, they're keen to explore the other bits so they can make the outcome even stronger.

USING INSIGHT TO DRIVE BUSINESS GROWTH

But of course, being found is just the beginning. Search success can create quick wins here, but it also leads to longer-term gains for the client through sustainable business growth.

And increasingly, as the search industry comes of age, that's what we're getting involved in. We may have started off in the server room, but these days, we're shown into the boardroom for a high-level debate about how to find, attract and keep customers.

In a recent client satisfaction call with the Head of Digital & CRM at one of our clients, he described us as *"Growth Engineers"*:

"You guys are digital at your core, you understand the future consumer. The people you have, the way they think and operate is so strong, so valuable.

"There's a lot of focus around growth...how to engineer growth for clients, it's what they are all looking for. The data is so powerful and underpins everything you do."

It's been quite a journey from the server room to the boardroom, from coding to mind reading, mixing art and science as we go. Who knows where it will take us next? Wherever we end up, we'll make sure we've made life better along the way.

55. PRINCIPLES FOR GROWTH

◀◀ REWIND

Are you suffering from a bloated keyhole? Are you in danger of being brought down by a profit vampire? Do you have any idea what we're banging on about?

We didn't either, until we had it explained to us – and it turns out we were at risk from both. Luckily, we got some brilliant advice about the right way to drive growth before we became our own horror story.

NAILING THE NUMBERS IN A PURPOSE-DRIVEN BUSINESS

Growing an agency isn't that hard. Well, OK, it's a bit hard. But it's not as hard as trying to grow a successful agency doing brilliant work which keeps your team motivated, your clients keen to recommend you, and generally makes life better. That's quadruple-hard.

It helps that we aren't focused on growing revenue at any cost, and that we're relaxed about putting people before profit. But clearly, if growth is our game, we need some sound commercial principles to ensure we're playing it for keeps.

Chief amongst these, for us, has been to build a balanced portfolio in which no single client is worth more than our profit margin. Without this balance, a big client could jeopardise what we do by putting us at financial risk, or by diverting attention from other clients or our people.

That might sound simple; indeed, for businesses that have lots of small clients rather than a few big ones, it might not even be a problem that needs solving.

But it's much trickier than it sounds. For example, what do you do when one of your clients is so happy with your work that they want to double their investment with you, taking them well over that profit-margin threshold we mentioned?

GETTING THE CLIENT-TO-PROFIT BUCKET RIGHT

We regularly have to ask ourselves this kind of question, and we haven't always known the answer. So, over the years, we've sought commercial insights from a number of experts; in particular, Caroline Johnson, a co-founder of The Clear Partnership[ii], and Chris Merrington, the founder of Spring 80:20[iii].

We first worked with Caroline back in 2010, at the very beginning of our growth journey, and we still use the client portfolio model she shared with us today. It's tried and tested, it's founded on sound commercial principles, and it's easy to understand. Here's how it works.

Your top 15 clients (in terms of revenue) should make up around 80% of your profit. And that profit should be balanced as follows:

- The top five should make up around 60% of your profit (c12% each).

- The next five should make up 25% of your profit (c5% each).

- And the next five should make up 15% of your profit (c3% each).

Or, to put it another way, using the client-to-profit bucket:

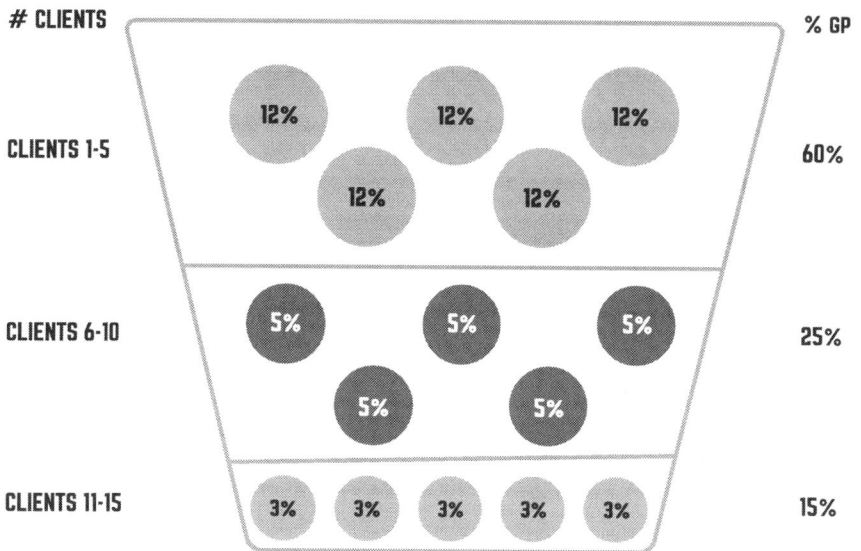

CLIENTS   % GP

CLIENTS 1-5   12% 12% 12% 12% 12%   60%

CLIENTS 6-10   5% 5% 5% 5% 5%   25%

CLIENTS 11-15   3% 3% 3% 3% 3%   15%

Using this model, you should be able to balance the risk between your five largest clients, provided that your profit margin is above 12% (most agencies aim for 15%). If your margin is less than 12%, you may either need to try and increase it (for example, through your pricing), or change the balance of your portfolio so that no single client can expose you to a loss.

The second group of clients (6-10 in terms of revenue) should be the ones which deliver opportunities for great work and the potential for growth.

Ideally, at least one of these would have the potential to move up into the first group, if one of the top five clients left or didn't deliver according to plan.

And the third group (clients 11-15) should offer you opportunities to experiment and innovate at a relatively low risk.

It's worth remembering that this isn't about your five biggest clients being your most important clients; they are all valuable in different ways. Recognising this also makes it easier to have your people working on lots of different opportunities, which is healthy for everyone involved.

BUILDING A BUCKET FROM A BLOATED KEYHOLE

Of course, the bucket (appropriately enough for a Brighton-based business) is the perfect scenario. However, it doesn't always work out that way. In fact, the first time we went through our profit portfolio with Caroline, we discovered that it was an entirely different shape.

Our biggest client was worth 40% of our profit. We had 11 clients in the middle, netting out at around 5% of our profit each, and our smallest three were at risk of being ignored, when in fact they were vital for us to maintain our balance.

The technical term for this, we gathered, is a 'bloated keyhole'.

And if that sounds a bit nasty, that's because it is; the potential impact of such a high profit-ratio client leaving is massive. It's not uncommon, but it's a highway to the danger zone.

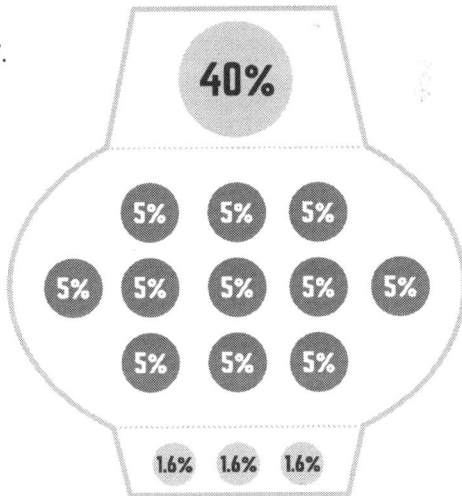

So, we set about changing the balance of our portfolio to make our business stronger – and narrowly avoided a disaster as, less than a year later, our 40% client decided to take the work we did for them in house. If we hadn't already turned our keyhole into a bucket, this could have wiped out our profit and potentially our business.

BEATING OFF THE PROFIT VAMPIRES

Chris Merrington has shared lots of great thinking with us over the years, but our all-time favourite is his theory of profit vampires. These are clients that suck the lifeblood of profit out of your business, often without you noticing.

According to Chris, who has worked with thousands of UK agencies,

"Every company I have worked with seems to have at least one profit vampire client, and many have several."

How does this happen?

- Sometimes it's a question of scope creep.

- Sometimes it's overservicing, driven by a fear of losing the business.

- Sometimes it's the result of pricing to win at the start of the relationship.

- Sometimes it's due to being seduced by the idea of having a trophy client on board.

- Sometimes, however unprofitable they may be, the team just love working with them.

Whatever the reason, it's up to you to take responsibility for talking about this with the client. They're unlikely to make it a priority themselves; why would they? The chances are they're among your happiest clients, largely because they're getting loads of your work for free.

But you need to make it your priority, because if nothing changes, you'll be forced to make your team and your other clients deliver extra profit to compensate for it. And without wanting to be all Hammer House of Horror about it, that's a spine-chilling thought.

For starters, you'll need to make sure you've got the relevant facts and figures to hand, so you're clear about the root cause of the problem – whether it's overdelivering or undercharging, for example. Once you know what you're dealing with, you can work out how to tackle it, and how best to negotiate the way forward.

We'll leave you with this quote from David Ogilvy, which we always keep in mind when negotiations are looming:

"Clients who haggle over their agency's compensation are looking through the wrong end of the telescope. Instead of trying to shave a few measly cents off the agency's fifteen per cent, they should concentrate on getting more sales results from the eighty-five per cent they spend on time and space. That is where the leverage is. No manufacturer ever got rich by underpaying his agency. Pay peanuts, get monkeys."[iv]

He may have written it more than 50 years ago, but we reckon he's still bang on the money.

BE SUPERENGAGED

Do you know the profitability of each of your clients or customers? And are you happy with it? Are they all making you money? You should aim to have a balanced client portfolio, where no single client is worth more than your profit margin. Try mapping yours out to see how things currently stand.

Are you clear about what your commercial principles are? Do you know what you're willing to compromise on, and more importantly, what you're not? Set your principles from the off – and stick to them, however tempting it might sometimes be to veer off to the wrong side of the margin.

YOU WIN SOME, YOU LOSE SOME

Like us back in the early days, many businesses have one dominant client. And that's all fine, just as long as it's all fine. But the minute something goes wrong (and there is always the potential for that to happen), it's not only that piece of client business that's at risk. Your whole business is at risk – including your other clients.

So whatever you do, don't put all your eggs in one basket. It's easy to be seduced by the money, but it's far far better to spread your risk for optimum security and reward. Easy to say, harder to do but believe us, well worth it.

FURTHER READING

Why Do Smart People Make Such Stupid Mistakes?
Chris Merrington, 2011

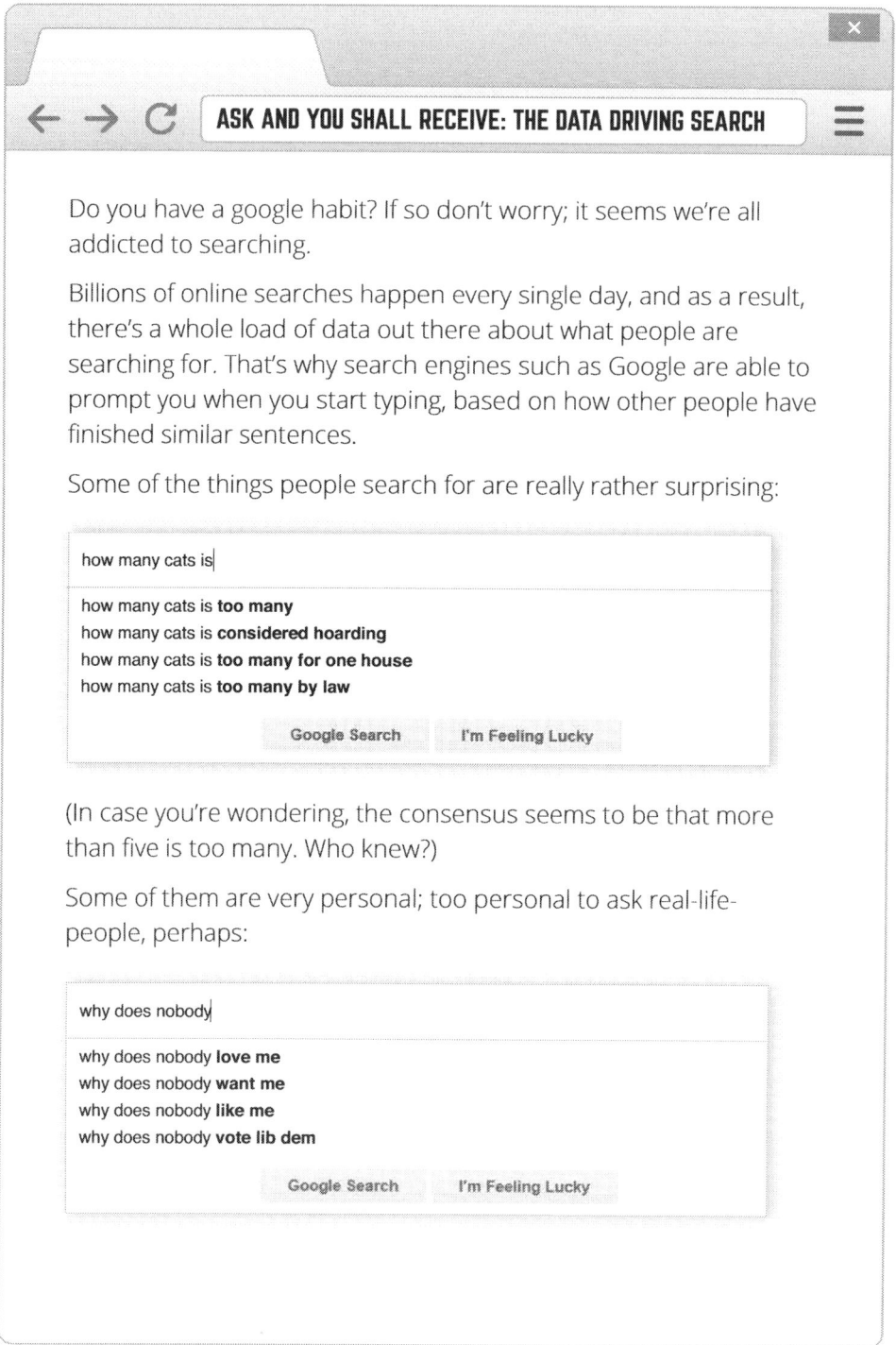

Do you have a google habit? If so don't worry; it seems we're all addicted to searching.

Billions of online searches happen every single day, and as a result, there's a whole load of data out there about what people are searching for. That's why search engines such as Google are able to prompt you when you start typing, based on how other people have finished similar sentences.

Some of the things people search for are really rather surprising:

how many cats is|

how many cats is **too many**
how many cats is **considered hoarding**
how many cats is **too many for one house**
how many cats is **too many by law**

Google Search   I'm Feeling Lucky

(In case you're wondering, the consensus seems to be that more than five is too many. Who knew?)

Some of them are very personal; too personal to ask real-life-people, perhaps:

why does nobody|

why does nobody **love me**
why does nobody **want me**
why does nobody **like me**
why does nobody **vote lib dem**

Google Search   I'm Feeling Lucky

But more often than not, a search is for a specific product or service, and so reveals a strong intent to purchase.

For example, if you're a fashion brand that sold maxi dresses in a size 18, you'd really want your website to appear on page one of the answers to this search:

> maxi dress size 18 with
>
> maxi dress with **sleeves** size 18
>
> Google Search   I'm Feeling Lucky

Likewise, if you're selling brogues, you would very much hope to show up in response to one or more of these:

> best brogues unde
>
> best brogues under **£100**
> best brogues under **200**
> best brogues under **£200**
> best brogues under **300**
>
> Google Search   I'm Feeling Lucky

So how do you make sure you're the answer to the questions your customers are asking?

That's where we come in.

56. DEFINING WHAT WE DO

◀◀REWIND

At the start, and for some time afterwards, we weren't clear enough about what we were doing, where we were going or how we were going to get there.

Jack, one of our founders, was the only person who could sell what we were offering, and the rest of us weren't entirely sure what that was. It was hard for us to create a unique offer that appealed to a strong base of clients, because we hadn't got it out of Jack's head and into a proposition that we could all understand.

Once we worked that out, the Propellernet journey really started. And we're continuing to move forwards, on our own unique path, as the world around us changes.

UNDERSTAND WHAT YOU'RE BRILLIANT AT, AND TELL THE WORLD

What we do, and how we talk about what we do, has changed a lot over the last 15 years. We started out as a search engine optimisation (SEO) agency; today we help our clients "Be Found".

Now, if you're involved in the digital world, or you just have a basic working knowledge of the English language, you might not think there's a lot of difference between the two. But in fact, the shift between these two propositions has been a deliberate, Darwinesque evolution that has made us stronger and fitter.

And there's a good reason behind our determination to evolve in this way. As we've explained, we don't have an exit strategy, and we're not for sale; we love what we do, and we want to carry on doing it. But that absolutely doesn't mean doing the same old same old until the end of time.

MORE IN CHAPTER 10

With new competitors, alternative technologies, changing social mores and other forces emerging at a frankly breathtaking rate, businesses that don't adapt are destined to go under. So, we've put aside time to prepare for change, and made sure we articulate these changes, so that everyone we work with – including our own team – is clear, and excited, about what we actually do.

FROM SEARCH TO 'BE FOUND' IN FOUR LEAPS

Six years into Propellernet, having previously described ourselves as a search agency, we decided we wanted to develop a more defined proposition. Something that would make new and existing clients want to work with us, and keep our people enthusiastic about working alongside us. Something that would set us apart from the pack in an increasingly competitive marketplace.

So, we worked with Doug Kessler at Velocity Marketing to define what we were particularly brilliant at. And here's what we concluded.

- Google was getting better at differentiating between the brands that *earned* their way to the top of their listings and those that were gaming the system.

- Savvy brands were starting to understand this and wanted to be among the former, not the latter.

- Our approach to search marketing, using talented PRs to earn coverage rather than buying it, was light-years ahead of most other agencies.

- And we were able to show clearly what we were doing, how we were doing it, and why it worked.

AUTHENTIC SEARCH

The result of this process was a new proposition, *Authentic Search*, which we felt shouted out our strengths and created new market opportunities. And if you'll excuse a moment of smugness, it was one of the best things we've ever done. (Thanks, Doug.)

Why? Because it was something everyone on the team could understand and buy into. It made it easier to explain what we did, and why we were different, to existing and new clients. It helped us to win new business, including a couple of big names on the high street. In short, it made life better for us on all fronts.

And it continued to do so for three or four years. But as time went on, we noticed that other agencies were starting to use similar language, talking about authenticity and more ethical approaches. Stealing our thunder? Perhaps – or perhaps they were just evolving too. But the bottom line was, our proposition was no longer unusual, and we risked getting lost in the crowd.

THE POWER OF SHARING (AND WHY IT DIDN'T WORK)

So, we pivoted. We spent some time thinking about what we were doing particularly well, and we concluded that our commitment to creating properly shareable content was something that marked us out.

At the time, social media and the behaviours associated with it were becoming more and more important, particularly the way that people shared stuff they liked. We felt there was a great opportunity to identify ourselves with this new way of behaving, by building it into our proposition.

As a result of this reflection, we developed a new potential proposition: *The Power of Sharing*. And we were very excited about this to start with. But this time, we didn't get to be smug, because it wasn't a winner; it didn't resonate with clients and our team didn't really see its value. So, we decided to pivot again.

INSPIRING SEARCH (AND WHY IT DID)

The good news is, the time we spent working through *The Power of Sharing* wasn't wasted. Although we ditched it as our proposition, we hung on to the belief that people share campaigns and content that makes them feel like they're in the know, or that makes them laugh, or is useful; stuff that inspires them in some way.

We also knew from crunching the numbers that the campaigns that generated the biggest impact were usually the most inspiring ones; our next proposition, we decided, needed to take us to inspiration and beyond. And so, from the ashes of *The Power of Sharing,* emerged *Inspiring Search*, based around a couple of core ideas.

Firstly, it encompassed the fact that inspiring websites, those that were alive with connections, were the ones that appeared in the most searches and deserved to be shared. And secondly, it put a marker down that, while being at the top of a Google search was important, being at the front of people's minds was even more so.

As well as playing to our creative strengths, *Inspiring Search* allowed us to have slightly different conversations with our clients about how we could deliver the biggest possible impact; conversations which we knew would also open up other areas of opportunity.

It also felt much more us, and we won a number of new clients, and started a lot of new conversations, on the back of it.

Interestingly, some of us (and some of our clients) regarded *Inspiring Search* as a natural next step from *Authentic Search*, while others thought it was something completely new. Either way, it went down a storm.

WHAT WE'RE BRILLIANT AT TODAY: *BE FOUND*

In the last year or so, we've gone back and revisited our proposition once again, on the basis that focusing on search no longer reflects the breadth of the work we're doing, or the impact that work is having.

We've realised that what we do isn't always about search marketing, or social media, or PR; in fact, it's greater than the sum of all these things. The benefit we create for our clients today is helping them to be found in today's vast digital space.

So that's our current proposition: *Be Found*. Right now, we couldn't be happier with those two words and what they represent. But we know that we wouldn't have got to them without exploring *Authentic Search*, *The Power of Sharing* and *Inspiring Search*. Each of these stages has fed into the next, and helped us refine not just what we do, but how we talk about it.

We're confident that we'll stick with *Be Found* for a while but, as before, we will build in regular pit stops to look at what we're offering as a business, and how we talk about it. And we'll be brave enough to fess up and take action if what we opt for isn't working out.

BE SUPERENGAGED

Are you clear about what you stand for? Do you know what your team and your clients think about your proposition? Does it define what makes you different?

Do you build in time for preparing for change? Are you making sure you're ready to deliver what your clients will want in future, as well as what they want right now?

Are you prepared to accept it when something hasn't worked, and learn from it?

YOU WIN SOME, YOU LOSE SOME

If you're not sufficiently clear about what you do, it's harder for clients to buy in to you. This can be a real issue in our industry, as the word 'search' means completely different things to different people; to some, it's just the tech side, whereas we expand it into PR, content and the rest.

As a result, we've sometimes found ourselves talking at cross-purposes when pitching for potential clients. One major holiday brand said, "We're impressed, but you're not really a search agency, are you?" And another travel company said, "These ideas are incredible, unlike anything we've seen from anyone else. But we're not sure we're ready for you yet!"

Our proposition wasn't clear enough about what we actually offered, which meant we weren't as good a match as they had originally thought. Interestingly, now they do know what we're about, they've been back in touch, one of them with a new brief.

FURTHER READING

The B2B Content Marketing Workbook, Doug Kessler, 2009

57. GETTING THE CLIENTS WE DESERVE

◄◄ REWIND

Like most start-ups, we didn't have a secure client base for a good few years. We pitched a lot and took on everything that came our way, playing the volume game to keep our numbers up and our panic levels down. As a result, we had a lot of small clients which we couldn't possibly service properly, let alone build into sustainable relationships that could flourish over time.

We also took on some clients whose values were light years from our own, who kicked us around like an end supplier, who expected the moon on a stick but not to have to pay for it. That was bad for our people, bad for our profit margins, and bad for our other clients, who got less time and attention as a result.

But once we were brave enough to be clear about the kind of clients we wanted, and confident enough to stick to our guns, everything changed.

> *People do not buy goods and services, they buy relations, stories and magic.*

Seth Godin, The Marketing Blog.

KEEPING THE BASTARDS FROM THE DOOR

If you've got this far, you've probably realised that we're a bunch of no-nonsense straight talkers, and never more so than when it comes to our views on client relationships. So, in the interests of honesty, and with apologies to anyone who finds it a bit on the feisty side, here's our one-line summary of how we approach new biz:

We don't want to work for bastards, so we won't.

But hang on, you may be asking, how can you afford to be so picky? Our answer, not surprisingly, is: how can we afford not to?

Our no-exit strategy means we need to focus on winning the right business, not the most business. Our people-first focus means we won't let our team suffer just to hang on to a piece of business. And our desire to build mutually-fulfilling relationships with the clients we have, means we don't want to take on new, overdemanding ones which will suck up all our time and energy. If that means turning business away, that's what we do.

MORE IN CHAPTER 10

MORE IN CHAPTER 6

We are so committed to this principle that we run every potential new business opportunity through a detailed checklist, and only take on clients who get a big bunch of ticks. Here are our criteria:

NICK THIS

- **Is there a decent brief?**
    - The client has issued a clear, written brief and/or we have got them to agree to our understanding of a verbal brief. The more we know about the company, product and challenge, the better job we can do.

- **Is there a clear budget?**
  - o The budget matches what the brief is asking for – we love smashing client targets, but trying to fulfil champagne tastes on lemonade rates is a bad place to start.

- **Are we excited by the opportunity?**
  - o We are enthusiastic about what this brief offers, which will drive us to deliver great work. Our people aren't precious; they get excited by lots of different kinds of work and industries, so this rarely holds us back.

- **Will we be able to do a brilliant job?**
  - o We have the resources we need to produce great work, now and in the future. There's no point taking a project on if we don't have the right people and skills to deliver it; we're not in the business of setting anyone up to fail.

- **Will we be able to deliver what we recommend?**
  - o There are no major restrictions on our ability to do great work. For example, we need to be able to implement our technical recommendations if we're to demonstrate the true value of what we do.

- **Will we have scope to work across the business?**
  - o The nature of the role means we'll be involved with people at all levels, including senior contacts. When you're spending significant amounts of the client's money, the right decision-makers need to be involved.

- **Will we be able to collaborate as equals?**
  - o The brief offers an opportunity for working in partnership, with all partners playing to their strengths, rather than within a client-supplier relationship, which too often leads to fear-based, reactive decision-making.

- **Will we be able to work constructively with other partners?**
  - o There is an opportunity to play nicely with in-house teams and/or other agencies. We can't stand inter-agency politics and prefer to build positive working relationships with our clients' other partners.

- **Do the numbers add up, and allow us to Make Life Better?**
  - o Where a procurement[v] team is involved, we have agreed our costing model before committing to the pitch, and factored in our determination to put people before profit.

- **Will our work have a notable impact?**
  - o What we can do in relation to the brief will resonate with potential customers and stand out in a crowded marketplace. And we will be able to collect and display the data to prove it.

- **Is the relationship sustainable?**
  - o The initial contract will be for at least one year, and ideally two or three – allowing us to demonstrate the full impact of what we do, and provide more certainty for everyone.

- **Is there potential for growth?**
  - o One-off projects will be considered on a case-by-case basis, but they will need to be sufficiently profitable. In these cases, a contingency should be included.

- **Are they bastards?**
  - o The client contacts are reasonable and logical, and their company culture is one that we can identify with. We're not interested in working with people or organisations that are unreasonable and chaotic. They take time and attention away from other clients and make life worse for all of us. Life's too short.

And whilst this may all sound a bit picky, it makes good business sense, for us and for the potential client. If a business is about to pay us a substantial amount of money to drive their brand forward, we need to make sure we're in the best possible position to deliver on that. If we can't, we'll save a whole heap of hassle by saying so up front.

So, whenever we're approached by a new client, we complete a scorecard based on these criteria. It's not a scientific process, but it's a useful one, which helps us to spot the right opportunities – or turn the wrong ones around, by using our feedback to revise the brief.

Sometimes we turn opportunities down without even going through the list. For example, there are certain industries we just don't want to be associated with, because of what they do, and these businesses always receive a polite *"Thank you, but no"*.

But sometimes, things aren't so clear cut... and when that happens, we involve the whole team in the decision.

CASE STUDY #1 WHEN THE TEAM SAYS NO, IT'S A NO

We were recently approached by a former client, who had taken up a senior position in a new organisation. And while the individual was keen to work with us again, and vice versa, their new industry was controversial.

To be clear, it's not that they were involved in anything dodgy. But we had a hunch that working with them might be a problem for some of our team and perhaps for some of our other clients. So we told our contact that, before committing to further discussions, we would need to talk it through with the agency as a whole.

And that's exactly what we did. We explained the opportunity and then gave everyone the chance to feed back anonymously on what they thought, covering:

• Whether they thought we should work with the organisation.

• Whether they, personally, would love or hate to work with the organisation.

• Any other thoughts they might have about the opportunity.

About three-fifths of the agency responded, with answers fairly evenly split between *for*, *neutral* and *against*. By adding the *for* and *neutral* responses to the two-fifths who didn't respond (who we assumed weren't bothered, one way or the other) it was possible to make a case for pursuing the opportunity. After all, only one-fifth of the agency were actively against it.

However, that one-fifth of the agency were *fiercely* against it, which wasn't something we felt we could ignore. As we were mulling over what do to next, I asked the question:

"What's more important, the engagement levels of 20% of our people, or the extra revenue?"

No prizes for guessing what happened next. Clearly, for us, the engagement of 20% of our agency trumped any potential revenue. We're proud of how engaged our people are – it's played a big part in our success – and we felt it just wasn't worth risking it for some extra cash.

And while our contact was disappointed, they clearly respected our honesty, and expressed a hope that we would work together again, on a personal level, in future. We hope so, too.

Not everyone here agreed with the decision that was made, but many did, including some of those who had voted *for*:

"Just struck by how awesome the agency response was and the overall decision-making process. Well done and thank you. Proud to be a member of the team."

"Just wanted to say thank you for organising this debate/ vote and for the way that you handled the whole thing."

Taking the time to make sure we only work with great clients has therefore been a massive part of our growth story. But even great clients can sometimes become problem clients (and very, very occasionally, toxic clients), doing damage under the table while you count the money on top.

CASE STUDY #2: SPOTTING UNDER-THE-TABLE DAMAGE BEFORE IT'S TOO LATE

Four years ago, our relationship with our biggest client, which had been the jewel in our crown (and was almost worth more than our agency margin) had started to lose its sparkle. In fact, it was actively making the (really quite big) team who worked on it unhappy. And eventually, it became unavoidably clear that we needed to find a way to get the jewel shining again, or take the crown off – and quickly.

It was the morning after a sixth round of creative presentations. Our team had presented to 14 stakeholders in a cramped room at the client's offices, an hour behind schedule, and were asked to speed through the presentation because people needed to get to other meetings. Those in the room showed very little interest, focusing instead on their smartphones and laptops.

It wasn't the first time this had happened, but there was worse to come. We'd spent hundreds of hours developing our ideas, but the feedback we got was completely contrary to the initial high-impact brief we'd received.

This meant that we'd wasted time (and money) on work that wasn't wanted or needed, something which was brutally brought home when one of the clients said, *"Can we focus on the most basic ideas, the ones that we can get signed off with no hassle?"*

Errrm, well, no, actually. That's not how we do things; it just won't get results.

So, the morning after that meeting, we got our team together and asked them to give us their views, based on their responses to the following statements:

- *We are doing great, high-impact work for Client X*
- *We have the potential to do great, high-impact work for Client X*
- *I enjoy working on Client X*

- *There is potential to enjoy working on Client X*

- *Our day-to-day contacts are challenging in all the right ways*

- *I am learning (loads)*

- *If we stopped working with Client X I would feel*

- *I am likely/unlikely to recommend that anyone else in this agency works for Client X*

- *Because...*

The feedback was overwhelmingly negative. Pretty much everyone involved felt that the relationship wasn't making either our clients' or our own lives better.

So, despite the financial and reputational value that this client brought to our business, we decided we had to let them go. As it turns out, they were feeling the same, and we have both gone on to bigger and better things.

Over the last decade, we've only reached this kind of crisis point with a client twice. On the second occasion, we were able to use the feedback we got from the team to have an honest conversation and reset our working relationship with them. We're now back on track to Make Life Better.

We've certainly taken David Ogilvy's home truth about clients on board; here it is, in full:

"Clients get the advertising they deserve. I have worked with ninety-six of them, and have had unique opportunities for comparing their attitudes and procedures. Some behave so badly that no agency could produce effective advertising for them. Some behave so well that no agency could fail to do so."

We believe you get the clients you deserve; and our people deserve nothing but the best. If that occasionally means making a tough decision to cut ties with a client, we tough it out.

BE SUPERENGAGED

Are you choosing the right opportunities and winning the clients you deserve? How do your business growth decisions impact your team beyond the bottom line?

Be honest with yourself – are you working with any bastards? Do you have any current relationships doing more business harm than revenue good? Try applying the relevant points of our scorecard to your current clients, and see how they measure up.

How do you deal with problematic business relationships?

YOU WIN SOME, YOU LOSE SOME

If you're focused on revenue, deciding to part company with a client is never easy. But it's entirely the opposite if you're focused on people, purpose and culture. It's also worth remembering that a problematic relationship with a particular client can have an impact on other clients too, taking additional time to handle and sapping energy all round.

And if you do decide to end a client relationship, the important thing is how you handle it. Here's what our experiences have taught us.

- *Don't rush, but do be timely. Dragging these situations on is a wellbeing killer.*

- *Talk to the client. They're human too and probably struggling as much as you are.*

- *Plan for the relationship to come to as positive an end as possible – or to turn it around.*

- *In the meantime, put your best people on replacing the revenue. You never know where the next opportunity may be lurking.*

FURTHER READING

www.themarketingblog.co.uk/2016/07/people-do-not-buy-goods-services-they-buy-relations-stories-magic-seth-godin/

TL;DR

58. FOR THE SKIM READERS AMONG YOU...

As in all service industries, our clients are pretty important; they are the lifeblood of our business. So, in order to Make Life Better for our people, we need to create sustainable growth that delivers ongoing success for our clients.

But that doesn't mean we see ourselves as their servants, or even their junior partners. We work with our clients as equals, fuelled by a determination to help them Be Found and to make their lives better, too. And if that sometimes means being choosy about who we work with, so be it.

END NOTES

i   *A great source of information like this is Internet Live Stats (www.internetlivestats.com). Prepare to have your mind blown...*

ii   *Caroline Johnson, Co-Founder, The Clear Partnership, a progressive strategy consultancy which equips marketing services businesses with the tools and know-how to be highly relevant, effective and profitable.*

iii   *Chris Merrington, Founder, Spring 80:20. A leading speaker and trainer, helping agencies and sales teams to be more successful, profitable and confident.*

iv   *Confessions of an Advertising Man, David Ogilvy, 1963*

v   *In many large companies, procurement teams are responsible for finding companies to pitch to them, and agreeing terms with the winner.*

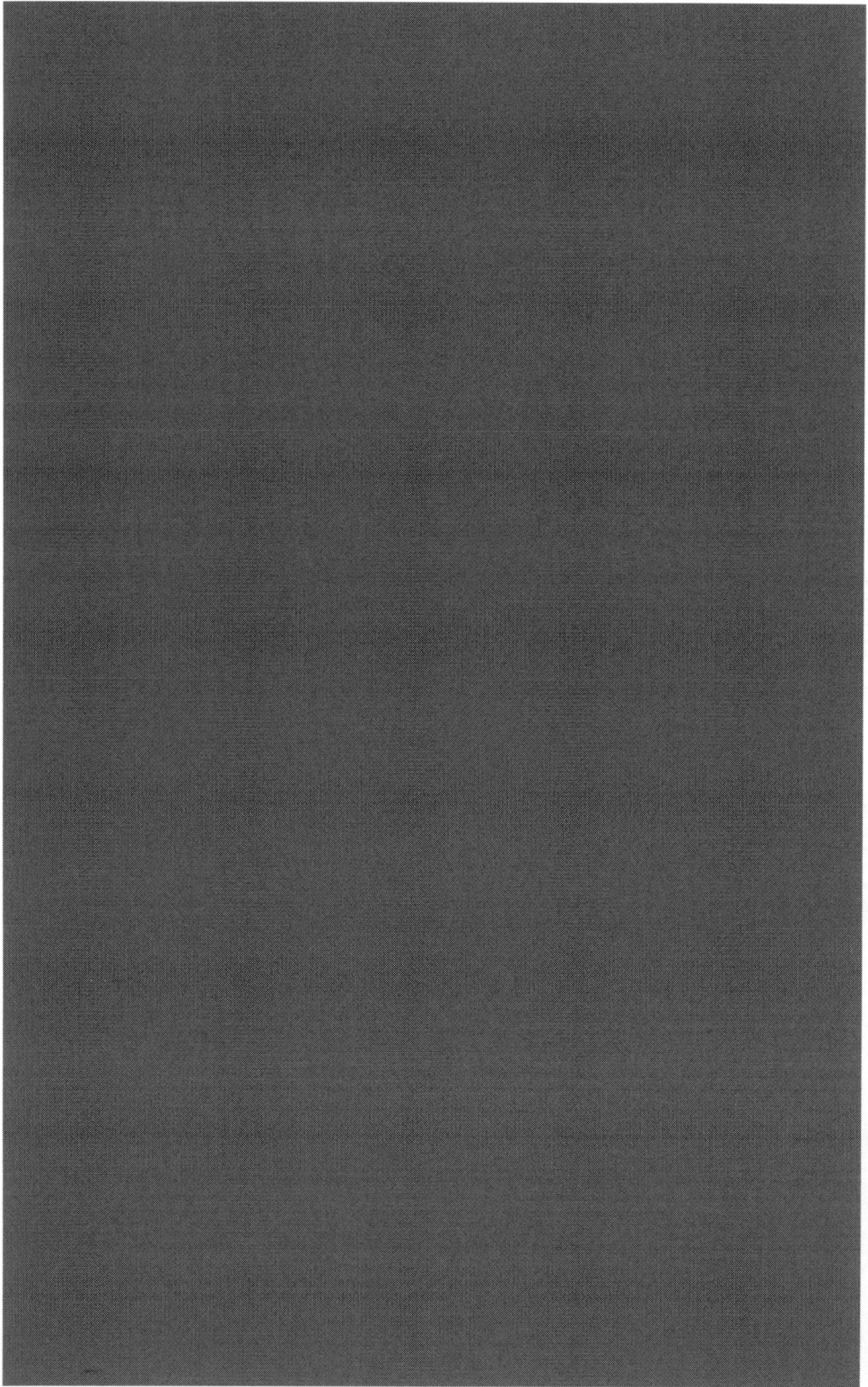

Section 9
WHAT'S NEXT?

59. THE FUTURE OF WORK

> " *We in the developed world are generally not working to survive. We have more than enough of everything we need. So much that we can actually afford to waste it... these days too many leaders of organisations seem to be wasting the goodwill of people. I wonder how long that can last until they can't afford to do it anymore.* "
>
> Simon Sinek, *Leaders Eat Last*

WHEN THE FUN REALLY STARTS

When we think about the future of our business, we think about the future of work...and we're facing a choice. We can look at it as a new set of opportunities, or a terrifying bunch of threats. You can probably guess which way we're going.

To be fair, it's hard to avoid the sense of impending doom. It feels like there's a fresh news story every day saying that loads of roles are going to be automated out of existence, that robots and algorithms are going to take over the world and steal our jobs, that our only friends will be mechanical ones. But can this really be true?

It's impossible to know exactly what's going to happen; as Nobel prize winning Danish physicist Niels Bohr stated rather amusingly back in the seventies, *"Prediction is very difficult, particularly if it's about the future."*

But we'd be naïve if we didn't think that automation is going to change things; it's happening right now. Here are just a few of the hundreds of clever ways that machines are already supporting or replacing humans:

- Planes are largely flown by artificial intelligence, with pilots doing the taking off and landing (which is about seven or eight minutes of the flight).

- Virtual assistants such as Siri, Alexa, Cortana and Google Assistant are helping us find what we're looking for using voice recognition or hands-free search.

- Online supermarkets remind us to buy kitchen roll.

- Amazon suggests books we might like based on what we've bought before.

- Social media apps use facial recognition to automatically tag people, based on knowing who your online friends are.

And that's just what's going on as we write this. A whole load of other potential workplace disruptors are being talked about with increasing frequency as this book goes to press (which may well be mainstream by the time you're reading it):

- Augmented reality and virtual reality
- Elon Musk's Hyperloop
- The four-hour working day as standard
- The sharing economy, the gig economy, the experience economy, the cryptocurrency economy...
- Smartphones, smart homes, smart cities...

One or more of these are likely to have an irreversible impact on the workplace. And we don't know which, or how many, or to what extent. (Someone who knows much more than we do is Klaus Schwab, whose book *The Fourth Industrial Revolution* makes some stark predictions for the future; have a look, if you're feeling brave enough).

But there's one thing we do feel certain about: we will need to have our minds open to a new kind of work. And instead of seeing that as a threat, our view is that we need to embrace it. We want people to be so superengaged that they will love going to work. It's not some crazy ideal, it's possible. We just need to make it more probable.

DOING THE WORK THAT ROBOTS CAN'T

To thrive in the workplace of the future, we'll all need to be prepared to adapt to changing circumstances and technologies, and to seize new opportunities as they arise. We'll need to be ready to improvise – to plan to improvise, in fact – so that we're rolling with, or leading, new developments in the workplace, rather than being caught out or left behind.

And we'll need to use our happy, engaged, creative minds to create new roles for the new future we're facing, which require the skills that machines lack. As humans, we excel in novel situations, solving problems we haven't seen before, based on context, environment and empathy with other human beings. These are things that robots and algorithms can't do (yet).

But this won't just happen; there is no magic engagement tree. As employers, we're going to need to instil these skills into our teams, and design roles to match. And we'd argue that focusing on engagement, through values such as innovation, creativity, adventure, fun and wellbeing is a great place to start.

Now, we would say that, wouldn't we? Well, yes, and not just because we think we know all the answers. We truly believe that these values help build a workplace culture that allows flexible, ideas-driven, non-automated minds to develop, and creates superengaged staff who will deliver a healthier bottom line.

And we're not the only ones. A recent study by the Department of Economics at the University of Warwick found that happiness led to a 12% spike in productivity, while unhappy workers proved 10% less productive. As the research team put it:

"We find that human happiness has large and positive causal effects on productivity. Positive emotions appear to invigorate human beings."

If they're right, we need to create jobs that will engage and invigorate us to do our best work; arguably, jobs with purpose. That's going to require leaders of organisations to take action: to stop wasting the goodwill of people and instead, create organisations designed to be enjoyable to work in.

And it's going to need to be based on motivating the stakeholders that make it all happen, not rewarding the shareholders on the outside.

CREATING A WORKPLACE NOW THAT'S FIT FOR THE FUTURE

According to responsive.org, who are looking to *"create a fundamental shift in the way we work and organise in the 21st century"*, the need for action is right now. Their manifesto highlights the change from the predictability of the past to the uncertainty of the future:

> ### *Everyone and everything is connected*
>
> *The world has become one giant network where instantly accessible and shareable information rewrites the future as quickly as it can be understood. Fuelled by relentless technological innovation, this accelerating connectivity has created an ever-increasing rate of change. As a result, the future is becoming increasingly difficult to predict.*
>
> *Meanwhile, most organisations still rely on a way of working designed over 100 years ago for the challenges and opportunities of the industrial age. Team structures support routine and static jobs. Siloed, command and control systems enable senior leadership to drive efficiency and predictability at the expense of free information flow, rapid learning, and adaptability.*

Responsive.org use the comparisons below to outline how future-fit businesses can respond to change and learn more rapidly. Their view is that basing business models on the predictability of the past is counter-productive, given the unpredictability of the future; If we take these on board, we have the potential to create more responsive businesses. Here's a hot- off-the-press example; we're currently experimenting with the idea

PAST
PREDICTABLE

FUTURE
UNPREDICTABLE

PAST (PREDICTABLE)		FUTURE (UNPREDICTABLE)
PROFIT	⟶	PURPOSE
HIERARCHIES	⟶	NETWORKS
CONTROLLING	⟶	EMPOWERING
PLANNING	⟶	EXPERIMENTING, IMPROVISING
PRIVACY	⟶	TRANSPARENCY

of moving from a line-management-based reporting structure to a coaching- and mentoring-based one. We're taking it slowly; it's a work in progress, but we think it could allow us to be more responsive to employee, client and workload needs. Watch this space.

There are many organisations who are already on the right path; just look at the list of Great Place to Work® winners, Fortune's 100 Best Companies to Work For, or any other employee engagement community.

The thing is, we need more of them. That's where you come in.

BE SUPERENGAGED

How future fit is your organisation? Have you looked ahead, and given some thought to what will be different – and how you need to plan for that change?

Do you have jobs that engage and invigorate people to do their best work? Could you?

YOU WIN SOME, YOU LOSE SOME

Rather than wasting our time worrying about whether the robots will steal our jobs, we're taking a collaborative approach to new technology. Like experimenting with AI to help us to become more effective, or taking the monotony out of some tasks (for example, by building key word lists or automating real time reporting), freeing up our super-sharp people to focus on the more strategic and creative parts of their jobs.

This in turn allows us to add value to clients rather than drowning in spreadsheets, which is much more fulfilling all round.

FURTHER READING

The Fourth Industrial Revolution, Klaus Schwab, 2016

60. OVER TO YOU

BUILD THE FUTURE
YOU WANT TO LIVE IN

Emmy-nominated writer and leading innovation thinker at the intersection of science and technology, Steve Berlin Johnson, suggests that we'll find the future *"wherever people are having the most fun."* [i] Sounds like our kind of guy.

But right now, the focus on fun and engagement is being buried under the overwhelmingly negative reports around levels of wellbeing. 50% of people report being exhausted at work. [ii]

And, according to Alex Kjerulf, Chief Happiness Officer at Woohoo Inc, too many people stay for too long in jobs they hate, with 25% of people saying they would like to quit their job tomorrow. [iii]

To the 25%, and the 50%, and anyone else who feels like they've had enough, we say, *"Don't quit!"*. Instead, stay on the inside, get involved, turn the problems into solutions. Don't spend your energy on job-hunting; invest it in exploring ideas and finding inspiration to tackle these problems. Whether you're a big cheese or a Babybel, you have a part to play.

We all need to work together to address the 70% of workers globally who are disengaged, those who are simply turning up hoping to make it through the day without getting fired. This isn't just an individual issue, it affects us all; how much potential and innovation are organisations missing out on, if so many of us are just going through the motions?

Margaret J Wheatly and Myron Kellner-Rogers wrote *A Simpler Way* over 20 years ago. The words they began with are as true now as they were then:

There is a simpler way to organise human endeavour. It requires a new way of being in the world. It requires being in the world without fear. Being in the world with play and creativity. Seeking after what's possible. Being willing to learn and be surprised...

The simpler way summons forth what is best about us. It asks us to understand human nature differently, more optimistically. It identifies us as creative. It acknowledges that we seek after meaning. It asks us to be less serious, yet more purposeful, about our work and our lives. It does not separate play from the nature of being... If we can be in the world in the fullness of our humanity, what are we capable of? If we are free to play, to experiment and discover, if we are free to fail, what might we create?

Margaret J Wheatly and Myron Kellner-Rogers

We can't afford to wait another couple of decades to address this; the right time is now. There are some big problems we have to solve on this planet[iv] and we need the ingenuity of the human spirit to be fully engaged to do so. How brilliantly could we be doing if that 70% were fully engaged too? And how can we make that happen?

Someone who had pretty firm views on this was Steve Jobs, who changed the way we interfaced with the world more than once (the 2001 iPod, the 2007 iPhone, the 2010 iPad...) As he said in his 2005 Stanford Commencement speech:

> *Your time is limited, so don't waste it living someone else's life. Don't be trapped by dogma – which is living with the results of other people's thinking. Don't let the noise of other's opinions drown out your own inner voice. And most important, have the courage to follow your heart and intuition.*
>
> Steve Jobs

Right on, Steve. We'd add, don't sit on the side-lines, full of fear, and let the future happen to you. Start today, be brave, and create the future you want to live in. It doesn't matter where you sit in your organisation; it's down to every one of us to take action. Let's superengage with everything we have and find out what we're capable of.

And if you're wondering where to start, as we did when we set ourselves the same challenge, keep reading. We've designed the next few chapters to be an easy-to-action, practical toolkit, which will help you start to understand the different levels of engagement and how to achieve them, based on the things we've got right (and wrong) along the way.

61. ENGAGEMENT TOOLKIT

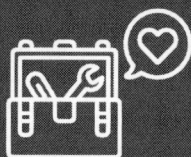

BRIEFING

THE THREE STEPS THAT WILL TRANSFORM YOUR ENGAGEMENT LEVELS

As we said all the way back in the Introduction, the world is in the middle of an engagement crisis, with recent research suggesting that only 30% of employees are fully engaged at their workplace[v].

In the intervening chapters, we've taken you on our journey from partial engagement to superengagement, sharing all our ups and downs along the way. Now, it's over to you.

Whilst we hope you've found the book interesting and entertaining, what we really want is for you to be inspired to take action, and to use engagement to transform your business' performance. So we've created a three-step *Engagement Toolkit* to help you do just that.

You'll find details of each step in the next three chapters, but here's a sneak preview:

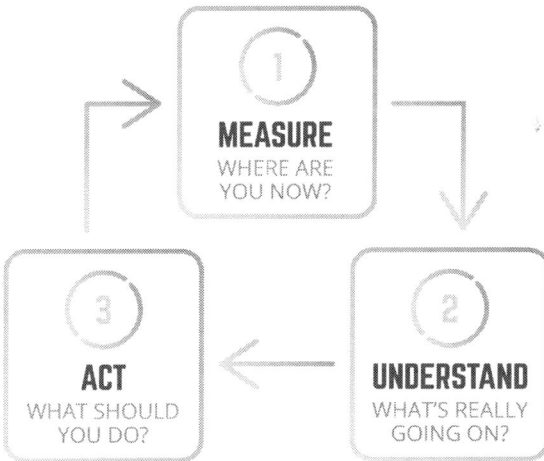

However, before you get stuck in, here are a few briefing notes, along with some questions to help you kick-start your thinking.

#1 IF YOU GET THE FOUR PRINCIPLES OF ENGAGEMENT RIGHT, YOU WON'T GO FAR WRONG

According to engagement experts Nita Clarke and David MacLeod,[vi] *"There is no 'one size fits all' approach and no master model for successful employee engagement".* However, their research has identified four common themes:

1. **Strategic narrative**: Visible, empowering leadership, which provides a strong strategic narrative about the organisation, where it's come from and where it's going.

2. **Engaging managers**: Bosses at all levels who can help their people focus, treat them as individuals and give them scope for stretch and development.

3. **Employee voice**: An organisation-wide understanding of the role played by employees in reinforcing and challenging views, both between functions and externally. Employees are not seen as the problem, but instead as central to the solution, and are involved, listened to and invited to contribute.

4. **Integrity**: Organisational integrity, in which the values on the wall are reflected in day-to-day behaviours. There is no 'say-do' gap. Promises that are made are kept, or an explanation is given as to why not.

> **Ask yourself:** *How do you feel your organisation operates within these themes? Is your engagement strategy clear? Are your managers inspirational and supportive? Does everyone feel they have a voice within the business? Do you keep your promises?*

#2 YOUR COLLEAGUES ARE UNLIKELY TO FEEL THE SAME LEVEL OF ENGAGEMENT AS YOU

Never assume that your view of the business is shared by everyone else. In most organisations, there is a significant variation between how different people experience the company as well as between their individual levels of engagement. It's the Rashomon[vii] effect in full flow. And a key factor is whether or not they hold a leadership position[viii].

We saw this for ourselves when we carried out our first *Culture Catalyst* employee engagement survey back in 2014. Although we felt we were performing pretty well in the four key areas, there was a big difference between the levels of engagement of our senior team and those of the rest of the business, with the leadership team scoring 17% higher overall (there was also a disconnect in the levels of understanding our purpose — more on page 399).

While this may be not unusual, it nonetheless highlighted a large crack in our business that we simply weren't aware of. It was only once we saw it, that we could try and fix it.

Ask yourself: *Are you guilty of assuming that your team members share your worldview? Do you have a sense that there is an engagement gap within your organisation? Have you asked?*

3 THE BEST WAY FORWARD IS TO ASK QUESTIONS – AND LISTEN TO THE ANSWERS

The Corporate Rebels 2017 report into trends that directly or indirectly influence employee engagement, *The Ugly Truth about the State of the Workplace,[ix]* found that:

- 61% feel their line manager doesn't listen to their opinions.
- 57% feel their values don't match with the organisation.
- 66% don't feel they can fully utilise their talents at work.

So, just to be clear, over half of employees feel like they're in the wrong place and aren't listened to, and two-thirds think they aren't able to make good use of their skills. Now that's what we call a waste.

Yet as we have shown throughout this book, questions are hugely powerful tools. Few of us have the magic skills of Derren Brown, or even Paul Daniels, but as we've shown, there's a simple way to find out what people are thinking or feeling: ASK THEM.

Of course, asking is only the starting point; you also have to listen to the answers, and then act on what you learn. And that, in a nutshell, is the process that the *Engagement Toolkit* will take you through.

Ask yourself: *Do you ask your employees their opinions? If so, do you listen to the answers, and act on them? If not, why not, what's holding you back?*

The overall conclusion from Corporate Rebels is that there is a lot of work to be done;

"Most organisations need a serious upgrade if they want to motivate and fully engage their employees."

Are you ready to upgrade? Then let's go.

62. ENGAGEMENT TOOLKIT: 1.MEASURE

WHERE ARE YOU NOW?

GETTING THE FIGURES THAT UNDERPIN THE FACTS

As you may have gathered, we love digging into the data. It helps you understand where you're at, which is mission critical; if you don't know where you're starting from, it's anyone's guess where you'll end up.

The first step in the *Engagement Toolkit* is therefore to measure your current levels of engagement. Sounds complicated? Well, it isn't (phew). It's a simple, five-stage process based around a variation of our old favourite, the Net Promotor Score® metric:

MORE IN CHAPTER 6

"On a scale of 1-10, with 1 being low and 10 being high, how likely would you be to recommend working at this company to others?"

So, using this question as a base, here are the stages you need to go through to get a 360⁰ view of your engagement status quo.

1. **Note your Self Recommendation Score**

   Start by giving your personal view. What score would you answer the question with?

2. **Estimate your Perceived Team Recommendation Score (average)**

   Next, make a rough estimate of the view of your team as a whole. What do you predict their average score would be?

3. **Find your Actual Team Recommendation Score (average)**

   Now you're ready to measure what they actually think. Set up a quick online survey,[x] send it out to your team and wait for the responses. Make sure you keep it anonymous and reassure respondents that you're looking for honest answers; you'll get better insights that way.

   Then work out the Average Recommendation Score, by adding up all the scores and dividing by the number of participants. And note down the three initial scores to compare them.

1. Self Recommendation Score	
2. Estimated Team Recommendation Score	
3. Actual Team Recommendation Score	

4. Assess your Recommendation Gap

So, how did you do? Was your estimate anywhere near the reality? Are you and your team feeling similarly engaged, or might there be a crack appearing?

5. Dig a bit deeper

Having got an engagement overview from the first four stages, it's worth digging a bit deeper into the reasons behind your scores. Without this information, you'll struggle when it comes to the UNDERSTAND step.

To do so, you'll need to ask some more nuanced questions, which align with the themes we've explored in *Superengaged*. It's still a very simple model, and there are considerably more questions you could ask to get a fuller analysis, but these will give you a good steer.[xi]

Again, all responses should be anonymous, and each answer should be based on a scale of 1 to 10, with 1 being low and 10 being high.

1.	*I feel aligned to the purpose and goals of this organisation.*	**PURPOSE**
2.	*I trust this organisation to behave in ways that are true to our values.*	**VALUES**
3.	*This is a psychologically safe place to work.*	**BEHAVIOURS**

4. *I feel valued in my role.*	**CULTURE**
5. *I know what is expected of me.*	**RETENTION**
6. *I have received the right training to do my job well.*	**DEVELOPMENT**
7. *This organisation is committed to supporting my work-life balance.*	**BALANCE**
8. *I feel suitably challenged in my role.*	**PERFORMANCE**
9. *Leaders are open and honest in their communications.*	**TRANSPARENCY**
10. *I have the opportunity to progress in this organisation.*	**PROGRESSION**

You can add an 11th question if you want to establish whether there is a gap between the leadership team and the rest of the business:

11. *Are you a member of the board or senior leadership team? Y/N*

You can either use another online survey, go to www.superengaged.co.uk to download, or copy the worksheet at the end of this book and give it to your team to fill in.

When all the answers are in, it's time to try and understand them. Move on to Step 2.

63. ENGAGEMENT TOOLKIT: 2.UNDERSTAND

WHAT'S REALLY GOING ON?

WORKING OUT WHAT THE NUMBERS MEAN

So, you've got your responses back – and hopefully not had too many nasty surprises.

You've been able to take an at-a-glance look at the gap between your perception and reality. And you may have been able to spot whether there are any engagement cracks between the leadership team and everyone else.

What else can the numbers tell you?

Your Actual Team Recommendation Score, as an average figure, gives you a broad picture of your engagement levels, but looking at the distribution of the scores will tell you more.

So, the next thing to do is allocate the responses across four bands: 6 or under, 7, 8 or 9, and 10. Then work out what percentage of your employees fall into each of these categories.

- **6 or below:** Not Engaged
- **7:** Partially Engaged
- **8 or 9:** Engaged
- **10:** Superengaged

It's a rough measure, but it will give you a top-line indication of how you're doing.

ASK YOURSELF SOME QUESTIONS TO HELP YOU UNDERSTAND

However, the numbers themselves only tell you half the story. So now you need to interrogate the data by asking yourself some questions about what the responses might mean.

Here are some suggestions:

- What about the responses surprised you?

- What is in line with your thinking?

- Is there a gap between your perception and other people's reality?

- Do you have any areas of weakness?

- What about these responses concerns you?

- What are you proud of?

- Are there any cracks between senior leaders and the rest of the organisation?

- How many people score as Not Engaged in your business? How do you feel about that?

- How many people score as Superengaged in your business? What does that say about your leadership?

- Overall, how are people experiencing working here?

- What should you do something about, right now?

- What could you celebrate right now?

FOCUS ON WHERE YOU CAN HAVE THE MOST IMPACT

With unlimited time, you could look to address all these lines of thinking. However realistically, you might need to prioritise. So, we suggest you go through these eight stages to work out which areas would deliver the biggest impact. This will add a level of qualitative understanding to the quantitative numbers you've already got.

Write down any questions that occur to you when looking at the responses.	*Jot your initial thoughts here*
1. Which three responses jump out from the rest? For example, are any of them significantly higher or lower than you thought they would be, or just not what you were expecting? If it isn't the first time you've done this, have any of your scores dropped noticeably since last time?	
2. With just these three responses in mind, think about what the people who work in your organisation might be feeling. How might things look from their point of view? What would they want you to prioritise?	
3. Think about what you would like to ask them about their experiences. What could you learn from them? Then invite a mixed group of people to meet with you, explain that you are curious about some of the survey results and want to understand more. Throwing in some food and beers often helps.	

4. When you meet, talk about what the survey revealed and explain what you'd like to know more about. Ask them some questions. Reassure them that they won't be judged on their answers. Listen to what they have to say. Take notes on what they say – and make sure you keep a poker face.	
5. At the end, ask them if they would like you to act on any of the points raised. What would they like to see happen next?	
6. Go away and think about what you heard, and discuss it with your senior team. What steps could you take collectively?	
7. Write to those who took part, thank them for their time and explain what you plan to do. Then tell the organisation what happened and what you intend to do next.	

CASE STUDY: ARTICULATING OUR PURPOSE

As we mentioned in the briefing, the first time we carried out our internal *Culture Catalyst* survey, we discovered a crack when it came to our purpose. The score from board members suggested a clear engagement with, and understanding, of Make Life Better; but it wasn't connecting with the rest of the business.

This forced us to think carefully about how we were articulating Make Life Better, how well it was understood, whether it was being brought to life within the business, and whether people could connect with and align to it in their personal journeys with us.

So we didn't hang about. We explored the issue across the whole company, through a range of conversations and workshops. It wasn't a quick win; it took time for everyone to understand what we were asking. But seeing how others had connected their own development to our purpose really helped people understand how it could help them too.

As a result, we made sure we linked back to our purpose at every touchpoint of our business.

When we decided on whether to take on a new client:

"Will we Make Life Better for them by working with them – can we do great work?"

When we thought about how to make our employees love coming to work:

"How can we improve the culture and behaviours that drive our organisation, to Make Life Better for the people who work here?"

When we approached a new piece of work:

"How can we Make Life Better for our client's customers who are searching online?"

And when we asked ourselves how we could support our community:

"How can we Make Life Better for those in need in Brighton, by focusing our efforts and maximising our impact?"

It seems so obvious now, but at the time, we were merrily working away, assuming everyone was on board, when in fact we could have been making our boat go so much faster. Imagine where you could take your business, just by asking some simple questions.

And when you've done so, it's time for Step 3.

THE DO'S AND DONT'S OF FACE-TO-FACE-FEEDBACK

DO

- ✓ Do make sure there are more of them than you.

- ✓ Do ask open questions and give everyone room to speak.

- ✓ Do reassure them that their answers will be anonymous outside the room.

- ✓ Do recognise that spilling the beans to the boss might make people feel nervous.

- ✓ Do promise that you won't act on ANYTHING people say, unless they specifically ask you to.

- ✓ Do tell them that you want to make things as good as they can be, but you need their honest input.

- ✓ Do ask them at the end what they'd like you to do next.

DON'T

- ✗ Don't interrupt.

- ✗ Don't close people down.

- ✗ Don't try to explain, defend or justify yourself or your organisation.

- ✗ Don't express disappointment or annoyance, even if it feels uncomfortable. Everyone's perception is valid.

- ✗ Don't break confidences after the session.

- ✗ Don't take any action without their permission – they will never trust you again if you do.

64. ENGAGEMENT TOOLKIT: 3.ACT

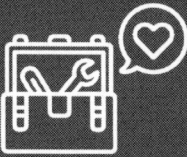

WHAT SHOULD YOU DO?

MAKING ENGAGEMENT HAPPEN

By now you should have a pretty clear view of how people feel about your organisation. But that's not enough, of course; the final, critical step is to act on what you've learned.

Over the years, we've discovered that the actions which move people from Not Engaged to Superengaged are directly linked to how much people feel acknowledged, valued and inspired:

- Making them feel **acknowledged** tends to move them from Not Engaged to Partially Engaged.

- Making them feel **valued** tends to move them from Not or Partially Engaged to Engaged.

- Making them feel **inspired** tends to move them up to Superengaged. And it doesn't get better than that.

So, how can you design actions that will help your people move along the scale?

The table overleaf suggests how people at different levels of engagement might be experiencing your company. It isn't a definitive truth; every organisation is different.

But it's a good starting point for identifying the feelings and opinions that sit behind engagement levels, which in turn will help you improve them.

Take a look and ask yourself, *"Is this like us or not? How are we the same, and how are we different?"* Use the blank version at the end of this chapter to complete your own table.

	NOT ENGAGED	PARTIALLY ENGAGED
1.PURPOSE *I feel aligned to the purpose and goals of this organisation.*	Not aligned to purpose. Just turning up, hoping not to get fired.	Some alignment to purpose. Understands goals but doesn't wholly agree with them or find them personally compelling.
2. VALUES *I trust this organisation to behave in ways that are true to its values.*	Sees values as a plaque on the wall at best. No understanding of values or what is valued. Lack of overall trust.	Believes values are evident beyond the plaque. Lack of match of the company values to personal values. Questionable level of trust.
3. BEHAVIOURS *This is a psychologically safe place to work.*	Sees conflict as a normal feature of the workplace. Believes addressing conflict is disregarded or depriori-tised. *"I cannot voice my concerns without fear of reprisal."*	Believes challenging the norm is not welcome. Feels conflict is sporadically / inconsistently addressed. *"I occasionally have the oppor-tunity to have my voice heard."*
4. CULTURE *I feel valued in my role.*	Thinks organisation has a high staff turnover with many negative leavers. Believes management writes off leavers as soon as they have resigned.	Considers staff turnover is badly managed. Experiences a lack of communication about leavers before they leave, which creates all-round awkwardness.
5. RETENTION *I know what is expected of me.*	Believes objectives are unclear and lacks an evolving job description (beyond role applied for).	Has some sense of what's expected individually but has no clear idea of how this fits into the bigger picture. Knows what they're doing, but not why they are doing it.
6. DEVELOPMENT *I have received the right training to do my job well.*	Considers there is no time or budget for training needs, or that the budget is the first thing to go when times get tough.	Believes training is focused on job skills in preference to cultural or personal development.

ENGAGED	SUPERENGAGED
Understands purpose and goals, which resonate strongly and are aligned to personal growth.	Aligned to purpose and goals and lives them out in unusual and motivating ways, creating new opportunities. A potential leader.
Feels values are evident and explicit, resonating on a personal level. Trusts the organisation.	Believes values are clear, engaging and alive throughout the business. Lives the values through daily practices and discussion. Feels trusted to do their job in the way they think is best.
Feels raising concerns is welcomed and made safe. Believes feedback is embraced, whether constructive or otherwise. *"I am actively invited to share my opinion."*	Thinks regular attention is given to how behaviour shapes the mood and culture of the business. Feels the culture enables conflict to be addressed in a positive way. *"Voicing my perspective is encouraged, celebrated and acted upon. I can see my impact on the business direction."*
Believes staff turnover is low. Considers leavers to be mainly positive, with professional relationships maintained.	Believes most leavers are positive and going on to a completely different role or career path. Considers leavers to be strong alumni for future growth.
Has clarity on what is expected in their role. Feels in control of their own career. Has the expectation and appetite to go beyond their core job role.	Shares the company's strategic expectations and is aligned to personal impact. Feels free to develop opportunities for new roles. Enjoys an abundance of career paths.
Considers the training remit expansive (culture, skills, management, personal) and continuous, on the job, as well as specific courses.	Has personal freedom and control of own training, alongside on-the-job and specific activities to broaden horizons, both personally and professionally.

	NOT ENGAGED	PARTIALLY ENGAGED
7. BALANCE *This organisation is committed to supporting my work-life balance.*	Believes the balance is not evident Feels obliged to work additional hours to those contracted.	Knows time out can be arranged in advance, but often at the expense of holiday or by making up time, despite over-delivering on contracted hours. Unable to disconnect enough to take more than a short period of time off, or constantly checking whilst away.
8. PERFORMANCE *I feel suitably challenged in my role.*	Subject to a hierarchical, annual, top-down appraisal, focusing on the past. Often exposed to (surprise) negative feedback, stored up for the annual event.	Works towards individual objectives with little idea of how this ties into the bigger picture. Given isolated goals, not integrated goals.
9. TRANSPARENCY *Leaders are open and honest in their communications.*	Feels there is no transparency. Believes that profit supersedes people, and that information relating to it, and decisions made because of it, are not shared beyond the shareholders. Is aware of, but not included in, top-down, behind closed doors conversations. Feels decisions are only shared once made. (Fear based)	Exposed to non-sensitive information, but is aware of a strict commercial line being drawn, with much of the information considered beyond their pay grade. (Parental)
10. PROGRESSION *I have the opportunity to progress in this organisation.*	Sees no route for progression, or doesn't understand how to progress. Feels stuck or just a number. Finds it hard to engage across the business, as it's not clear who people are, let alone what they do.	No idea if role is critical to the mission of the organisation. Sees others in this role move forward but doesn't know how to do the same. No clear plan.

ENGAGED	SUPERENGAGED
Feels trusted to do what is needed within working hours. Is able to take advantage of a variety of different working patterns. Takes and enjoys holidays. Is eligible for sabbaticals at certain points in time.	Enjoys the flexibility to bring life and work into harmony. Is supported by the right kit, the right access to different places to work and the right focus on outcomes not hours at a desk. Is able to plan in and take holidays and sabbaticals, in the knowledge that time out is considered as important as time working. Returns from time away with new energy and new ideas.
Understands the point of their role and how it fits into the overall organisation. Given regular and connected feedback to enable better performance.	Benefits from a focus on organisation and team, as well as on individuals. Has regular 121s and quarterly appraisal/ progression conversations, focusing on the future. Given peer-based feedback in person (not second hand). Has developed a coaching mind-set.
Shares in the good stuff. Benefits from a culture which celebrates when appropriate but doesn't share bad news, for fear of stressing people out. (Protective)	Enjoys complete transparency in terms of strategic goals, KPIs, commercials and decision making. Has ready access to information, including commercial position. Knows everyone is aware of important issues, and is collectively part of bringing ideas and action into being. Benefits from uncompromising honesty. (Brave)
Understands clearly how to progress in the organisation. Has a plan with milestone achievements and regular updates to keep on track. Focused.	Fully understands progression goals and how to reach them – and has the tools at their disposal. Feels they are in the driving seat. Believes everyone is valued. Benefits from regular time earmarked for collective reflection and public celebration of achievements and progression.

Once you've filled in your own table, you'll have a clear sense of the levers that shape your culture and drive engagement in your organisation.

You can then use these as a base for working with your team (at all levels) to identify strategies to shift people along the engagement scale.

Feel free to use the **NICK THIS** ideas and **BE SUPERENGAGED** questions to help you identify the best approaches for your circumstances.

You'll find the questions at the end of each chapter in this book to help you. You can also find a range of other tools to support you at *www.superengaged.co.uk*.

It's this kind of thinking that has enabled us to grow in ways we never imagined. To reach unheard of levels of engagement, and deliver highly impactful work. To triple our margin, quadruple our revenue and generate 10 times more profit in just ten years.

What could it do for you?

OVER TO YOU

What would your people be experiencing at each of these levels of engagement? (You can use the blank table on the next page as a starting point).

1.PURPOSE

I feel aligned to the purpose and goals of this organisation.

2. VALUES

I trust this organisation to behave in ways that are true to its values.

3. BEHAVIOURS

This is a psychologically safe place to work.

4.CULTURE

I feel valued in my role.

5.RETENTION

I know what is expected of me.

6.DEVELOPMENT

I have received the right training to do my job well.

7.BALANCE

This organisation is committed to supporting my work-life balance.

8.PERFORMANCE

I feel suitably challenged in my role.

9.TRANSPARENCY

Leaders are open and honest in their communications.

10. PROGRESSION

I have the opportunity to progress in this organisation.

NOT ENGAGED	PARTIALLY ENGAGED	ENGAGED	SUPERENGAGED

END NOTES

i   *www.ted.com/talks/steven_johnson_how_play_leads_to_great_inventions*

ii   *Bruce Daisley, EMA VP Twitter.*

iii   *Alex Kjerulf, Chief Happiness Officer at Dutch company Woohoo Inc, world-leading experts on happiness at work. Kjerulf has set up a site to help you work out if you should quit your job tomorrow... check out www.internationalquityourcrappyjob-day.com and take the 10 question test "to give you some indication of whether it's time to quit."*

iv   *According to a Business Insider report, the 10 biggest work problems that are concerning millennials (who are the future of our workforce, after all) are: 1. Climate change and destruction of natural resources. 2. Large scale conflict and wars. 3. Religious conflicts. 4. Poverty. 5. Government accountability, transparency and corruption. 6. Safety, security and wellbeing. 7. Lack of education. 8. Lack of political freedom and political instability. 9. Food and water insecurity. 10. Lack of economic opportunity and unemployment. uk.businessinsider.com/world-economic-forum-world-biggest-problems-concerning-millennials-2016-8/#10-lack-of-economic-opportunity-and-unemployment-142-1*

v   *Figures taken from Gallup research, as quoted in Glenn Elliot and Debra Covey's 2018 book Build It: The Rebel Playbook for World-Class Employee Engagement. engageforsuccess.org/the-four-enablers*

vi   *engageforsuccess.org/the-four-enablers*

vii   *The Rashomon effect occurs when the same event is given contradictory in-*
      terpretations by different individuals involved. The effect is named after Akira
      Kurosawa's 1950 film Rashomon, in which a murder is described in four mutually
      contradictory ways by its four witnesses.

viii *Culture Catalyst survey overviews since 2014.*

ix   *corporate-rebels.com/research*

x   *Google has a tool for this, called Google Forms, or try any of the cloud-based*
      services out there like Survey Monkey, Wufoo or Typeform.

xi   *These questions have been developed in conjunction with Ian Scott, MSc, from*
      Then Somehow and the Royal Statistical Society. They are proven predictors of
      engagement, used in over a million multinational surveys over the last 25 years.
      When scored highly, they individually and collectively, consistently and extremely
      accurately, point to superengagement. NB There is some considerable overlap
      with questions asked in many other studies. For example, Gallup research asks
      a question around being appreciated and being able to do your best work, and
      MORI research asks respondents to score knowing how you can develop, both of
      which have been shown to successfully indicate levels of engagement.

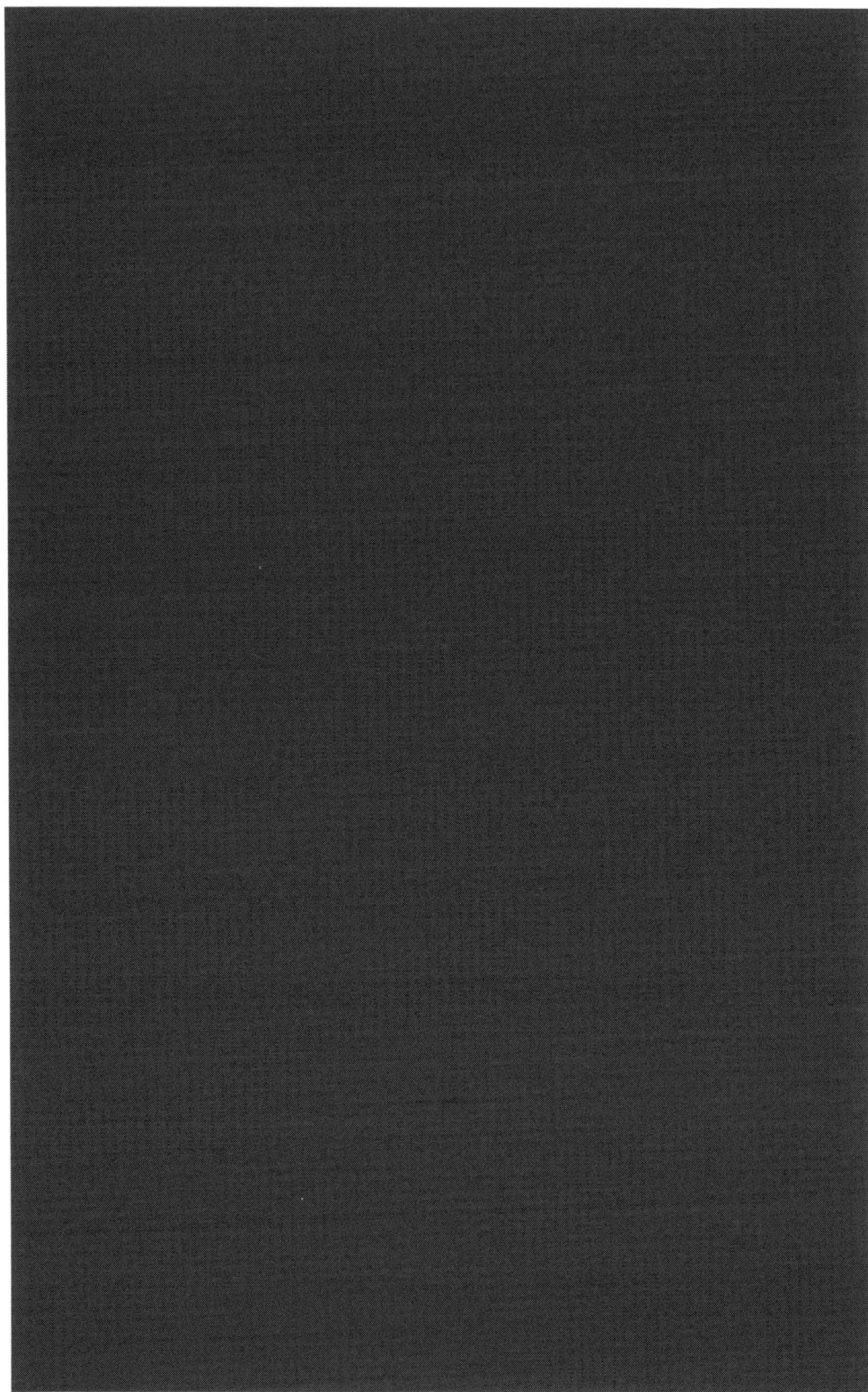

Section 10

KEEP ON DREAMING

65. THE PROPELLERNET MANIFESTO

*Our 15-point plan
for superengaging the world*

1. **Make engagement a priority**
   If you're looking to drive your business's performance and profits, treat your engagement levels as seriously as your margins. The more engaged your teams are, the more ingenuity they will bring into the heart of your business, and the higher your commercial gains will be.

2. **Know why you exist**
   Have a clear purpose. It enables you to make sound, coherent decisions, for the overall good of the organisation, rather than focusing on short-term business gains. In the same way that music without soul is just noise (© funkmaster Nile Rodgers), business without purpose is just admin.

3. **Bring your values out to play**
   If your purpose is what you're working towards, your values are how you'll get there. Choose ones which create a strong cultural force that will drive your organisation forward. People have well-honed bullshit detectors, so values need to be worth the brain-space they occupy, and to be lived to be believed.

4. **Get your people happy**
   Very simply, happy people do better work than miserable people. It's not rocket science – but it's surprising how rarely it's factored into the business plan. So, make sure you make them feel welcome both before they arrive and on their first day, set them up to succeed, celebrate their achievements and support them through any tough times.

5. **Be clear about your expectations**
   Putting your people first doesn't mean letting them do whatever they want; they aren't assets to be sweated, but they do need to add value. Make it clear what you expect from them, both in terms of business performance and social behaviour. Then put the tools, culture and support in place to help them deliver.

6. **Encourage your people to switch off**

   As well as giving people the tools to succeed, you need to help them feel free to unplug; your P&L will thank you for it. Check that they're managing their workload; be flexible around working hours; help them keep their free time work-free and insist they take their holidays. In return, you'll get inspired, energised colleagues who might just light up the world.

7. **Recruit slowly and personally**

   Recruit at haste, repent at leisure. If you employ the wrong person, it can cost you 15 times their salary to put right. Instead, view recruitment as an ongoing activity, and build relationships today with people who might be a great fit in the future. You never know when the time will be right.

8. **Plan to lose your best talent**

   People will leave, life will go on, the world will keep turning. It's better to plan for it than ignore it and end up in a panic replacement scenario. People who say goodbye on friendly terms become a powerful part of your alumni, and act as advocates for your brand and business. The good ones never really leave you, anyway.

9. **Don't be afraid to be transparent**

   Honesty really is the best policy. If you're open about everything, right down to your profits, rumours don't have space to breathe. And the more information you share, the more people can grab opportunities and tackle any problems together. It's surprising, perhaps, but there's safety in sharing numbers.

10. **Let your team have a say in who you work with**

    If you're working on something you can't engage with, it's hard to produce brilliant work. Fortunately, the opposite is also true. So, ask your people if there are clients or sectors they'd like to work with, then enlist their help with making it happen; it's a shortcut to enthusiasm and commitment.

11. Say no to bastards

Never put toxic client revenue before your people. Unreasonable, demanding clients who want the moon on a stick for free are not worth having. They will drive value out of your business, suck the life out of your strategy, take their toll on your team and take your attention away from more worthwhile clients. Don't think *"How can I afford to be so picky?"*. Think *"How can I afford not to?"*

12. Build climbing frames instead of career ladders

In traditional hierarchies, senior roles are scarce, which makes career progression difficult for all but a few. Instead, create innovative, flexible career paths, which are open to non-traditional growth as opportunities arise. By enabling people to blaze their own trails and bring in their side hustles, you'll create an inspiring group of entrepreneurial thinkers and doers, who will grow your business as they grow their careers.

13. Create something bigger than yourself

Community matters. Yes, you need to focus on the business at hand, but it's also worth lifting your head up from time to time and thinking about how you could contribute to the world outside your window. It will enthuse and engage your people and is likely to be some of the most rewarding work you do.

14. Build a bucket list business plan

Put any scepticism to one side and try to imagine the spirit of teamwork and loyalty that you could unleash by making your team's dreams part of your business plan. Not to mention the new commercial opportunities that you could generate along the way. Don't believe us? Prepare to be amazed.

15. Act like there's no exit

Whatever your plans for the business, try approaching it as if you will never leave; as if there were no exit, no prospect of a sale and no retirement date. It will transform the way you work day-to-day and will help you build a brilliant future, and Make Life Better, for everyone.

THE PROPELLERNET MANIFESTO

OUR 15-POINT PLAN FOR SUPERENGAGING THE WORLD

1. MAKE ENGAGEMENT A PRIORITY

No 2. KNOW *why* YOU EXIST

3.

BRING YOUR VALUES OUT TO PLAY

4. GET YOUR PEOPLE HAPPY

5. BE CLEAR ABOUT YOUR EXPECTATIONS

6. ENCOURAGE YOUR PEOPLE TO SWITCH OFF

7. RECRUIT SLOWLY & PERSONALLY

8. Plan to lose your best talent

11. SAY NO TO BASTARDS

9. DON'T BE AFRAID TO BE TRANS-PARENT

10. LET YOUR TEAM HAVE A SAY IN WHO YOU WORK WITH

12. BUILD CLIMBING FRAMES INSTEAD OF CAREER LADDERS

14. BUILD A BUCKET LIST BUSINESS PLAN

13. CREATE SOMETHING BIGGER THAN YOURSELF

15. ACT LIKE THERE'S NO EXIT

66. DREAMING BIG

> *The future belongs to those who believe in the beauty of their dreams.*

Eleanor Roosevelt, First Lady, diplomat, and one of Gallup's Top 10 Most Widely Admired People of the 20th Century.

DREAM ON, DREAMERS

So, looking into the future, what are we dreaming of?

That we achieve our core ambition, and Propellernet becomes the best place to work in the world.

That our engagement levels stay super-high, and our 15-year experiment in putting people first goes from strength to strength, providing a springboard for more creativity and innovation, more adventures and more fun.

That we continue to deliver a culture that evolves and evolves, bringing in new people who share our vision and values and want to take them forward, throwing ourselves into the bends of change, embracing the challenges and engaging all the way.

That we keep planning to improvise, and ignite more dreams, engaging our people to take risks, do the best work of their lives and take what they've learned into other opportunities, achieving collectively more than we could ever do individually or apart.

That the ripple effect of Make Life Better reaches far and wide, not just through our team and our clients but also the creative mavericks and progressive thinkers who have a backstage pass to our business, hanging out at the Foundry to engage in animated discussion, exchange ideas and let serendipity in.

That Dream Valley remains a platform for transformation, allowing us to work collaboratively to design a positive future, and to connect ideas that will lead to even more innovation, pushing the boundaries of exploration as we go.

That we continue to win awards for the way we work as well as the work we do, and that we are invited to tell the story of how we do it all over the world.

That more great clients knock on our door asking to work with us, and that none of them are bastards who detract from the stars, so we can focus on solving problems and creating value for clients and their customers alike.

That our technology business continues to revolutionise the way people work, with www.coveragebook.com, www.answerthepublic.com and www.answertheclient.com being just the first stage of our mission to Make Life Better in the PR industry, in marketing and in every creative field.

That our housing renovation project helps more people onto the housing ladder, delivering more starter homes for people in our community and helping tackle the housing crisis, alongside our fundraising efforts in support of Brighton Housing Trust.

That our safari project snowballs (sandballs?) so that as well as driving traffic to Wild Dog Safaris, we open up awareness of the whole of Namibia, supporting the growing eco-tourism industry and helping safeguard the future of native animals.

That the Red Stars go stratospheric, perform at Burning Man and inspire a raft of spin-off creative pursuits that bring more light into the world. And that we build up an audience of over 100,000 followers for the online web series W.A.R.S and Netflix want to buy it. And win a BAFTA. An Oscar. A cabinetful of Oscars.

You can dream, right?

Experience has shown us that it's worth dreaming big, and that weaving our dreams into our business plan helps make sure they come true. We can promise you that this kind of thinking will open up opportunities that you wouldn't have seen before, boosting your performance and profits along the way.

It's engaging just thinking about it. Superengaging, in fact.

And so to our dreams for you. We're dreaming that this book has inspired you, and that it continues to inspire you. That it ignites conversations with others and that you pass our message on – adding to the ripple effect of Make Life Better, flowing out into the wider world, further than any of our dreams would let us imagine.

What are you dreaming of?

67. THE LAST WORD

OVER TO THE TEAM

As a people-first business, it feels only appropriate that we let our team have the last word. Here's what inspires them about working with us:

"Freedom. Adventure. Creating futures. Challenging ourselves and our expectations. It's not 'Why?' it's 'Why not?' and laughter aplenty."

Nikki

"Doing something different nearly every day and calling it work."

Louise

"Having a job in line with my interests and feeling grateful that I'm excited waking up on Monday mornings because of the people I work with."

Will

"Working hard and enjoying every moment of it!"

Tallulah

"The agility to build solutions around our clients' needs without being restrained by silos or egos."

Tobit

"Learning from smart people. Being in a great environment where you can be yourself. Power ballads. '80s buddy cop movies."

Randip

"It's quite a thing to find a workplace that really cares for its employees – and even rarer to find one which shows that same level of care for contractors and freelancers (like me)."

Oliver

"Weird enough to come up with brilliant ideas, brave enough to put them forward and nice enough to work as a team to make them reality."

Robin

"Always saying yes and seeing where it takes you."

Jim J

"A place where the minutiae of everyday life can be transformed into something inspiring – and where curiosity definitely didn't kill the cat."

Chloe

"Taking risks and defying the conventional. Collaboration and creativity. Sea air and beach walks. Giving something back and not giving up!"

Corryn

"Working for a company that cares about employee lives inside and outside of work."

Jake

"The implausibly random conversations that lead to ground-breaking brand-shifting work."

Jenny

"Allowing the numbers to give people the freedom to be creative."

Simon

"Helping to deliver exceptional campaigns steeped with insight and technical excellence, with plenty of fun to celebrate."

Colin

"A strong workplace culture that always puts people first."

Tuna

"People who maintain a childlike sense of wonder and don't take things for granted, because absolutely anything can be an inspiration."

Stephen

"Juggling multi-coloured plates and making magic."

Lucy

"Using technology, data and creative in combination to reach people in a meaningful way and change behaviour. Basically, mind control."

Jim K

"Working with lovely people every day, for a company which supports its staff to always chase their dreams."

Amanda

"The amazing combination of passion, honesty, creativity, knowledge, open minds, good coffee and having fun, just for the fun of it."

Jo

"Getting to work with extremely talented people and being given the freedom to be creative."

Dave

"You never fail, you only find 10,000 more ways that don't work."

Harry

"Make Life Better isn't just a tagline, it defines everything we do. I'm honoured to be part of a team making themselves and the world better."

Joe

GRATITUDE

THANK YOU

There are so many people who have contributed ideas, critiqued content, created the memories and supported me along the journey of telling the Propellernet story.

My personal support: my husband Neale, who has put up with my *Superengaged* obsession, patiently waiting whilst I start scribbling down an idea that's just popped into my head (often in the middle of a meal, a conversation or the night). He keeps my feet on the ground and makes me laugh, always.

My everyday inspiration: the brilliant and bonkers team at Propellernet, all of whom feature in the book, and without whom it wouldn't exist. Keep those stories coming.

My backroom team: Cathy Halstead and Wayne Fick. An alchemic combination of wit, intelligence and creativity. THE best editor + art director team I have worked with – and I've worked with some amazing ones.

My confidence boosters: Louise Greeves, Stefan Hull, Hannah Harris, James Sandford and Jo Kirrane. At the beginning, you encouraged me and made me get on with it. In the thick of it, you kept me on track, providing insightful comments, the occasional comedy dig and many improvements along the way. You'll never know how much your support mattered.

My reality checks: all the lovely people who gave me their feedback. In particular, a big shout out to Steve Stark, who stopped me in my tracks and made me dig deep into the full story a couple of times, and to Henry Stewart, who was so generous with his ideas when I occasionally got stuck.

My promoters: everyone who wrote a review, particularly before launch – it's a big ask to read a 400-page book when it's still a bunch of PDFs in Dropbox. Your generous comments made me smile.

And finally, of course, Jack Hubbard, Jim Jensen and Gary Preston. You started this. We've had a riot in the last decade and I'm chuffed to have had the pleasure of capturing it. Thank you.

APPENDIX

SUPERENGAGED

/ˌs(j)uːpərɪnˈɡeɪdʒd/

adjective: superengaged

According to engagement experts
Then Somehow, a superengaged employee:

- Knows their organisation cares for its people and is doing its utmost to ensure their emotional and psychological wellbeing.

- Has complete faith that the organisation will tell them the truth, while being faithful to its own core principles (which, in turn, they feel deeply aligned to).

- Feels genuinely challenged, with the appropriate training and support to take on those challenges, and has a clear sense of how they will progress.

Engagement can mean different things in different organisations. Virgin Atlantic will have different points of engagement to MI5 – defining your own is an important step on the journey. By way of examples:

Engage for Success.
Employee engagement is a workplace approach resulting in the right conditions for all members of an organisation to give of their best each day, committed to their organisation's goals and values, motivated to contribute to organisational success, with an enhanced sense of their own well-being.

Institute of Employment Studies.
A positive attitude held by the employee towards the organisation and its values. An engaged employee is aware of business context, and works with colleagues to improve performance within the job for the benefit of the organisation. The organisation must work to develop and nurture engagement, which requires a two-way relationship between employer and employee.

HR Zone.
Employee engagement is the emotional attachment employees feel towards their place of work, job role, position within the company, colleagues and culture and the affect this attachment has on wellbeing and productivity. From an employer's point-of-view, employee engagement is concerned with using new measures and initiatives to increase the positive emotional attachment felt and therefore productivity and overall business success.

Advita Patel,
Communications Specialist, Nuclear Decommissioning Authority.
Definition of employee engagement can vary depending on where you work or what the organisational focus is. However, for me it's quite simple – excellent employee engagement is when colleagues give their very best every day to deliver great results for their organisation. One thing to remember is that every employee is different but they all have something that motivates them to continue being the best – and a good business leader would work hard to discover what that motivation was!

Amanda Coleman,
Head of Corporate Communication at Greater Manchester Police.
Engagement is about interacting and involving people in the organisation. It can be about employees or service users. In both cases it requires some active listening and an ongoing commitment to continue the conversation in good times and when under pressure. This is taking communication to a different level that meets the expectations of people.

Within Greater Manchester Police this means developing a continuous conversation with people in communities across the region. Practically, there are public meetings and local discussions as well as daily social media conversations and webchats with key personnel. Decisions and developments are explained and where possible people can make their views known about the proposals. It is a similar approach to employee engagement which is focused around providing a flow of information and the ability for people to get involved at all levels. We provide opportunities to quiz senior leaders, to make suggestions about developments and to prioritise face-to-face discussions.

The term engagement can mean many things to many people. It is essential that an organisation has a clear understanding of what it means and how that will drive the development of the business. Effective engagement needs involvement from people at all levels of the organisation so understanding what it means can help the right things to be implemented. Developing engagement is simple but it is not easy for businesses.

ENGAGEMENT – DIGGING A BIT DEEPER – TOOLKIT

These 10 questions can help you to understand more about you team's engagement levels. Each answer should be based on a scale of 1 to 10, with 1 being low and 10 being high. For the most insightful feedback, all responses should be anonymous.

Please allocate a score of between **1** and **10** for the extent to which you agree with these statements, with **1 being low** and **10 being high**.

PURPOSE
I feel aligned to the purpose and goals
of this organisation.   1   2   3   4   5   6   7   8   9   10

VALUES
I trust this organisation to behave in ways that
are true to its values.   1   2   3   4   5   6   7   8   9   10

BEHAVIOURS
This is a psychologically safe place to work.   1   2   3   4   5   6   7   8   9   10

CULTURE
I feel valued in my role.   1   2   3   4   5   6   7   8   9   10

RETENTION
I know what is expected of me.   1   2   3   4   5   6   7   8   9   10

DEVELOPMENT
I have received the right training to do my job well. 1   2   3   4   5   6   7   8   9   10

BALANCE
This organisation is committed to supporting
my work-life balance.   1   2   3   4   5   6   7   8   9   10

PERFORMANCE
I feel suitably challenged in my role.   1   2   3   4   5   6   7   8   9   10

TRANSPARENCY
Leaders are open and honest in their communications. 1   2   3   4   5   6   7   8   9   10

PROGRESSION
I have the opportunity to progress in this organisation. 1   2   3   4   5   6   7   8   9   10

Are you a member of the Board or
Senior Leadership team?   YES   NO

Printed in Great Britain
by Amazon